Discipleship:

Essays in Honor of Dr. Allan Coppedge

Matt Friedeman, Editor

TELEIOS PRESS

Francis Asbury Press

Cover design and book layout by Two Cups Creative.

First edition 2017

ISBN: 9781547099870

Printed in the United States of America.

To all who have learned more about Jesus' desire and method
to make disciples from the example, teaching, writings and
discipleship groups inspired by Allan Coppedge.

Contents

Preface xi
Matt Friedeman, Professor of Evangelism and Discipleship, Wesley Biblical Seminary

A Tribute to Beth Coppedge xvii
Mary Friedeman, Homeschool Mom of Six and Children's Pastor

Discipleship and Scripture

1 Discipleship and the Bible: Foundations 1
John N. Oswalt, Asbury Theological Seminary

2 Discipleship and the Gospel of Mark 13
Dennis Kinlaw (1922-2017), Former Chancellor/President Asbury College, Founder of the Francis Asbury Society

Discipleship and Theology

3 Discipleship and Personal Holiness 25
Christopher T. Bounds, Chair of the Department of Christian Studies and Philosophy, Asbury University

4 Discipleship and Self-Giving Love 45
M. William Ury, National Ambassador for Holiness, Salvation Army

Discipleship and the Church

5 Discipleship and the Growing Church 65
Rurel and Lisa Ausley, Crosspoint United Methodist Church

6 Discipleship and Multiplication 77
Wes and Joy Griffin, International Leadership Institute,

7 Discipleship and Conflict 91
Stan Key, President, Francis Asbury Society

Discipleship and Mission

8 Discipleship and Compassionate Ministry 103
Matt Friedeman, Professor of Evangelism and Discipleship, Wesley Biblical Seminary

9 Discipleship and Preaching in a Global Context 121
Timothy C. Tennent, President, Asbury Theological Seminary

10 Discipleship and Family 131
Tim Philpot, Fayette Circuit (KY) Family Court Judge

11 Discipleship as a Lifestyle 149
Robert Coleman, Professor, Disciplemaker, Author

12 Discipleship and Orality 159
William A. Coppedge, Missionary

13 Church History's Greatest Missed Opportunity 173
Thane Hutcherson Ury, Scholar in Residence for Intercultural Studies Asbury University

Preface

Matt Friedeman, Professor of Evangelism and Discipleship,
Wesley Biblical Seminary

Most of us who know Dr. Allan Coppedge recognize that he has always seemed to have had a serious interest in small group discipleship. But there was a genesis to this emphasis in his life. He was teaching Old Testament in Medellin, Colombia, at the One Mission Society seminary. Al testifies that "after I had been there a little while it suddenly dawned on me that I was a missionary that told people I was going to the mission field to fulfill the Great Commission but I wasn't doing anything directly to make disciples for Jesus."

As Dr. Coppedge relates, the Spirit started speaking to his spirit. Disciples needed to be made.

Al talked back. "I don't know how to do that."

The Spirit seemed clear: "Why don't you invite four or five guys out of your class to discover what it means to be a disciple."

"But I've never been in a discipleship group. What would I do?"

"Well, you've got Dr. Robert Coleman's book The Master Plan of Evangelism; you can start and walk through it with them. The biblical passages are there..."

"Well, Jesus (exasperated), I don't know how to do this..."

"You start, and I'll show you what to do."

So, says Coppedge, "I started... and God met with us."

God has been meeting with Al Coppedge and his rotating cast of "four or five guys" ever since. These "four or five" typically turn around and meet with four or five guys, who, not unusually, begin meeting with four or five guys, and...

Dr. Allan Coppedge enjoyed a thirty-three year career at Asbury Theological Seminary as the Beeson Professor of Christian Theology, teaching in the areas of Wesley Studies and Systematic Theology (Emeritus). He received his Ph.D. from the University of Cambridge in Historical Theology. In addition to post-doctoral research on American Methodist history and theology at the Johns Hopkins University, his education includes a Th.M., Asbury Seminary, a B.D. (Honors), University of Edinburgh, and a B.A., Emory University.

For a number of years, Dr. Coppedge served as Academic Dean and Professor of Old Testament at the Biblical Seminary of Colombia, South America, where he was under appointment as a missionary with OMS International. He has experience as a pastor in both Georgia and Kentucky, and has done extensive preaching in Central and South America as well as Scotland and England. For a brief time he worked with The Navigators in San Antonio, Texas. He is a member of the North Georgia Conference of the United Methodist Church.

Dr. Coppedge has served as the President and one of the founders of The Barnabas Foundation, an organization for the promotion of discipleship ministries in the Wesleyan tradition. The Barnabas Foundation was assigned to promote discipleship ministries in seminaries, colleges, local churches and mission organizations and accomplished that goal, with the greatest concentration of disciplemaking taking place at Asbury Theological Seminary.

Dr. Coppedge has written numerous academic articles and materials for discipleship purposes—most significantly, the following books:

- *Shaping the Wesleyan Message: John Wesley in Theological Debate* (Evangel Publishing House, 2003) is a description of the theological debates over predestination and Christian perfection among the Arminians and Calvinists of the eighteenth-century Revival. This is a volume not only of theology but also of how theological issues were decided in that era.
- *The Biblical Principles of Discipleship* (initially Zondervan/1989, now re-released under Teleios Press 2017). This book lays out the biblical and theological foundations for discipleship ministry and the clear contemporary implications for continued use.
- *In His Image: A Workbook on Scriptural Holiness* (coauthor, Providence House, 2000). Penned with Bill Ury, this interactive workbook focuses on intimacy with God and how to reflect His nature.
- *Portraits of God; A Biblical Theology of Holiness* (InterVarsity, 2001). Coppedge thoroughly examines one of the key ideas of his professorial career – the roles, or portraits, of God. These eight portraits point the way to a more thorough conception of God and its implications for the pursuit of a holy life.
- *The God Who is Triune (*IVP Academic, 2007). This volume tackles the biblical doctrine of the Trinity including attributes, roles, freedom and providence but, most helpfully, the necessity of beginning with Jesus to know the Father and Spirit.

Dr. Coppedge is married to the former Elizabeth Kinlaw. The Coppedges have four children: Katy Beth and Cricket who were born in Colombia, South America, and William Asbury and Susannah who were both born in Kentucky.

I have wanted to compile this *festschrift* honoring Al Coppedge for a long time. A few years ago, he had a serious heart attack and I thought that day that perhaps we had missed the opportunity to honor this mentor to so many. Later, a friend started a similar project but lost momentum; to then initiate another attempt seemed a potential collegial affront. It began to look like a well-intentioned endeavor would never came to fruition. But one day, late last year, a voice seemed to say, "Now." My friend whose similar project was stalled gave the green light to proceed.

The first task as editor of such a volume is to ask, "Who are potential writers?" While I am sure I unintentionally omitted some people who should have been included, for the most part I identified cherished colleagues, friends, and family of Dr. Coppedge who had the ability to produce an essay within the necessary time frame. Many of these contributors are some of the most cherished names in the Wesleyan world and certainly the Asbury community. I assembled a "dream list" while resigning myself to the likelihood that not all of them would be able to participate.

I was wrong.

With one solicitation email and a couple days' response time, nearly everyone I had contacted enthusiastically reciprocated: Coleman, Oswalt, Tennent, Ury, Bounds, and on the list goes. Cricket Albertson even edited a sermon on the topic of discipleship from her grandfather and Coppedge's father-in-law, Dr. Dennis Kinlaw (whose funeral is tomorrow, as I write this).

It was the easiest job I ever accomplished; gathering this noteworthy and prominent list of participants required little more than a single electronic missive. Everyone I contacted wanted to honor this man. They couldn't seem to say "yes" fast enough. Potential contributors were not confined to the academic community, though many are professors in Christian higher education. Allan Coppedge didn't disciple people merely for college and graduate level schools, nor is discipleship a primarily academic undertaking. So it seemed appropriate, in celebration of Dr. Coppedge's legacy, to broaden the perspectives of this volume beyond the academy.

The result is a wide continuum of styles. Authors were asked to choose a topic on the theme of discipleship. As editor, I have attempted[1] to cluster the articles to enhance the continuity of the reader's experience.

In addition to the generous efforts of the contributors themselves, I would like to express appreciation for the assistance of several other people. Editing expertise was provided by my wife Mary, my daughter Hannah, and my son Elijah. Brad Easley and Bryan Easley at Two Cups Creative designed the cover and formatting. My dear colleague at Teleios Press, David Phillips, handles the publishing responsibilities. Thanks to Francis Asbury Press for their kindness and support in this endeavor. If, for some reason, there is disappointment with this work, the editor bears that burden.

Essays in this volume include:

A tribute to Beth Coppedge: We acknowledge the vital role played by Al's wife and helpmate, Beth Kinlaw Coppedge, a formidable disciplemaker in her own right. I have written a volume titled *Discipleship in the Home* but would have gladly

1 With the help of Asbury Seminary student and son Elijah Friedeman

never written it if I could have read Al and Beth on the topic. Instead of writing the book, they chose to inculcate the very best of their joint discipleship ideas in the hearts and minds of their own children. What an incredible legacy those children are having around the world! Beth has also poured her life into the Titus Women ministry and is a beautiful articulator of truth from the pulpit in a variety of venues. My wife Mary, who was in a discipleship group with Beth in seminary, handles this tribute.

Discipleship and Scripture: The essays on discipleship begin, most appropriately, with the Bible. John Oswalt's and Dennis Kinlaw's submissions are placed side by side, the former addressing the topic across the canon and the latter using the gospel of Mark. These two scholars have lived so much life together and been a part of so many joint projects that it is fitting to position their contributions together. Further, due to Dr. Kinlaw's illness when this *festschrift* was in progress, his granddaughter has written a beautiful tribute to her father and his son-in-law in his stead.

Discipleship and Theology: Asbury University's Chris Bounds provides an insightful presentation on sanctification, and Bill Ury delivers on a theme that was central in Dr. Kinlaw's life as well as his own – that of self-giving love. Together they enable us to consider theological implications for discipleship.

Discipleship and the Church: Rurel and Lisa Ausley were participants in the early years of the Coppedges' discipleship ministry at Asbury Seminary. They describe how this seminal experience has impacted their pastoral ministry. Wes and Joy Griffin write about their passion for international discipleship and multiplication, sparked at the Coppedge fire. Stan Key, current president of the Francis Asbury Society and brother-in-law to Al Coppedge, addresses the necessary topic of discipleship and conflict.

Discipleship and Mission: Discipleship should be a ministry that impacts culture. I write about the non-negotiable aspect of compassionate ministry in biblical discipleship. Asbury Theological Seminary president Timothy Tennent addresses preaching in the global context. Judge Tim Philpot considers discipleship and the family, and Dr. Robert Coleman speaks to his lifelong passion for the discipleship lifestyle, a truth he has long embodied. Al Coppedge's son Billy, missionary to Uganda, talks about discipleship and orality: how some cultures need to hear the message in an oral story pattern if they are to absorb it well. And to cap this section off, Hutch Ury discusses Christian history's greatest missed opportunity.

"God designed life to be lived in a certain way," Al Coppedge has taught his students for years. The challenge, according to the good professor, is to recognize that "The sooner He's directing our life the better we will be able to get His best." His best involves being the disciple God wants us to be and, consequentially, turning about and making disciples. This Dr. Allan Coppedge has most admirably done. But he probably won't rest until you, dear reader, do it, too.

Jackson, Miss.
April, 2017

A Tribute to Beth Coppedge

Mary Friedeman, Homeschool Mom of Six and Children's Pastor

I first became aware of Dr. Allan Coppedge when he spoke about discipleship at Asbury College, where I was a student. I had never experienced the kind of spiritual nurture he described, but I longed to. My time at Asbury had already whetted my spiritual appetite and I wanted growth and accountability. At the end of his message, Dr. Coppedge invited anyone who was interested in pursuing discipleship to visit his office at the seminary across the street. As much as I desired to be part of a discipleship group, I was too timid to actually follow his advice. I now know that he would have welcomed me and connected me with a group of likeminded young women, but the thought of navigating the halls of an unfamiliar institution in search of an esteemed professor whom I didn't know proved too daunting.

Fast forward a few years. I arrived at Asbury Theological Seminary as an incoming student. Almost as soon as I arrived on campus, I began hearing about the Barnabas Foundation. The fall retreat was probably my first personal exposure to Beth Coppedge; she was warm and welcoming, but I was more than a little in awe. I signed on to the covenant and found myself in a discipleship group with several other women.

Within just a few weeks I began to date my now-husband, who happened to be part of Al Coppedge's discipleship group. That got me on the Coppedges' radar screen for sure! Little did Matt realize his mentor would take such an active interest in the girl he chose to date, but of course Al and Beth realized how consequential the choice of a mate is for spiritual vitality and Kingdom purposes. So they did a little investigation to see just who was this young lady who had caught the eye of one of their own. Since I had spent the previous three years at Asbury College and we knew some of the same people, it didn't take long for them to gather the necessary intel. Fortunately, I passed the test, and the rest is history!

Over the ensuing months, I had numerous opportunities to visit the Coppedges' home and experience Beth's gracious hospitality. I was especially struck by the way she interacted with her children—bringing Jesus into the most practical aspects of sibling harmony, delighting in the joy of motherhood, and celebrating a child's "Jesus birthday" with fanfare...and a cupcake.

The next fall—as a newlywed—I became part of Beth's discipleship group. During that year, I got to know her as a woman with a sensitive heart and a passionate love for Jesus. Gentle, yet fierce when it comes to the things of God. Beth was definitely Mary to my Martha, because my natural disposition is not akin to that of my biblical namesake. It was instructive for me, as a "doer," to see someone who could become so lost in love at the feet of Jesus that—by her own admission—she sometimes had to scramble to figure out what to fix for supper!

Beth nurtured us with Scripture, encouragement, and practical advice. She introduced us to books and authors whose messages inspired and challenged. Through Beth I discovered Isobel Kuhn, whose *Green Leaf in Drought Time* is my all-time favorite missionary book—a treasured volume which I have re-read, recommended, loaned, and gifted countless times in the last three decades.

Matt and I were especially influenced by Al and Beth's parenting. I grew up in a Christian home where we were taught the Bible and saw faith lived out. But the intentionality in discipleship that I observed as they sought to raise "Jesus boys and girls" made a huge impression. When our first child arrived several years later, the memory of their example set us on a path of family discipleship that has blessed us immensely and eternally impacted the trajectory of our children's lives. Watching Katy Beth, Cricket, Billy, and Susannah faithfully following Jesus to fulfill the Great Commission was an encouragement and inspiration as we began to raise our own rapidly growing brood.

Beth also provided a model of effective ministry, vital to me as a young wife heading with my husband into full-time Christian service. She and Al are an example of husband and wife serving the Kingdom as a team. They bring different gifts and strengths to the work to which the Lord has called them, and each values the other's contributions. I also saw firsthand the importance of hospitality. The Coppedges' home was a hub of ministry, and Beth selflessly threw wide the doors. I realized how an open home, centered on Christ, can be powerfully used by the Lord. Beth enfleshed for me what has become my vocation as well—ministry in and through the family. While nurturing her children spiritually, Beth engaged them as co-laborers in loving service to others. In this way, Kingdom work strengthened the family unit and cultivated in the children a natural affinity to love and serve God. This pattern provides an instructive antidote to ministry models that set ministry demands and family concerns in opposition to one another, often leaving brokenness in their wake.

In recent years, I've had the pleasure of seeing the women of my own church—precious sisters in Christ—get to know Beth through the *Come to the Fire* conferences. The same passion for Jesus that I first knew in a circle in her living room now radiates and inspires as she speaks to hundreds of women.

Sharing the Savior's love is a lifestyle for Beth. She has a hunger and thirst for the things of God and a winsome yet ardent way of delivering His truth. Her heart for the Father enables her to see everyone she meets with His eyes, so that even the most mundane encounter becomes an opportunity for redemption.

A volume commemorating discipleship in the life of Al Coppedge is also a celebration of this remarkable woman and their unity in faithfully doing the works of the One who sent them.

Discipleship and Scripture

Chapter 1
Discipleship and the Bible: Foundations

John N. Oswalt, Asbury Theological Seminary, Wilmore, KY

Tribute

Al Coppedge and I first met at an Evangelical Theological Society meeting in Philadelphia in 1968 or 1969. Although we were not together very long at that time, there was an instant affinity between us. Thus, when he joined the faculty of Asbury Theological Seminary in 1976 (I having been a member since 1970), it was almost immediate that we began to meet together weekly for prayer and fellowship. I don't remember who suggested it first, but I suspect it was Al. Since that time, 40 years ago, we have been prayer partners. When I became president of Asbury College (now Asbury University) in 1983, he was the one (apart from Karen, my wife) to whom I could unburden myself, knowing two things: that he would bear the burden, and that he would keep my confidence absolutely. We have wept together, we have travailed over each other's children together, and we have had some prayers answered in ways that left us wondering, but through it all we have rejoiced in shared faith, in victories won, in children saved and called, in a deep and blessed bonding. I was teaching in Jackson, Mississippi in 2008 when the word came late one evening that Al had suffered a possibly terminal heart attack. I sat on the edge of the bed and was overcome with almost uncontrollable sobbing. When I asked myself what that was about, I realized that apart from Karen, Al was the person in all the world to whom I was closest.

There is so much about Al for which I am grateful. I am grateful for his abiding love for God expressed in his commitment to prayer and Bible study. I am grateful for the way in which he and his wife Beth have parented their children, raising up godly offspring. I am grateful for his commitment to people, as seen in his work in discipleship through the Barnabas Foundation which he created and managed. I am grateful for his commitment to a soundly Biblical Wesleyan theology, especially as seen in his preaching and teaching ministry, but also in his major books on the subject. But, of course, in the end I am forever grateful that he has befriended me.

Essay

Although discipleship is not an exclusively Biblical concept, being a practice that is found around the world, it is a profoundly Biblical one. This is so because of the nature of the Biblical God. Discipleship is at bottom a matter of relationship, and whatever else the God of the Bible may be, he is profoundly relational. Recent studies have focused on this significant difference between the Biblical Yahweh, the Three-In-One, and the Muslim Allah, the unitary monad.[1] Allah seeks no relationship with his followers, whereas Yahweh is constantly seeking such a thing. Although the Bible does not explicitly answer why this should be so, virtually everyone who has inquired into the subject has concluded that it is precisely because there is relationship within the Godhead himself, between Father, Son, and Spirit, and he wishes to extend this blessing to all persons everywhere. Indeed, the Bible being true, this explains why discipleship should be a worldwide phenomenon. Relationship is the central character of the Creator, so it is not surprising that relationship should be a central factor in the human experience, and that relationship should be at the heart of the way in which we learn.[2]

The Nature of Biblical Revelation

This truth forms the foundation for our understanding of discipleship, and it is that aspect which I wish to consider in this study. Some may argue that we have no concrete evidence of the actual practice of discipling until relatively late in the Biblical experience. So we have the reference to Elijah calling Elisha to follow him (1 Kings 19: 19-21), and Isaiah referring to his disciples (Isaiah 8:16). But the foundational concept goes back to the nature of the Bible itself. The Bible is unique among the world's holy books, in that it is built upon narrative accounts of God's interactions with particular groups of people at particular points in time and space. It is not primarily composed of a collection of divine declarative statements about reality and the nature of things, as the others are. Where such declarative statements exist, as in the prophets, for example, they are still delivered in, and are inextricable from, very particular social contexts.

What are we to make of this? Upon reflection, the point becomes clear. Yahweh has chosen to reveal truth about himself and his creation only in the context of relationships with actual human beings. This is already hinted at in the third chapter of the Book when we learn that it was Yahweh's habit to walk with his creatures in

1. Nabeel Qureshi, *No God But One* (Grand Rapids, MI: Zondervan, 2016).

2. This is a point that should be paid more attention to as learning by machine assumes a larger and larger place in education. Enthusiasts for this mode argue that more and deeper relationships are possible in on-line classrooms than in physical classrooms. However, the very way in which this latter approach is described, "face-to-face learning," suggests that there may be a major component missing in on-line education.

the garden in "the cool of the day." Some might dismiss this as only a naïve tale, but the profound content of that chapter as it reflects on the nature of sin, its effects on human relationships as well as divine ones, and its tragic consequences, argues against mere childish naiveté. Instead, we have here an introduction to the mode of revelation that will characterize the Book from end to end: God teaches in the context of face-to-face relationships. Thus, when we do the same thing we are only replicating what the Creator had done and does.

The Importance of "Walk"

In this regard, the Bible's use of the word "walk" in both its verbal and nominal forms is very important. The majority of the term's occurrences in the Bible, in both the Old and New Testaments, are metaphorical, nearing three quarters of the total: that is, "walking" refers to one's manner of life. For instance, the apostle Paul enjoins the Ephesian Christians to "walk worthy of your calling" (see also Col. 1:10; 1 Thess. 2:12). What is he saying? He is saying that they should continuously conduct themselves in such a way that they will bring honor to their faith, and to their Savior. But what kind of a "walk" is that? It is one that looks like the Master's walk! If Jesus is "walking" one way, and we his followers are "walking" in another way, there has been a disconnect somewhere.

This idea of a "walk" that reflects that of the master reaches far back into the Old Testament. The first occurrence of such a usage is found already in Genesis 5, where we are told that Enoch "walked[3] with God" (5:22, 24). We are not given much context to know exactly what is intended by such a statement, and it is made even more tantalizing by the enigmatic "and he was not because God took him" that concludes 5:24. But whatever else is connoted, it surely speaks of an ongoing relationship with God that was reflected in the quality of Enoch's life. The NIV translation "walked faithfully" is an attempt to capture some of that idea. A similar occurrence is to be found in the description of Noah in Genesis 6:9. Here the content of the "walking" with God is made clearer by the context. We are told that Noah was a man who did what is right, and in so doing was "whole [Heb. *tamim*] in all his generations" [author's translation].[4] In short, to walk with God was not only to learn what is right but also to find the strength to do it. But more than that, it was to become a whole person: all that we are meant to be as humans.

3. The form of the Heb. word (hithpael) suggests continuing reiterated action. So this was not a one-time or momentary behavior, but one that was ongoing.

4. The Heb. word translated "whole" here is tāmîm which means to be complete and unblemished. While the common modern translation "blameless" (i.e. "without defect") is not incorrect, it plays into a certain kind of theology that suggests we can have a great deal of blame-worthy behavior in our lives while still being "blameless" in God's eyes through the blood of Christ. Surely none of us will ever be able to stand before God on the basis of our own behavior. On the other hand, to suggest, as this theology too often does, that the quality of our lives is only a secondary matter is equally wrong.

The same constellation of thought is found in Genesis 17:1 where Yahweh calls upon Abram to "walk before me and be whole [Heb. *tamim*]." The context of this passage is very important. It is the next thing said after the announcement of Ishmael's birth at the end of chapter 16. There Abram had attempted to fulfill God's promise of a son in his own way and in his own strength. The result had not been blessing for the world, but only a deepening of the curse, as is always the result when we attempt to do God's work in our intellect and our strength. Now, thirteen years later, Yahweh directs Abram to walk in a manner that fulfills God's direction for life. If the patriarch will do so, he will be all that God intended a human person to be; he will be whole. But again, how is this to be accomplished? It is by "walking" in God's presence: "before me." It is a personally-directed process, with progress toward a goal in mind. The evidence that Abram will commit himself to this regimen is that he submits to the mark of circumcision. Once again, the proximity to chapter 16 and Ishmael can hardly be coincidental. Abram is submitting his human vitality, as symbolized in his sexual powers, to the control of God. Of course the world's problem is not resident in the male genitals; rather, it is in the unsurrendered will. Thus, it is the "heart," the center of the personality for both males and females, that must be circumcised (see Deut. 10:16). My right to myself has to be cut off once forever but also every day.

What is being talked about in Genesis 17 is discipleship. Yahweh is inviting Abram into a committed relationship with him in which Abram will mimic Yahweh's manner of life and behavior. In doing so, Abram will be achieving God's goal for all humans: that we will be whole and complete, exactly what God imagined for us. This statement does not envision perfect performance, or a restoration of Adamic perfection. What it does see is humans who are delivered from neurotic self-reference, who are genuinely free to give themselves away for others without asking what is in it for themselves, who can deny themselves for the sake of the best both in themselves and others, persons who though damaged in a variety of ways are yet able to live out the eternal mandate to love God with every faculty they have and their neighbors as themselves. This is humanity as it was meant to be. What a thought!

This must be the goal of discipleship at its heart. We are concerned with enabling men and women to walk with God in life-transforming ways. We must never seek to produce clones of ourselves. God forbid! But we must constantly point past ourselves to the glorious vision of "God-like-ness." That goal is only achieved when God's character and nature are made so clear and so compelling that being like him becomes the most desirable thing in the world.

"Walk" As a Means of Learning: God is trustworthy

In Genesis 24:40, Abraham gives testimony to his servant Eleazar that he has indeed carried out God's call to discipleship when he says that the God "before whom I have walked" will make the servant's journey a success, leading him to a wife for Isaac. What has Abraham, the disciple, learned while "walking"? He has learned that God is faithful and can be depended upon. In many ways this is the most basic and most necessary truth for life that is "whole": Yahweh can be trusted! The snake attacked God's trustworthiness in the Garden, and everything has been in peril since. Down in the very depths of our being, where it was for Job, we must believe that whatever happens, God can be trusted. What that means is the unshakable confidence that God is good and is for us.

Most Christians do not really trust God because they have never been taught how to walk closely enough with God to allow him to demonstrate his trustworthiness to them. They have never allowed him to maneuver them into the kind of tight place from which they cannot extricate themselves. They have never *had* to rely on God. Thus, when their worlds truly do fall in on them, as they will, these people do not know whether God can be trusted or not. Psalm 46:10 says, "Relax, and discover that I am God" [author's translation]. That's what a committed disciple knows from experience. If Yahweh is indeed God, and if he can be trusted absolutely, there is nothing that cannot be ventured at the Master's direction.

God is Gracious and Kind

There is another feature of the Abraham narrative that may speak to the nature of discipleship as it is conceived of in the Word. Twice in this narrative we find occurrences of the unique Biblical word *ḥesed.* They are the earliest occurrences in the Bible. They are found in the mouths of first Lot (Gen 19:19 NIV, "kindness") and then Eliezer (Gen 24:12 NIV "kindness"; ESV "steadfast love"; 24:14 NIV "lovingkindness"; ESV "steadfast love"). This word is unknown outside of the Bible yet it occurs more than 275 times in the Bible with about three-quarters of them referring to God (see for instance Ps. 136, where it occurs in the refrain of every verse [KJV "mercy"]). It appears to have been coined by the Hebrews to express the new idea of a God who will show deep and abiding love consistently, particularly to those who do not deserve it.[5] So who coined it? Is it possible that it was Abraham, as he reflected on the undeserved love that he had experienced from God as he walked with him? I strongly suspect that it was. Part of the reason I think such a thing is because of the two mouths in which the word first appears. What do Lot and Eliezer have in common? Or rather, *whom* do they have in common? It is Abraham. In short, what Abraham had learned in his walk, he had communicated to these two who quite literally walked with him. This is discipleship in practice.

---

5. Because the word frequently occurs in the context of covenants (see 1 Sam 20:8-16) it was originally thought to have arisen particularly in that context. It is now believed to have had a wider usage, as in seen in the two passages cited above.

Covenants Provide Specific Content for the Walk

Without Obligation

This idea of a God who calls persons into a walk with him provides the Biblical rationale for discipleship. The content for the walk is provided in the covenants, culminating in the Sinai covenant. While some believe that there was an implicit covenant that Yahweh made with Adam, the evidence for this is equivocal at best. The first indisputable covenant between God and humans is the Noahic covenant. There Yahweh does not merely promise not to destroy the earth with water again, but legally binds himself with repeated covenant terminology (Gen 9:8–17). What is significant here is that all of the obligation is from the God-ward side. This is one more indication that the basis for all divine-human relationships is found in God's free giving of himself to us.

The second covenant is the Abrahamic one (Gen 15:18–21). The divine promises found in chapter twelve of Genesis were entirely reliable, but they were not stated in terms of a binding covenant. Here the covenant language and symbolism is fully engaged: Yahweh commits himself with covenant oaths that the large family he has promised to Abraham will possess the land of Canaan. Again, there is no obligation from Abraham, from the human side. All of the obligation for fulfilling the terms of the covenant is on Yahweh's side. In Genesis 22, subsequent to the sacrifice of Isaac, this covenantal promise is amplified to include all that was said in Genesis 12. Of particular importance in the context of the sacrifice of Abraham's son is the promise that through Abraham's "seed" all the nations of the earth would be blessed, the means of which would be the yet-further covenant with David. As previously, there were no requirements placed upon Abraham. To be sure, in chapter 17, as discussed above, Abraham and his descendants were to bear the mark of circumcision, but this was more of a sign of acceptance of God's offers than a commitment to a particular pattern of behavior.

It is only with the giving of the Sinai covenant that human obligations to behave in certain ways come to center stage. Why is this? Why did it take so long for God "to get around to this"? I think the answer is to be found both in the nature and the wisdom of Yahweh. He *is* the giving God. This is so hard for us to accept. Our deep consciousness of our estrangement from him (note that around the world people are inclined to offer sacrifices to placate whomever they conceive to be in charge of the cosmos) means that we deeply distrust him, being sure he is "out to get us." So Yahweh had to work diligently through the generations of Abraham, Isaac, Jacob, and Joseph to try to demonstrate that this is not so. He is not out to get us, but is for us. He does not wish to take from us, but to give to us. Joseph expressed just how deeply he had gotten that point in his response to his brothers in Genesis 50:19–21. His brothers, sure that with their father dead their powerful brother would now take vengeance upon them, contrived a lie that their father had requested Joseph to have mercy on them. Joseph, seeing straight through the lie, said, "'Don't be afraid of me. Am I God, that I can punish you? You intended to harm me, but God intended it all for good. He brought me to this position so I could save the lives of many people. No, don't be afraid. I will continue to take care of you and your children.' So he reassured them by speaking kindly to them" (NLT). Note that the last sentence contains the very same words that God spoke through Isaiah to the discouraged and frightened exiles in Babylon, certain that they had sinned away any grace they might have had from God (Isa. 40:1). As with Joseph's brothers, God was not out to get the exiles. They had suffered enough. Rather, as Yahweh intended to do good to the brothers through Joseph, so he intended to do good for the Judean exiles.

This willingness on God's part to offer himself in the beginning without demanding a return obligation is an important point for us as we seek to disciple others. Sometimes, fearful of being found guilty of "bait and switch" practices, we are very careful to outline for prospective disciples just exactly what will be expected of them in the relationship. Maybe we ought to begin by demonstrating our obligations to them before we begin to expect very much of them. Will some take advantage of us, and later on try to resist any obligations? Well, that is what we humans have been doing for millennia, so it should probably not be a surprise. But in the end such persons will probably self-select themselves out of the program. It is better to risk some potential misunderstanding and a certain fuzziness in the relationship than to compromise in any way the truth of God's nature as the Self-giving One.

Sharing the Holy Character

In his wisdom, God understood that there is only so much we humans can understand or receive. Thus there is nothing about the holiness of God in the book of Genesis. That was much too far up the learning curve for it to be introduced too early. At that point it was more than enough if humans could learn that he really can be trusted, and thus believed, and thus obeyed. If they could be brought along that far, *then* he could begin to demonstrate to them just who it was that was inviting them into a trusting, believing, obedient relationship. With the foundation securely established, then he would begin to give them the stupendous news that he is absolutely OTHER than this world, and that to live in relationship with him was more than merely saying, "Oh yes, that sounds like fun." Indeed, we will have to discover that there is a deep antipathy in us to allowing him to be completely OTHER in our lives, for that means that he is completely beyond our power to manipulate him. But that discovery was *far* down the road for Abraham in Haran, as it is for the average new believer in Christ, and God was not about to bring the whole salvation enterprise into jeopardy by throwing Abraham "into the deep end of the pool" at the outset.

But in God's purposes there had to come a time when his followers began to realize who this trusty "God of the fathers" really is and what the implications of that reality are for us humans. We see the beginning of this realization taking place in Exodus 3 when Moses, the 80-year-old dropout, stepped aside to see a bush that burned but was not consumed. Out of the bush came the personalized command, "Moses, take your shoes off because the ground you are standing on is holy." What is the significance of that statement? This was not a sanctuary that had been duly dedicated and appointed. This was an ordinary place with ordinary dirt. But there was something about the Being that spoke out of that bush that automatically "infected" whatever was around it. That is holiness indeed.[6] Then when the voice identified itself as belonging to the "God of your fathers," Moses covered his face in fear. "Is the one we have thought of as our family god, our own rabbit's foot, as it were, the Holy One?" This was the revelation that came to Moses in that moment. We can imagine him saying to himself, "What have we gotten ourselves into?" How little he knew!

The Significance of the Sinai Covenant

But who exactly was this HOLY ONE? For 400 years the Hebrew people had lived in one of the most polytheistic cultures the world has ever known. Whatever of their earlier faith they may have retained, it was certainly thoroughly permeated with an Egyptian worldview. What was that worldview? Here are just a few of its tenets: 1) This world is all there is to reality, thus it is divine. 2)That being so, there are as many gods as there are psycho-socio-physical powers in this world. 3) It is possible to manipulate this world and its gods through sympathetic magic to get what I want and need from it. 4) Since this world is an endless cycle, coming from nowhere and going nowhere, there is no purpose in life other than survival with a maximum of comfort, pleasure and security, all of which are dependent on the acquisition of power. 5) Right and wrong are entirely relative to a given situation, and have no basis in the nature of reality. Does this all sound somewhat contemporary? It is not because I have intentionally framed the statements for that effect. Rather, wherever and whenever people begin with the premise that this world is all there is to reality, as we in the post-World War II West have come to do, these

6. "Holy" refers to that which is other than the norms of experience or existence. In and of itself, it has no moral or ethical connotations, but refers to "the other" which because it is out of the ordinary provokes feeling of unease all the way up to terror. But the Hebrews learned that there is only One Being in the universe who can rightly be called "holy." The gods are not really other, but are simply representations of the ordinary forces of this world. This is especially obvious in the practice of idol-making: the divine is represented with natural objects shaped into a human likeness. That is not other. But Yahweh is not this world and cannot be represented by anything in this world. He is truly OTHER, and is thus the only one who can rightly be called holy. But if there is only one holy being, then there is only one holy character: his! That is the function of all the covenants, and especially the Sinai Covenant: to teach us humans the character of the Holy One.

concomitant understandings will result.

So how was Yahweh to correct all of that wrong thinking? And it was wrong. The startling thing is that to start with that wrong premise is to end up with wrong thinking at every turn. That view of reality and its concomitants is not partly wrong and partly right, it is entirely wrong! This world is not all there is to reality, and it is not divine. There are not many gods, but One. God cannot be manipulated through magic, but can only be surrendered to and trusted. There is a goal for this life: abundant life beginning now and extending into eternity. There is purpose in life: sharing the character of the creator. There are absolute ethical values that are rooted in the very nature of the cosmos as Yahweh designed it to be. The acquisition of personal power is finally terribly corrosive; it is in the voluntary surrender of power to our loving God that we are enabled to find abundant life.

So again I ask, how was God to correct the wrong thinking (and living) that had sprung from all those years of exposure to Egyptian thought? Should he drop a book of true theology on the Hebrews in their brick-pits? Hardly! These were uneducated slaves. What would they have made of complex theological reasoning? Nothing! So what did God do? He graciously delivered them from their bondage, and then invited them into an exclusive covenant with himself. Would they like to be his exclusive people and have him for their exclusive God? Of course they would; they had seen that the mighty gods of Egypt were not competent to even appear in the same arena with him.

The Nature of the Commandments

But what would such an exclusive relationship entail? It would mean that in turn for the covenant Lord's care, protection, and provision (the very things that had been demonstrated on the journey to Sinai [Exod. 16–18]), they would commit themselves to act in the ways he dictated. But what about those dictates? Where did they come from? Were they simply arbitrary demands from a heavenly tyrant? They were not, as is made abundantly clear in Exodus 19 and Leviticus 19. In Exodus 19 Yahweh was carefully preparing the people to say "Yes" to the invitation to enter into a covenant with him. The first step was intellectual preparation in which God reminded the people what he had done for them and then promised that they would become his own special possession: "a holy nation and a royal priesthood" if they would accept the covenant (Exod. 19:5-6). But that word "holy" raises an interesting question: "holy" in what sense? Surely they were not going to become transcendent beings like God. So how are they going to become "other"? Would that be a label statement that they belonged to the Holy One? Or would there be an observable change in their behavior? Leviticus 19 answers the question in a definitive way. The chapter begins with the unequivocal demand, "You must be holy, because I, Yahweh, your God, am holy" (19:1). What follows is a concise summary of all of the covenant requirements. In short, to be holy is to fulfill certain ceremonial, civil, and ethical behaviors. Why is that? A moment's reflection answers the question. We must live in these holy ways, because these behaviors reflect the holy character of God! We are not expected to share his transcendent essence, but we are expected to share his transcendent character!

So why the covenant? It was a learning tool, a discipleship tool, if you will. The people learned the character of reality, of the God who is reality, by living it out, by *walking it out.* They learned that there is no other God than Yahweh when they could not worship other gods. They learned that he is not this world when they could not make idols. They learned that God cannot be manipulated in magical ways when they could not use his name in magical ways, etc. But they also learned how deeply Yahweh values persons: their property, their lives, their sexual integrity, their reputations, etc. Fully six of the ten commandments that form the basis for the rest of the covenant stipulations have to do with our treatment of other people. But this is in a covenant with God. What does religion have to do with the way we treat others? In fact, Yahweh is showing his people his heart. He is not about himself but about others, and people who walk with him in holy fellowship cannot be about themselves either.

Thus, the covenant was the culmination of God's attempt to show the world who he is, what reality is, and what we, his creatures, were meant to be. By placing the laws in the context of a mutual covenant, their significance was deeply altered. There are other, older law codes found elsewhere in the ancient Near East. Several of these even purport to come from a god. But none of them put the laws into the context of a covenant. In them the motivation for obedience is coercion: do this, or else. Here the motivation is quite different: your God has graciously delivered you and invites you into an exclusive relationship of blessing; your part is to do what pleases him. It is interesting that what is often translated as "to obey" in English is actually "to listen to the voice of" in Hebrew.[7] That gives the concept a different feel, doesn't it? Rightly or wrongly, "obey" carries with it the connotations of demand and coercion, whereas "listen to the voice of" carries much more of the connotation of an intimate personal relationship. That conveys something of what the covenant is about. Yahweh is inviting us into a committed walk with him wherein we listen to his voice guiding us, and as we do so we are coming to a deep and abiding understanding of who he is and what he longs for, for us.

Here, then, are the foundations for discipleship as it is played out in the rest of the Bible. To be a disciple is walk with one's teacher, to learn by doing, to listen to his voice. It is to learn in the context of a relationship. Here, while there is, to be sure, a transfer of information – knowledge – there is also a deepening perception of how that knowledge relates to the business of living, how it relates to other knowledge, how it is to be rightly utilized, when its use would be unethical,

7. See Dennis F. Kinlaw, *This Day With the Master* (Grand Rapids, MI: Zondervan, 2002), 12/9.

etc. In short, it is in the context of discipleship that knowledge becomes wisdom. That takes place as a disciple participates with the master in the living out of his or her knowledge, with the eventual result that, almost imperceptibly, the relationship shifts from disciple-master to friends.

With this foundation in mind, it comes as no surprise at all that the Second Person of the Trinity, when asked the rather inane question, "Where do you live?" answers "Come and see" (John 1:39). The answer is not about information, but is an invitation. So also, it is no surprise that the beginning of Jesus' saving ministry on earth was to walk along a beach one day and to say to some young men at work, "Follow me" (Mark 1:16-18). Nor is it surprising that he should spend a night in prayer before reaching a decision on the select few with whom he would become intimate (Luke 6:12-16). Isaiah had said centuries before, "Bind up this testimony of warning and seal up God's instruction (*torah*) among my disciples." He knew that the ultimate impact of his ministry depended on the success of his discipling ministry. Clearly, Jesus knew that the same was true for his ministry as well. Discipling was that important; it still is, for it is written into the very fabric of reality.

Chapter 2
Discipleship and the Gospel of Mark

Dennis Kinlaw (1922-2017), Former Chancellor/President Asbury College, Founder of the Francis Asbury Society

Tribute by Cricket Albertson

I have the privilege of being Al Coppedge's second daughter. In our home, discipleship was a way of life. Groups of seminary students came weekly to meet with my father and mother; sometimes three different groups would meet in our home each week. My sister and I knew what that meant: clean up the kitchen quickly, straighten the living room, help mama with the younger two kids, and scoot upstairs to do our homework unobserved. I remember flipping over the banister and sneaking downstairs, trying desperately not to be seen by the seminarians in the good living room. We knew that our dad was investing in the lives of younger men so that they would be equipped to share Jesus with even more people, and we felt that was a worthwhile investment–even if it meant an invasion of our home. As we watched, we found that our father's investment paid off; we began to see young men and women travel out from Wilmore, Kentucky, to all kinds of interesting places with the purpose of making disciples for Jesus around the world. We felt it was an honor to be part of such an enterprise.

After college, I found myself following in my father's footsteps. I attended seminary and took every class he offered, discovering from him a love for theology, church history, and biblical studies. After seminary, the Francis Asbury Society hired me as an assistant to my grandfather, Dennis Kinlaw; he needed help with theological projects, and, on my father's recommendation, felt I would be a good fit. Thus, I embarked on an eighteen-year discipleship adventure with my grandfather. He invested in me as if I were worthy of investment, and when I became a mother (three times over) he thought that just multiplied the value of his investment.

In honor of my father, I have edited one of my grandfather's sermons which he preached at Asbury College in 1974. This message explores discipleship from the context of the book of Mark and provides the foundation for discipleship, which is knowing who Jesus really is and knowing who we really are. It seemed a fitting way to pay tribute to my father, whose commitment to discipleship came out of his love for Jesus and his acknowledgement of the Spirit's transforming power in his own life.

Sermon

Preached at Asbury College
April 1974

I want to call your attention to a passage of scripture found in the last paragraph of the first chapter of Paul's letter to the Corinthians, beginning with verse 26:

> "Brothers and sisters, think of what you were when you were called. Not many of you were wise by human standards; not many were influential; not many were of noble birth. But God chose the foolish things of the world to shame the wise; God chose the weak things of the world to shame the strong. God chose the lowly things of this world and the despised things—and the things that are not—to nullify the things that are, so that no on may boast before him. It is because of him that you are in Christ Jesus, who has become for us wisdom from God–that is, our righteousness, holiness and redemption. Therefore, as it is written: 'Let the one who boasts boast in the Lord.'" (1 Cor 1:26-31 NIV)

I would like to pick out particularly verse 29, which is a pivotal conclusion in the paragraph: "so that no human being might boast before him." There are other translations that translate that verse, "so that no flesh might glory in the presence of God."

Recently, I was invited to speak in the seminary chapel, and I considered what I would say to young men and women who were studying for the ministry that would be of profit to them. As I prayed about it, the thing that interested me or the burden that came to me was the matter of Christian discipleship. What is a disciple? Who is a disciple? What does it mean to be a disciple of Jesus Christ? To prepare myself for that assignment, I thought that I would take one of the gospels and read it very carefully, working my way through one gospel to see how Jesus dealt with the issue of discipleship from the calling of his twelve disciples until the resurrection. I suppose I chose Mark because it was the shortest of the four gospels. I wanted to be able to sit down and read it through from beginning to end at one sitting without stopping. I wanted to get in my mind the content of that little book, particularly as it related to the subject of discipleship.

There is something beautiful about the way God will open up a verse so that it just stands out and one can say, "This is my verse for the day. This is my verse for the year. This is the word on which I live at this moment." It is even a better thing when a paragraph just comes alive, and the parts of it all fit together. When one can understand a whole chapter, it is great, but when the whole structure of a book can be seen, it is far greater and helps the reader see the world from God's perspective. Every person ought to work towards seeing the big pictures so that we can see things whole, because there are things that can be seen only when we look at the totality of the text that could never be seen clearly when we look at any one part.

As I worked my way through the book of Mark, I began to understand something of the sequence and logic of the book; in the process, two things stood out brilliantly and dramatically. The first one I had seen before, but it came home to me afresh. That is the beauty of scripture; it keeps opening to us in deeper and deeper ways. Mark, in writing his gospel, is concerned about one question—who is Jesus? In his opening paragraph, a group of Jews gather around John the Baptist with the question in their minds, "Is this the Christ?" John turns the attention from himself to Jesus; Jesus is the bridegroom and John simply bears witness to him. Carefully, deliberately, and dramatically, Mark builds his case to prove Jesus' identity as the Messiah. He is the one to whom John the Baptist describes in this way: "the straps of whose sandals I am not worthy to untie" (John 1:27).

Mark builds the suspense for eight chapters of his gospel in good Hebrew fashion. There are many scholars who do not believe that each gospel was written by a single author. They think, rather, that the gospel stories are bits of tradition that were collected and somebody, perhaps not even an eyewitness, took these bits and pieces and put them together like beads on a string, so each gospel is put together of various bits and pieces of stories from Jesus' life, but they are not whole units composed by single individuals. As I lived with the Gospel of Mark, the unity of the book became clearer and clearer, and the single authorship of it seemed obvious as the case unfolded to answer the question of "Who is Jesus?" Mark answers this question as powerfully as he can.

Mark does not make his case in the way a lawyer or a philosopher would do it. Our tendency is to take our basic principles and lay them down logically and build discursively until finally we can draw the conclusion that we think should be drawn from the data. That is not the way a good Hebrew did things. In fact, there is a vast difference in the way a Hebrew mind works and a Greek mind, and it is demonstrated in the way they would argue a case. When a person came to Jesus and asked him a question, he did not start into a logical discourse. Instead, he told a story. The Hebrew mind illustrated truth rather than rationally discussing it. Jesus painted a picture in the mind of his listeners, which is better than a thousand logical discourses.

Mark, in good Hebrew fashion, begins to build his case, not discursively, but rather, picture by picture by picture by picture. Each one is given to provoke the question, "Who is Jesus?" In his very first chapter, Mark just plunks the reader headlong into his argument. Jesus sits at the synagogue at Capernaum, and he finds a man who has an unclean spirit, and he speaks to the man with the unclean spirit. The unclean spirit is expelled from him, and the man is set free. Then Jesus begins to teach the people who have gathered at the synagogue, and they are astounded, for they have never heard a man who spoke like Jesus. The people begin to ask the question, "Who is this man?"

After that visit to the synagogue, Jesus and his newfound disciples go with Peter to his home, and Peter's mother in-law is sick with a fever. Jesus sees her and lays his hand upon her; the fever is driven away, and she made well. She gets up and serves them, and one can imagine these disciples saying, "We knew John, and he was a great prophet, but he never did anything like this. It seems that no matter what the problem is, Jesus is the answer!"

Then, before the disciples know what is happening, a man comes running to them, and to their astonishment and terror, he is a leper. He does not, in good leper fashion, run in the other direction and say, "Unclean! Unclean!" He draws near to Jesus and falls on his knees in front of Jesus. I am confident that the disciples scattered, watching from a distance to see what Jesus would do. Jesus does the unthinkable and reaches out and lays his hand on the man. The leper is confident that Jesus has the authority to make him clean; he only wonders if Jesus wants to make him clean. Jesus does want to make him clean, so he touches the one no one else would touch, and the man is cleansed of his leprosy.

Then Mark paints another picture of the Sabbath. Jesus is teaching, and some men bring a paralytic to him. They lift the tiles from the roof, and he is lowered until he lays on the ground in front of Jesus. Unperturbed, Jesus looks at the paralytic and declares that his sins are forgiven. The Pharisees and the scribes are indignant and ask among themselves, "Why does this fellow talk like that? He is blaspheming! Who can forgive sins but God alone?" (Mark 2:6). Jesus recognizes their thoughts and responds to their anger with the power to forgive sins and heal the body. He instructs the man to get up and walk. His sins are forgiven: "I want you to know that the Son of Man has authority on earth to forgive sins" (Mark 2:10).

Following this is the story of the man with the withered hand. Again, on the Sabbath the Pharisees are watching to see if he will heal on the Sabbath. Jesus asks the man to hold out his hand, and as he does so his hand is made perfectly whole. The people go away wondering, "Who is this man?" and "Where does he get his power?" Jesus stands in his own synagogue, and as he speaks, the people watch him in awe. They know his family, his mother and brothers, and they cannot understand the source of his power and wisdom.

Mark continues his string of stories; one night the disciples are crossing the sea, and a massive storm arises, and they come to Jesus who is sleeping in the boat, and say, "Teacher, don't you care if we drown?" He simply arises, looks at the waves, turns to the wind and says, "Quiet! Be still!" (Mark 4:38-39). The stormy night becomes instantly calm, but as the waves subside, a tempest begins inside the boat, in the hearts and the minds of the disciples as they look at each other and wonder, who is this man—a man that even the winds and waves obey?

Through all Mark's stories, he is declaring to the reader that Jesus is perfectly able to meet every human need that arises. Never has there been a man like this man. He heals the sick, cleanses the leper, raises the paralytic, and calms the storm. There are a few parables that Mark records, but only a very few. Almost all the first eight chapters of Mark give witness to the miraculous power of Christ to meet every human need. As each story is given, the disciples' or the crowd's reaction is recorded. The people wonder about his ability to forgive sins; they are confused by his healings on the Sabbath; they cannot understand his power over evil spirits, and they marvel at his ability to calm the storm. The Pharisees and the Herodians come together and declare that Jesus is dangerous and must be eliminated, but the common people listen to Him and declare that he had done all things well (Mark 7:37). After this declaration, Jesus turns to his disciples and says, "Who do people say I am?"

They replied, "Some say John the Baptist; others say Elijah; and still others, one of the prophets."

"But what about you?" he asked. "Who do you say I am?"

Peter answered, "You are the Messiah" (Mark 8:27-29). This story is the climax of that first part of the book of Mark, halfway through the book. Jesus asks the ultimate question of every disciple-maker, "Who is Jesus?" Jesus has been with the disciples these three years, and they have had an opportunity to see him in all different situations with all different people. In that moment of illumination, Peter turns and says, "You are the Messiah" (Mark 8:29). When Peter spoke, I am sure he spoke not only for himself, but he spoke for the eleven with him.

Mark does not linger or explain this pivotal moment in his book. He moves quickly and dramatically to the next big question, but Mark is convinced his readers understand who Jesus is. The first lesson is learned; he wants to begin to answer the second question. I believe that the first step in being a disciple of Christ is to know who *he* is—who Christ is. No person will ever follow him fully until they have some grasp of who Jesus really is, and no person will ever give themselves totally, irrevocably, and completely to him until they know what Mark knew: that Jesus is the one who is sufficient for every human need. He is the All-Sufficient One.

Immediately after that confession, a dramatic change occurs in the book. Before Peter's declaration, Mark has been telling these stories about who Jesus is. They have tumbled from him in quick succession, stacking up the data, but immediately after Peter's confession, the emphasis is different. Instead of an almost third-person atmosphere in which Jesus is detached from the twelve, performing his acts for their benefit as well as for others, now he reaches out his arms and draws the twelve into an intimacy with him that they have not known before. Now that they know him, his teaching begins. He begins to instruct them, not in *who* he is, but in *why* he came. The mystery of his mission begins to be his burden with the twelve. Now, that they know who he is, he wants them to know what is going to happen to him. He lets them know that they will go to Jerusalem, and his enemies will make him suffer; they will beat him and crucify him. He will die. Peter takes him aside and rebukes him. Jesus is now introducing them into the mystery of his mission, and Peter cannot comprehend or else cannot bear to hear it. Jesus looks at him and says, "Get behind me, Satan! You do not have in mind the concerns of God but merely human concerns" (Mark 8:33).

Jesus continues his teaching by taking three of his disciples up on a mountain, and when he gets them up on a mountain, he is transfigured before Peter, James, and John. He is transfigured before them, and to their astonishment, awe, and (I am sure) terror, they look and see Moses and Elijah standing with Jesus. Moses, the architect of Israel's religion, that man who talked face to face with God and did not die; and Elijah, that stormy old prophet, who brought God's word to the nation of Israel and was carried to heaven in a chariot of fire. To their amazement, Moses and Elijah talk with Jesus, and it is crystal clear to Peter, James, and John that Jesus is greater than even Moses and Elijah, the two greatest prophets in Israel's history. All that they had confessed about Jesus is true; he is the Holy One of God, the Son of God, the Christ, the Messiah, the Savior.

Now the disciples are on the inside of the secret of Jesus' identity. As they start down the mountain, Jesus again tells them what is going to happen. He tells them that he must go to Jerusalem, suffer and die, but he also tells them that he will rise from the dead. Then he instructs them not to tell anyone about the Transfiguration until he has risen from the dead. Just like a bunch of systematic theologians, the disciples huddle up and discuss what "rising from the dead" could possibly mean. When they get to the foot of the hill, there is a great commotion. Jesus walks straight into the commotion and finds that his other nine disciples are at the heart of it. He asks the crowd about the problem. A troubled man comes and says, "Teacher, I brought you my son, who is possessed by a spirit that has robbed him of speech. Whenever it seizes him, it throws him to the ground…I asked your disciples to drive out the spirit but they could not" (Mark 9:17-18).

Jesus replies, "You unbelieving generation, how long shall I stay with you? How long shall I put up with you? Bring the boy to me" (Mark 9:19). The father brings his son, and his son is set free and healed.

Notice how these three stories after Peter's declaration answer a completely different set of questions with a completely different set of stories. Instead of stories about dramatic acts of Christ and his adequacy, Jesus tells Peter to "Get behind me, Satan" (Mark 8:33). To the three on the mount of transfiguration, he tries to explain to them what it meant for the Son of Man to be rejected. To the disciples confronted by the spirit-possessed boy, Jesus calls them "unbelieving generation" (Mark 9:19). They are confused and afraid about the message of his mission.

Their consternation continues as they walk down through Galilee toward Jerusalem; they come to the end of the day when Jesus turns to His disciples and says, "What was it that you were arguing about on the road?" (Mark 9:33). And they look at each other and blush, and Peter, so eager to speak before, now is strangely silent. James and John, intimate in the deeper things, look at each other and have nothing to say. Jesus knows what they were discussing; they were talking about who would be the greatest in Jesus' kingdom. While Jesus is going to Jerusalem to a cross, they are looking for a way to get a throne and a crown.

The disciples' performance gets even worse. They come to Jesus for approval after forbidding a man to cast out demons in Jesus' name. Jesus rebukes them, and declares that those who are not against him are for him. Jesus knows that any man who met human need in Jesus' name is not an enemy.

They bring children to Jesus, and the disciples send the parents away, declaring that Jesus does not have time for children. Jesus rebukes them and says, "Let the little children come to me, and do not hinder them, for the kingdom of God belongs to such as these" (Mark 10:14). James and John ask Jesus a question: "Let one of us sit at your right and the other at your left in your glory" (Mark 10:37). He says, "You don't know what are asking. Can you drink the cup I drink or be baptized with the baptism I am baptized with?" (Mark 10:39). He explains that they would drink the cup of suffering that he would drink, but they did not understand. Jesus turns and says to them that all of them will forsake him; and although they all deny that they will abandon him, that is exactly what happens in the Garden of Gethsemane.

The difference in the stories in Mark is amazing. In eight chapters, Jesus demonstrates his adequacy, and then for seven and a half long chapters the disciples demonstrate their inadequacy. There is little discussion of their inadequacy until they come to believe that Jesus is the Christ, and no person will ever know their own sinfulness and inadequacy until they come to saving faith. I am firmly convinced that the first step in discipleship is to know who Jesus is, and the second step in discipleship is to find out who we are. We must understand that he is enough for every situation, and then we must recognize our inability to meet the needs of human life. No human flesh will be able to boast in itself. It is not what we do that has significance; it is only what he does.

Mark drives this lesson home with the story of the Transfiguration. Why does he name Peter, James, and John when he takes them up on the mountain? I think he wants us to see clearly the three best of his disciples. It was these disciples who asked for the best seats in his kingdom, who denied him and fled from him when the soldiers came to arrest him later in the Garden of Gethsemane. Mark names Peter at the denial of Jesus in order to press home the point that all of the disciples had the same problem—the same problem as all of us. There are no exceptions. The best among us are no better than the worst. The strongest are no better than the weakest, and Peter failed just like all the rest. The very best of the flesh is not enough. Mark even goes so far as to tell the story about the young man in the linen cloth who flees naked from the soldiers in Gethsemane. Tradition holds that the young man was Mark, himself. Mark wants to be sure his readers know that he is no exception; he flees just like all the disciples (Mark 14:51). When the resurrection comes, two points are crystal clear: the complete adequacy of the Savior and the total inadequacy of His disciples.

If the story had stopped there, Mark would be a rather miserable book, but it does not stop there; Mark sets the scene, and the other gospels and Acts finish it. Luke tells about how the disciples go to Jerusalem, and after Jesus ascends, they meet in an upper room for prayer and confession, intercession and repentance. Having now seen themselves clearly, I am sure they recount all the events in Mark's gospel with a sense of their own inadequacy and sin. On the tenth day the Holy Spirit comes, anoints them, and fills them, and after that, they suddenly understand the cross and the resurrection. When people turn and begin to ask questions, Peter, whose denial was more pointed than any other disciple, stands up and explains the purpose of Jesus' death and resurrection, and the one whose understanding has been so dim blazes forth with the Spirit of God. For the first time, he can really see and understand. Filled with the Spirit, the disciples are ready to take the Kingdom to the world in the name of the Savior. They are powerless in their own human flesh, and they are now aware of that powerlessness, but now they also know Christ's resurrection power. Going into the temple they meet a beggar and they say, "Silver or gold I do not have, but what I do have I give you. In the name of Jesus Christ of Nazareth, walk" (Acts 3:6). Impotence becomes power through the gift of the Holy Spirit.

The carnal spirit has been cleansed and has now become one of sacrificial devotion. Before the resurrection and the infilling of the Holy Spirit, the disciples all forsake him. In Acts 4, the disciples look into the faces of the people who crucified Jesus, and without fear say, "Which is right in God's eyes: to listen to you, or to him? You be the judges! As for us, we cannot help speaking about what we have seen and heard" (Acts 4:19-20). Fear gives way in the courage of the Holy Spirit.

The reader may ask why Mark did not record the dramatic change that occurs after the resurrection and the giving of the Holy Spirit. That is the question that came to my mind. Why is Mark so incomplete? Then I realized Mark is not incomplete. In the opening paragraph of Mark, John the Baptist states, "'After me comes the one more powerful than I, the straps of whose sandals I am not worthy to stoop down and untie. I baptize you with water, but he will baptize you with the Holy Spirit'" (Mark 1:7-8). Then Mark records Jesus' baptism and the coming of the Holy Spirit on Jesus. "Just as Jesus was coming up out of the water, he saw heaven being torn open and the Spirit descending on him like a dove. And a voice came from heaven: you are my Son, whom I love; with you I am well pleased" (Mark 1:10-11). In the opening paragraph of Mark, he spells out the answer to the basic problem of discipleship that the book displays so dramatically.

Do you understand why we talk about the need for the infilling of the Holy Spirit? After a person has been converted, they must come to know who the

Messiah is and who they are, and then they must experience the fullness of God's living, quickening, Spirit within. No person is adequate until there has been in his or her life a personal Pentecost, too.

Thursday night before the cross, Jesus and his disciples are in the Upper Room. He is talking personally with his twelve disciples. It is the scene of greatest intimacy between the disciples and Jesus that the gospels record, and what does Jesus say? "I will ask the Father, and he will give you another advocate to help you and be with you forever—the Spirit of truth" (John 14:15-17). Jesus knew he had to leave his disciples, but he also knew the Father would send One to take his place. He instructs his disciples to wait for him in Jerusalem until he comes. The disciples have loved Jesus and found him to be adequate for every need; and now they will be given the Spirit of Jesus so that his adequacy can be within them.

Let me ask you, have you had John the Baptist's promise fulfilled in your life? "He will baptize you with the Holy Spirit" (Mark 1:8). What's the proof of the baptism of the Holy Spirit? It is the end of our own self-will and our attempts to meet the needs of the world on our own. It is the cross! As we die to our own will, we begin to know the Spirit's divine power. We begin to live as true disciples of Jesus Christ, filled with his Spirit and sharing his love.

Discipleship and Theology

Chapter 3
Discipleship and Personal Holiness

Christopher T. Bounds, Chair of the Department of Christian Studies and Philosophy, Asbury University

Tribute

As a student at Asbury College, earnestly seeking the experience of entire sanctification, I heard from my college mentors that Al Coppedge was "the person" at Asbury Theological Seminary I needed to know. I was not disappointed.

When I started Asbury Theological Seminary, I intentionally took Al for all my basic theology courses and joined a Barnabas group. Al made systematic theology come alive for me. With logical precision, he helped me see the profound coherence of Christian faith, inflaming my mind. More importantly, he fueled my heart through the profound love of God radiating from his life and lectures. He modeled for me how Christian theology can bring head and heart together in the love and awe of God. In my Barnabas group, I learned spiritual discipline, having the classical Wesleyan means of grace habituated into my life. I saw in Al the disciplined Christian life I so desired for my erratic and disordered spiritual practices.

However, while Al helped shape the direction of my life, planting the seed of doing a Ph.D. in systematic theology, and establishing spiritual disciplines in my life, it was his clear, winsome, and wise teaching on entire sanctification that influenced me most. I came to the seminary thirsting for entire sanctification. To my great disappointment, few of my professors ever addressed the subject; if they did, they talked about it as an experience late in Christian life. My zeal to experience this work of grace in college began to wane in seminary. Thankfully, Al frequently discussed it and challenged his students to experience it now in life, rather than later. Al's exhortations kept the fire burning and led to my own experience of sanctification my last year of seminary.

As the years have passed since my seminary days, Al has continued to play a significant role in my life, opening doors for me in ministry, teaching and scholarship. He has always been a source of godly encouragement and support. I am deeply honored to have this opportunity to contribute my chapter to this volume. Thank you for the many ways you have shaped my life in Christ.

Essay

"Holiness unto the Lord" is a phrase deeply rooted in the American Wesleyan tradition. This phrase not only states what God requires of us, but it also points to a beautiful possibility and hope in the present life – God can make us holy.

As Christians, we recognize that the deepest longing of the human heart is to be fully devoted to God. Within each of us is the desire to love God without reservation, to live in faithful obedience to Him, and to give ourselves in love and service to other people, just as Christ did. This is the human yearning for holiness.

Every Christian knows this longing. It wells up inside of us at different times and in various ways. It comes to us in quiet moments of personal devotion or public worship when our soul experiences God's holy presence. It arises in moments of frustration when our best intentions to follow Christ falter and we fail God once again. It comes to us in moments of weariness from the unresolved conflict between our sinful impulses and the desire to follow God's will. It arises in moments when we serve others but recognize that our service is motivated by selfish ambitions. As we go through life, there are inevitable moments in which our heart's cry for holiness clearly comes to the fore.

This longing should not come as any surprise to us. In explaining the two greatest commandments and the summation of Old Testament law, Jesus taught that we are created by God to love God with all of our being and to love our neighbor as ourselves. Holiness is "nothing more and nothing less" than the fulfillment of Jesus' teaching here. Because we are made in the image and likeness of God, even though marred by sin, by God's grace we are capable of reflecting divine love and walking in the righteousness of love.

As Christians, therefore, we find ourselves in a frustrating predicament. One part of us longs to give ourselves completely to God and others in love while another part, propelled by the natural inclination of our heart, seeks our own selfish ends. As such, we find that we do not have the internal power and resources to follow Christ fully. No amount of human willpower can bring about the love for which we are made. We may desire to truly be Christians, but we do not have the power to live the life to which we are called.

At this point, a question arises. Is there something God can do in our present lives to liberate the holiest longings of our heart? Is there grace available through the life, death, resurrection, and exaltation of Jesus Christ and the outpouring of the Holy Spirit that can heal the distorted conditions of our lives? Is it possible for God to replace our "bent toward sinning" with a propensity to love God and neighbor, empowering us to walk in the righteousness of love? The good news of Jesus Christ and the message of the Wesleyan tradition is that God can set us free to love and walk as faithful disciples of Jesus Christ.

In what follows, I want to explore the beauty and hope of holiness in this life as understood in our Wesleyan tradition. To do so, I will first examine what "Holiness unto the Lord" is and how Christians experience this work of grace from the larger context of the Wesleyan tradition. My purpose here is to help us see the similar yet nuanced ways the Wesleyan message of holiness is taught practically and theologically in our larger tradition. Second, I will identify the core beliefs of Wesleyan thought on holiness, essential to the understanding and experience of entire sanctification, which is the centerpiece of Wesleyan teaching on personal holiness. Finally, I will explore the Wesleyan approach to discipleship and its role in the experience of holiness.

Wesleyan Teaching on Experience of Personal Holiness

Theologically, personal holiness is couched in the language of sanctification. Expressed in the most general terms, sanctification addresses the Holy Spirit's entire work of transformation in our lives from the moment we are born again until we experience glorification in death. The ultimate end of the Spirit's work is to restore the full image of God in us, making us like Christ.

When the Spirit takes residence in our lives, He begins the process of transforming our attitudes, interests, and actions, while confronting us with an internal principle of selfishness and sin, persisting stubbornly in us. This is "initial" and "progressive" sanctification. While it may be described in different ways, Wesleyans believe the Spirit can (1) conquer this principle or deliver us from this principle, (2) thereby enabling us to love God with our whole heart and our neighbor as ourselves and (3) making possible our complete obedience to God's revealed will.[1] Over the course of Church history this work of the Spirit has been called "Christian perfection," "perfect love," "baptism of the Holy Spirit," "entire sanctification," and "fullness of the Spirit." However, the work of sanctification does not end here. Over time, as we continue to submit to the Spirit, our love deepens and our knowledge and understanding of God's will increases, thereby bringing us into greater conformity with Christ until we reach "final sanctification" in glorification at death.

While every Wesleyan tradition has a basic schema of initial, progressive, and entire sanctification, there are differences in the way they nuance their definitions of entire sanctification and in their teaching on how a person experiences it. These differences are rooted primarily in how high a view of entire sanctification they

1. There have been a number of ways the deliverance from inward sin is described in the Wesleyan tradition. Some have described it as an "eradication of the sin nature," "a cleansing from inward sin," "freedom from all inward rebellion," "the full restoration of the moral image of God," "the removal of the principle of sin," etc. Regardless of how it has been described, the Wesleyan tradition has taught that Christians can be freed from the inner propensity to sin, the drive to assert personal will and desire against God's will. As such, the Christian can be freed from the constant struggle between "the flesh" and "the Spirit," where the basic orientation of the Christian's life is obedience to and love of God.

have—how high they set the bar—as well as their understanding of how God's grace works to bring about entire sanctification. In what follows, I will outline the three primary positions in the larger Wesleyan tradition, as well as a fourth position that has often been taught in our tradition but never formally stated in Wesleyan denominations. With these four positions, I will attempt to sketch a spectrum of understanding, beginning with the most optimistic and concluding with the most pessimistic.

"The Shorter Way": Now by Total Consecration and Faith

The most optimistic view on holiness teaches that Christians can experience entire sanctification now, in the present moment, through an act of entire consecration and faith, whereby believers surrender their lives to the lordship of Christ and trust God to purify and empower them. Entire sanctification is a simple synergism in which the Christian's work of consecration and faith is met immediately by the Holy Spirit's work of deliverance from the inner propensity to sin and empowerment to walk obediently in the love of God and neighbor.

What makes this position unique in the larger Wesleyan tradition is its understanding of the ability Christians have to consecrate themselves and exercise faith. Every believer has an inherent power, either as a gift of prevenient grace, regenerating grace, or as an uncorrupted part of free will, to do the human work required in entire sanctification.[2] From the moment of conversion, any Christian can appropriate entire sanctification. Because the Holy Spirit is always ready to respond to a personal act of consecration and faith, only ignorance on the part of a believer, an unwillingness to surrender fully to the Lord, or a lack of will to believe become the root causes for not experiencing entire sanctification. Believers, therefore, can determine the moment they are entirely sanctified.

As such, this teaching makes a distinction between entire sanctification and Christian maturity. It is possible for a person to be freed from inward and outward sin, perfected in love, and empowered for ministry, but not have the knowledge, wisdom, and experience necessary for Christian maturity, resulting in sins of ignorance. Yet a Christian cannot become fully mature without the experience of entire sanctification. A believer can know what to do in a given situation, but not have the power or proper motivation to execute it in a way fitting with spiritual maturity.

Traditionally, this view has been termed the "shorter way" for its emphasis on the immediacy of the experience of entire sanctification, not having to wait any

2. Charles Finney is an example of a holiness evangelist in the nineteenth century who denied original sin and taught that this power to exercise faith is naturally inherent in each person apart from grace.

significant length of time to experience after conversion. Primarily associated with the teaching of Phoebe Palmer and the American holiness movement, this position can be seen in Keith Drury's Holiness for Ordinary People and in Allan Brown's "How to Be Entirely Sanctified," and is the position expressed in the Articles of Religion of The Wesleyan Church and the Church of the Nazarene.[3]

"The Middle Way": Seeking Until You Receive

The next view on holiness in the Wesleyan tradition affirms that entire sanctification takes place in a Christian's life through personal consecration and faith. It also makes a distinction between Christian maturity and holiness. However, unlike the "shorter way," it does not believe that faith necessary to appropriate entire sanctification is a power inherent at any given moment in a believer's life. Rather, sanctifying faith is a gift of grace, a grace with which a Christian can choose to cooperate or not. The grace capable of creating this faith often requires more grace than is made available at conversion.

John Wesley's teaching on levels or degrees of grace and faith is at the heart of this teaching. Wesley taught that a person is fully dependent on God's grace for the work of salvation, even for saving faith. At each stage or level of progression in the way of salvation, more grace is needed to move forward. For example, Wesley taught that prevenient grace given to every person enables a person to respond to grace, but this prevenient grace does not give a person the power to exercise faith to appropriate the new birth. To prevenient grace given to all, more grace has to be added to create the possibility of saving faith. This grace comes through the various means of grace, most notably through the preaching of the gospel, but also through other "instituted" and "prudential" means, such as prayer, Bible reading, fasting, and Holy Communion. Through participation in the means of grace, grace capable of creating saving faith can be communicated, with which a person can choose to cooperate or not. In the same way, to the grace made available at conversion, more grace must be given in order to make possible the creation of faith necessary to appropriate entire sanctification.

From this perspective, Christians actively seek entire sanctification, availing themselves of the various means of grace and waiting for God's grace capable of creating faith to appropriate it. Thus, a person cannot experience entire sanctifica-

3. Keith Drury, *Holiness for Ordinary People* (Indianapolis, IN: Wesleyan Publishing House, 1983; reprint 1994), 71-88; Allan P. Brown, "How to be Entirely Sanctified: Four Easy Steps for Christians," *God's Revivalist and Bible Advocate* 124, no. 6 (September, 2012), 1-4; and "Article of Religion VIII: Personal Choice" in *The Discipline of the Wesleyan Church 2000* (Indianapolis, IN: Wesleyan Publishing House), ¶ 224. A close reading of this article indicates that the prevenient grace given to all of humanity empowers a person to exercise saving faith, needing no additional grace, making possible the exercise of faith for salvation an inherent power within an individual. If this is true for conversion, it would appear to be true for entire sanctification as well.

tion at any given moment, but only in those times and places in which God's grace creates such faith. For example, while Wesley describes faith that sanctifies entirely as a trust that "God hath promised it in the Holy Scripture," that "God is able to perform" it, that "He is able and willing to do it now," and "that He doeth it," he makes clear that it is a "a divine evidence and conviction"—it is a faith that God creates and enables through the means of grace.[4] Entire sanctification ultimately happens when God makes possible grace to experience entire sanctification. God's timing plays a central role in personal holiness. Because grace is the "unmerited work" of the sovereign God, he decides how he works in any given moment.

Among the various Wesleyan models, this teaching may be called the "middle way," navigating between the simplicity of the "shorter way" and the arduous nature of the "longer way," addressed in the next position. The "middle way" is seen in Steve DeNeff's *Whatever Became of Holiness?*, J. Kenneth Grider's *A Wesleyan-Holiness Theology*, in some of John Wesley's more optimistic pieces like "The Scripture Way of Salvation," and also can be argued as a possible interpretation of *The Wesleyan Church's Articles of Religion*.[5]

In the history of the Wesleyan tradition, the "middle way" is often the default position for Christians holding to the "shorter way." When the "shorter way" has not immediately brought about entire sanctification in people's lives, the "middle way" position guides practical counsel. For example, when people have consecrated themselves fully to Christ and they have done all they know to do to appropriate entire sanctification and it still remains unrealized, they are counseled often by Christians in the "shorter way" to keep seeking this experience earnestly until God brings it to them. Consciously or unconsciously, there is the recognition of the role of God's timing in this experience. This is seen clearly in Keith Drury's book *Holiness for Ordinary People* where he articulates the "shorter way," but in his practical instruction for "seekers" of entire sanctification advises them to keep seeking it in the various "means of grace" until God brings it.[6]

"The Longer Way": A Long Process of Growth

In contrast to the previous two positions, the third Wesleyan position on personal

---

4. John Wesley, "The Scripture Way of Salvation," *The Works of John Wesley*, VI: 43-54.

5. Steve DeNeff, *Whatever Became of Holiness?* (Indianapolis, IN: Wesleyan Publishing House, 1996), 125-137; J. Kenneth Grider, *A Wesleyan-Holiness Theology* (Kansas City, MO: Beacon Hill Press, 1994), 367-468; "Article of Religion XIV: Sanctification: Initial, Progressive, Entire" in *The Discipline of the Wesleyan Church 2000*, ¶ 238. A close reading of this article affirms a progressive sanctification leading to the experience of entire sanctification. Progressive sanctification is described as a daily growing in grace. While not explicitly stated, this growing in grace may indicate the need for more grace to be added to the grace given in conversion in order for a believer to fully surrender to Christ and exercise faith to appropriate entire sanctification, pointing to the "middle way."

6. Keith Drury, *Holiness for Ordinary People* (Indianapolis, IN: Wesleyan Publishing House, 1983; reprint 1994), 114-125.

holiness emphasizes that entire sanctification happens most often in a Christian's life after a long journey of dying to self, following many years of spiritual development. There are Christians who will realize entire sanctification in the present life, but most will not experience it until just before death or at the point of death. A belief in the persistence and stubbornness of original sin forms the heart of the doctrine, a recalcitrance overcome only gradually through significant growth in grace, personal denial, and spiritual development.

The analogy of a slow death is one of the most well known descriptions of this view, an analogy emphasizing the complementary nature of process with an instantaneous moment. In a slow death, there is a long process leading to the point of death, often a painful and arduous one. Nevertheless, there is a point in which a person dies. While this view does not deny the possibility of a short process and early death, or the exercise of personal faith in appropriating entire sanctification, its focus is on the long progression. While the moment in which a Christian dies completely to self is always the goal in the present life, the process leading to the goal is preeminent.

Furthermore, while there are exceptions, many who adhere to this doctrine of holiness equate entire sanctification with Christian maturity or closely link them. This is in contrast to the teaching of the "shorter" and "middle" ways. John Wesley's high view of Christian perfection comes to the fore, a perfection in which a believer has "the mind of Christ" in speech, saying what Christ would say, and in action, doing what Christ would do.[7] Furthermore, the fruit of the Holy Spirit is always being fully manifested the Christian life, so that the believer is always joyful, always giving thanks, always loving to the fullest extent possible. The movement toward this state of perfection generally occurs by gradual growth in grace, wisdom, knowledge, experience, and the practice of spiritual disciplines. As such, entire sanctification is not really a possibility for new converts, but only for those who have diligently followed Christ for many years. Entire sanctification is ultimate spiritual maturity.

In the Wesleyan tradition this view has been called the "longer way," because of its focus on an extended process in the realization of entire sanctification. Wesleyans who subscribe to the "longer way" include Thomas Oden in *Life in the Spirit:*, Randy Maddox in *Responsible Grace*, and John Wesley in his more pessimistic

---

7. John Wesley, "The Character of a Methodist," *The Works of John Wesley*, VIII: 341-344. If a Wesleyan holds to this as a definition of entire sanctification, the person must realize that this goes beyond the common understanding of entire sanctification as defined in our paper. It must also be noted that Wesley at times defines Christian perfection in ways that encompass Christian maturity and at other times in ways that do not.

writings, such as "Brief Thoughts on Christian Perfection."[8] This is the dominant understanding of entire sanctification in the Wesleyan tradition today.

The Keswick Way - Sanctification from Willful Sin with Momentary Lapses

Standing close to but falling outside the Wesleyan tradition, Keswick teaching asserts that a Christian can be free from intentional sin, living a life of obedience to God, but will never be completely free from original sin in the present life. The Christian will persistently struggle with an inner attitude of rebellion, selfishness and pride. This is more than external temptation, but an internal bent to sinning that persists throughout mortal life. Believers can live above the sin nature, but cannot be free from it; they can be victorious over sin in any given temptation, but will continue to live with an internal struggle until glorification in death.

The Keswick perspective often teaches that intentional sin is an exception rather than a norm of Christian life. It embraces the Johannine teaching, "those who are born of God will not continue to sin, because God's seed remains in them; they cannot go on sinning, because they have been born of God," while realizing that "if anybody does sin, we have one who speaks to the Father in our defense – Jesus Christ, the Righteous One."[9] While a believer will have strongholds of sin broken and patterns of sin ended, because of ongoing internal conflict, the possibility of willful sin and the probability of occasional sins remain.

Some forms of Keswick doctrine teach that victory over intentional sin happens in conversion, while most forms emphasize a "second work of grace" experience. For those traditions that describe an experience subsequent to salvation, terms like "the higher Christian life," "the deeper Christian life," or "the Spirit-filled life" become ways to talk about the life of holiness.

Contemporary Christian leaders who hold this view include Bill Bright, Ian Thomas, and John Stott. The most prominent example of Keswick teaching on holiness is Campus Crusade for Christ's tract "Have You Made the Wonderful Discovery of the Spirit-Filled Life," which is the subsequent tract to "Have You

8. Thomas C. Oden, *Life in the Spirit* (Systematic Theology, Vol. 3) (San Francisco: Harper-Collins Publishers, Reprint Edition, 1994), 226-257; Randy Maddox, *Responsible Grace: John Wesley's Practical Theology* (Nashville, TN: Kingswood Books - An Imprint of Abingdon Press, 1994), 176-190, 201-215; and John Wesley, "Brief Thoughts on Christian Perfection," *The Works of John Wesley*, XI: 446. In these thoughts, Wesley states, "As to the time, I believe this instant generally is the instant of death, the moment before the soul leaves the body. But I believe it may be ten, twenty, or forty years before. I believe it is usually many years after justification; but that it may be within five years or five months after it, I know no conclusive argument to the contrary."

9. I John 3:9 and I John 2:1 (TNIV).

Heard of the Four Spiritual Laws."[10]

In many ways the Keswick position resembles Wesleyan teaching, except for its view on the intractability of original sin. In the nineteenth and twentieth centuries, there was significant interaction and cross-pollination between Wesleyans and Keswicks. Both traditions were intimately involved in the American holiness movement. Therefore, while the Keswick view is not an official view held by Wesleyan denominations, its teaching on holiness continues to exist among Wesleyan preachers and laity.

Wesleyan Core Beliefs: Personal Holiness as Taught and Experienced

Through my cursory survey, we see the major Wesleyan traditions on sanctification. Each position, in its own way, takes the work of personal holiness seriously. The Wesleyan tradition manifests itself historically in the "shorter," "middle," and "longer" ways, while flirting at times with Keswick teaching. Denominations claiming to be heirs to John Wesley express their doctrines of entire sanctification in one or more of these ways.[11]

At this point I want to clarify Wesleyan teaching on personal holiness by identifying five core teachings that not only describe "Holiness unto the Lord," but also give guidance to its experience in present life. These ideas express common ground between the positions.

1. Wesleyans Believe in Redemption from Inward and Outward Sin in the Present Life: Perfect Love

Wesleyans believe in personal redemption from inward and outward sin in the present life. One of the clear distinctives common to the three Wesleyan traditions, setting them apart from other evangelical teachings, is the depth in which sin is addressed. Not only do Wesleyans believe Christians can be liberated from intentional sin, being empowered to live lives of obedience to Christ, but they also teach that through the work of the Holy Spirit believers can be set free from the inner

10. Robert McQuilkin, "The Keswick View of Sanctification," *Five Views of Sanctification*, ed. Melvin Dieter (Grand Rapids, MI: Zondervan,, 1987); "Have You Made the Wonderful Discovery of the Spirit-filled Life" at http://www.greatcom.org/spirit/english/; Major W. Ian Thomas, *The Saving Life of Christ and the Mystery of Godliness* (Grand Rapids, MI: Zondervan, reprint 1987); John Stott, *Baptism and Fullness: The Work of the Holy Spirit Today* (Downers Grove, IL: Intervarsity Press, second edition , 1976).

11. The United Methodist Church's Confession of Faith, Article XI "Sanctification and Christian Perfection" in *The Book of Discipline of The United Methodist Church 2004* (Nashville, TN: Abingdon Press, 2004) is ambiguous enough to allow all three Wesleyan-Arminian interpretations of entire sanctification. This confession of faith comes to The United Methodist Church through her merger with The Evangelical United Brethren Church in 1968.

propensity to rebellion, selfishness, and pride and have their hearts oriented in love to God. As such, the Wesleyan teaching on sanctification goes beyond a simple affirmation of deliverance from intentional sin.

There have been a number of expressions used by Wesleyans to describe the inward freedom from the power of original sin. Negatively, "eradication of the sin nature," "overcoming the sin principle," "cleansing from original sin," and "deliverance from inward rebellion" have been some of the popular ways this work of sanctification has been described. Positively, "baptism of the Holy Spirit," "infilling of the Spirit," "perfect love," "full salvation," and "second blessing" have been some of the descriptions used to define this work of sanctification. Regardless of language used, all convey a redemption from that part of human existence that sets itself up against the rule of the Holy Spirit in the Christian life, a liberation from the "old man" that cries out "I won't" and/or "I can't" to the call of discipleship.[12]

However, the end of entire sanctification is not freedom from known sin. Sometimes the Wesleyan tradition has been so focused on being free from sin, it believes this is the end of sanctification. The end of entire sanctification, however, is love. The ultimate purpose of inward sanctification is "perfect love," a love of God with all "heart, soul, mind, and strength" and the "love of neighbor as self," fulfilling the two greatest commandments. The inward sanctifying work of the Spirit removes the spiritual obstacles to the heart's orientation of love for God and neighbor. Although the Wesleyan tradition has called this "perfect love," it does not denote a static state but rather a dynamic reality, deepening and maturing over time, never reaching an end in development in present or future life.

2. Wesleyans Believe in Grace and the Means of Grace

The Wesleyan understanding of holiness emphasizes grace as the basis for sanctification and articulates clearly the means of grace. Entire sanctification is a gift of grace. It is not something we can generate, produce, or bring about in ourselves. It is God's work. All three Wesleyan views in various ways presume the total dependency of humanity upon God's grace in salvation. If restoration of the image and likeness of God in human beings is going to take place, God must take the initiative and do the work through grace. In articulating prevenient, convicting, justifying, regenerating, and sanctifying grace, all three positions explicitly teach or imply an order of salvation in which growth in grace or the communication of more grace must take place to progress in the way of salvation. To the grace given in prevenient

---

12. Until we have a clearer understanding of what essentially the sin "nature" is, we can use a variety of expressions to describe our redemption from it. For example, the sin "nature" has been defined at times as a physical or spiritual substance attaching itself to the soul or body, sometimes as the absence of the reign of the Holy Spirit in human life, and other times as the corruption of the image of God in humanity, etc.

grace, more grace must be given in order to be saved; once regenerated, more grace must be given to progress in sanctification; once progressing in sanctification, more grace must be given to experience entire sanctification; once entirely sanctified, more grace must be given to continue the work of renewal in the image and likeness of God.

If humanity is completely dependent upon God's grace for salvation and sanctification, the question must be raised, "How does God communicate or channel saving and sanctifying grace to human lives?" The Protestant tradition has emphasized the marks of the Church – the preaching of the pure word of God, the due administration of the sacraments, and the community rightly ordered – as the divinely-appointed means. Through communication of the Gospel, participation in the sacraments, and being a part of the Body of Christ through a local congregation, Protestants traditionally believe that God imparts grace that seeks to bring conviction of sin and faith to unbelievers, confirm new Christians in discipleship, and transform them progressively into the likeness of Christ. People cannot be spiritually regenerated, be converted, or grow in sanctification apart from these means.

John Wesley explicitly reiterated the Protestant marks as the means of grace and made them requirements for Methodists, as well as recognizing other means of grace such as "works of mercy."[13] Through these means, Wesley believed and observed that grace capable of saving and sanctifying a person occurs. The Holiness movement in the nineteenth century, while not explicit in its understanding of the means of grace, began to see that through camp meeting preaching, "Tuesday Morning Meetings for the Promotion of Holiness," Christian literature, intercessory prayer, and the practice of Christian disciplines like fasting and Bible study, people experienced repentance, faith, conversion, and sanctification.[14] These became venues, means of grace, through which God works to transform human lives. For example, The Wesleyan Church in her Articles of Religion does not formally express an understanding of the means of grace apart from baptism and Holy

---

13. John Wesley, "Minutes of Several Conversations," *The Works of John Wesley,* VIII: 322-24. Among the instituted means of grace, Wesley lists prayer, reading the Scriptures, Holy Communion, fasting, and Christian conferencing. Among the prudential means of grace, which consisted of rules for ordering the Christian life, Wesley lists his famous instructions of "doing no harm," "doing good," and "attending all the ordinances of God."

14. Unfortunately, the danger in emphasizing the means of grace is that they become an "end" in themselves and not a "means." Also, John Wesley, as the Protestant tradition in distinction from Roman Catholic, did not believe that grace is automatically communicated through the means of grace. In regard to the means of grace another issue worth exploring is whether or not God ordains for "a season" a particular method of evangelism or discipleship as a means of imparting saving and sanctifying grace, such as the altar call in the nineteenth and twentieth centuries. A similar issue is whether or not God ordains a particular place and time as a means of imparting saving and sanctifying grace, such as historic revivals like Cane Ridge, Kentucky, and the Great Awakenings in American history. If so, what might God use in the twenty-first century? When and where?

Communion, yet through her membership standards requires members to participate in many of the historic Wesleyan/Methodist/Protestant means of grace.[15]

From a Wesleyan perspective, participating in the means of grace is essential because of a person's complete dependency upon grace to bring about spiritual transformation in attitudes, interests, and actions. Although the means by which God communicates grace is not always clear in different Wesleyan traditions, they each affirm an order of salvation that teaches that to the grace given in any moment, more grace is necessary to progress in the way of salvation. This grace primarily occurs through the means of grace.

3. Wesleyans Believe in Entire Consecration and Faith

The Wesleyan doctrine on sanctification believes in personal consecration and faith as the means of appropriating entire sanctification. While there may be differences in the three Wesleyan positions understanding on the place of consecration in the order of salvation and how grace works to make faith possible, they each affirm the necessity of both actions for the experience of entire sanctification.

For example, differences exist regarding personal consecration in the teaching of John Wesley, who represents the "middle" and "longer" positions, and Phoebe Palmer, who represents the "shorter" view. Wesley assumed entire consecration on the part of Christians at or before the experience of conversion. It would be difficult for Wesley to conceive of individuals being born again apart from full consecration. Palmer, on the other hand, saw entire consecration as an act of a believer subsequent to conversion and an essential element in appropriating entire sanctification. Yet, while there are differences between their teachings, each one has as a prerequisite the necessity of a person's full surrender to Christ in the experience of entire sanctification. If a person is going to be entirely sanctified, then entire consecration, full surrender, must take place.

At this point, it is helpful to clarify that while entire consecration is essential to the realization of entire sanctification, it is not the equivalent of it. A truly Wesleyan view affirms that it is possible for a Christian to be entirely consecrated to the Lord and not entirely sanctified. A believer must still exercise faith in order to appropriate entire sanctification. However, a believer cannot experience entire sanctification without full surrender to Christ.

Again, the differences in the understanding of faith and the work of grace in the creation of faith for entire sanctification exist in each Wesleyan tradition. The

---

15. "Article of Religion XVII: Sacraments: Baptism and the Lord's Supper" in *The Discipline of the Wesleyan Church 2000*, ¶ 242; In reading the Articles of Religion, while grace is presumed to be the basis for the way of salvation, the means of grace are never articulated formally beyond baptism and holy communion, ¶¶ 210-250. However, many of the traditionally recognized means of grace are specified in the Covenant Membership Commitments, ¶¶ 260-286.

"shorter way" sees faith as inherent in every Christian either as a gift of prevenient grace or regenerating grace. From the moment of conversion, it is within the power of any believer to do the human work required to exercise faith to appropriate entire sanctification. The "middle way" does not believe that faith necessary to appropriate entire sanctification is a power inherent at any moment in a believer's life. Rather, faith is a gift of grace given as God determines with which a Christian can choose to cooperate or not. The grace capable of creating this faith requires more grace than is made available at conversion. The "longer way," much like the "middle way," teaches that faith necessary to appropriate entire sanctification is a gift of grace given subsequent to regeneration, although generally only after a long process of growing in grace. While recognizing their respective understandings of faith, however, all three Wesleyan positions emphasize that entire sanctification does not happen apart from faith.[16] If a person is going to experience entire sanctification, the exercise of sanctifying faith is necessary.

In the history of Christianity, God has used all three views to bring Christians into personal holiness. In God's providential care, he has used the "shorter," "middle," and "longer" ways to move people toward entire sanctification. However, with this said, one of the chief contributions of the holiness movement and the historic position of Asbury Theological Seminary and Dr. Allan Coppedge is the strong belief that entire sanctification should be experienced sooner rather than much later in life. A Christian does not have to wait a lifetime to "grow into" personal holiness.

4. Wesleyans Believe in Assurance of Entire Sanctification

The Wesleyan understanding of holiness provides a basis for verifying the personal experience of entire sanctification. Sometimes in the Wesleyan tradition there have been attempts to declare Christians entirely sanctified too hastily, either as a result of a deficient view of entire sanctification or as an attempt to strengthen faith in entire sanctification. For example, if a Wesleyan sees entire sanctification as simply entire consecration, then the Wesleyan may ask if a Christian is fully surrendered to Christ and assume entire sanctification if there is a testimony to such personal consecration. A person may be fully surrendered, however, and not have faith to appropriate entire sanctification. In another example, if a believer goes to the altar

16. Presently, these issues of grace, faith, the means of grace, and their interrelationship have not been fully developed in The Wesleyan Church. Without more attention to these areas, the possibility of losing the Wesleyan distinctives on sanctification remains a threat, at least on a practical level. These are the key issues in pastorally guiding people who are earnestly seeking entire sanctification and not experiencing it. Without a clearer theological view on these areas, the threat for pastors is to reduce entire sanctification to entire consecration or to see it simply as freedom from willful sin or to cause people to abandon the doctrine and its possibility altogether because they cannot provide adequate counsel for earnest seekers who have not experienced it.

seeking entire sanctification, the person may be instructed to testify to this work of grace as a way to strengthen faith. In subsequent days, however, the Christian may realize that entire sanctification has not happened.

At their best, each of the Wesleyan traditions has emphasized both a subjective and an objective process for personal examination to see if entire sanctification has occurred. These traditions all have roots in John Wesley, who provided practical advice for the discernment and verification of entire sanctification.[17] The objective process is a personal examination by Christians of their hearts and motives. Steve DeNeff, in an update to Wesley's questions, gives us examples of this inquiry: Is my conscience clear? Is my religion an obsession or a hobby? Do the people closest to me see this holiness in my life? Do I have power over sin? Do I have perfect love? Do I have genuine joy?[18] This objective inquiry is found in questions posed by Keith Drury: Have I made a total consecration to Christ? Do I have power over willful sin? Have I experienced a distinct increase in love for others? Is obedience the central focus of my life? If Christians cannot honestly answer these questions positively, most likely entire sanctification has not happened.[19]

To the objective witness, there is the subjective witness of the Holy Spirit. In this form of verification, the Holy Spirit testifies to the believer's heart that entire sanctification has happened. So, a Christian may ask, "Do I have the witness of the Holy Spirit that entire sanctification has been wrought in my life?" Just as a believer can have "an inward impression upon the soul" that she is a child of God, she can also have a similar witness in the experience of entire sanctification. However, it is possible for Christians to have entire sanctification and not have the internal witness of the Spirit.

Thus, through this objective and subjective process, Wesleyans can help Christian seekers prayerfully discern whether entire sanctification has happened in their lives and assist them as they grow in the way of holiness.

5. Wesleyans Believe in Continued Temptation and Infirmity, Continued Dependence upon Christ

Once a person experiences entire sanctification, Wesleyans affirm that there is never a state in present life where Christians are immune from temptation, are without need for the continual grace of Christ and the means of grace, or are ever completely free from sins of infirmities. The Wesleyan tradition has argued consistently that there is no state of sanctification or depth of holiness in present life that makes a believer immune from temptation. Wesleyans hold that the ongoing

---

17. John Wesley, "Further Thoughts on Christian Perfection," *The Works of John Wesley*, XI: 414-427.

18. Steve DeNeff, *Whatever Became of Holiness?*, 141-150.

19. Keith Drury, *Holiness for Ordinary People*, 89-95.

struggle between the Spirit and "the flesh" can be broken in entire sanctification, but that does not mean that such believers are without any occasion for struggle. Being free from the nature of sin does not mean there is no occasion for temptation or the possibility of falling into sin.

Throughout life, believers are continually dependent upon God's grace for maintaining and walking in entire sanctification. John Wesley compared this unceasing reliance to a vine connected to a branch. As long as the vine has connection to the branch, the nourishing sap flows into the vine. If the vine is severed from the branch, it withers and dies. In the same way, a Christian must be linked continually to Christ, continually dependent upon Christ for the grace necessary to walk in inward and outward holiness. Ongoing grace is necessary to believers and, as such, Christians must avail themselves of the means of grace.[20]

Closely connected to these points is the idea of sins of infirmity. While Wesleyans believe in liberation from intentional sin and original sin, they also believe that Christians cannot be free from mistakes in judgment, from clouded understanding, or from ignorance. As Wesley taught, even when God restores the moral image in entire sanctification, the natural and political images remain marred until glorification. Thus, while Christians can have the right motivation behind their actions, the impetus of love, and the empowerment to do God's will, the perfect fulfillment of action is impaired because understanding, judgment, and knowledge are impaired. Entirely sanctified believers continue to fall short of God's perfection and need Christ's atoning work to apply to their infirmities, and they need forgiveness for wrongs committed against God and others due to the impaired moral and natural image.[21] As such, there is the need for Wesleyans to pray the Lord's prayer daily, and when they have offended another person, unintentional or not, they need to go and seek forgiveness and reconciliation.

Wesleyan Discipleship and Personal Holiness

While some latitude of expression exists in the Wesleyan tradition, there is an identifiable core of beliefs defining the Wesleyan tradition on sanctification. It has a clear understanding of what "Holiness unto the Lord" entails in present life through the work of the Holy Spirit: a Christian's liberation from intentional sin, making possible a life of obedience to Christ and a freedom from an inner propensity of rebellion, selfishness, and pride, orienting the heart to God and others in "perfect love." This work happens through personal surrender to the lordship of Christ and the exercise of faith in Christ to sanctify. Consecration and sanctifying faith are a gift of God's grace and necessitate active participation in the means of grace. Once

---

20. John Wesley, "Plain Account of Christian Perfection," *The Works of John Wesley*, XI: 443.

21. John Wesley, "Christian Perfection," *The Works of John Wesley*, VI: 1-22; see also his sermon, "On Perfection," *The Works of John Wesley*, VI: 411-424.

entirely sanctified, the Wesleyan tradition believes Christians can know they have experienced personal holiness through the witness of the Spirit. Finally, it recognizes there is no depth of sanctification in present life that sets Christians free from temptation, makes them independent of God's sustaining grace, or frees them entirely from sins of infirmity.

In this last section, I want to explore the role discipleship plays in the experience of entire sanctification. At the end of his life in an expression of mature thought, John Wesley wrote a sermon entitled "Causes for the Inefficacy of Christianity." He asks, "Why has Christianity done so little good in the world? Is it not the balm which the great Physician has given to men, to restore their spiritual health?" Wesley answers by identifying the primary reasons inhibiting the Gospel from having maximum impact in Christian lives: absence of sound doctrine, lack of accountable discipline, and the neglect of self-denial.

Wesley organized his whole method of discipleship in society, class and band meetings to address these three deficiencies in the church of his day. Education in holiness doctrine, disciplined participation in the means of grace, and the active practice of self-denial still mark discipleship in the Wesleyan tradition.

Wesleyan Discipleship and the Role of Doctrine in Personal Holiness

Wesley believed that Christianity is the cure for the sin-sick soul. However, its strength diminishes significantly if the Gospel's full teaching is unknown. He states, "I am bold to affirm, that those who bear the name of Christ are in general totally ignorant, both to the theory and practice of Christianity; so that they are 'perishing by thousands' for lack of knowledge and experience … of justification by faith, the new birth, inward and outward holiness."[22] Wesley makes clear that if holiness is not preached, if it is not communicated or taught, then it will not be experienced in human life. To refrain from teaching personal holiness in "theory and practice" is to withhold the "balm which the great Physician has given to men, to restore their spiritual health."[23]

Wesleyans believe sound Christian teaching on holiness is an essential means of God's grace by which Christians experience increasing degrees of sanctification. Therefore, central to discipleship is biblical, theological and practical grounding in personal holiness. Instruction through Bible study, theological training, personal testimonies, and wise counsel serves two primary purposes.

First, while belief in entire sanctification may seem simple enough "on the face of it," there is a deep and pervasive skepticism about it in the American Church. Even in traditional Wesleyan denominations, cynical attitudes about its possibility

---

22. John Wesley, "Causes for the Inefficacy of Christianity," *The Works of John Wesley*, VII: 281-290.

23. I am indebted to Dr. Keith Drury for his thorough reading of a preliminary draft of this paper that resulted in constructive comments integrated into the body of the paper.

persist. Even though evangelicalism talks about spiritual transformation in Christ, it places focus on justification and forgiveness of sins. Salvation becomes primarily a ticket to heaven.[24] When sanctification is taught, it is portrayed as a slow and gradual process in Christian life, with little emphasis or expectation of a sudden, decisive intervention of God that radically alters people's lives, much less setting them free from the power of sin and orienting their hearts in love of God and neighbor. Because of these reasons and others, holiness theology has "fallen on hard times," resulting in greater difficulty for people to believe that God sanctifies entirely in a decisive moment.

People therefore need an immersive teaching experience on personal holiness, not just an occasional discussion or reference to the topic in preaching or conversation. Discipleship in the Wesleyan tradition grounds Christians in the biblical foundations of holiness, its theological understanding, its historic witness in church history, and its experience in believers. As Christians seek the experience of entire sanctification, discipleship leaders provide discerning guidance as personal issues and questions arise. While it is tempting to see knowledge of personal holiness as a purely cognitive experience, the Spirit works through it to tear down the recalcitrance of the human heart to the love of God and neighbor and works to build faith to believe that Christ can truly sanctify human life.

Second, teaching in the context of discipleship empowers the Spirit's work of progressive sanctification beyond entire sanctification, enabling Christians to experience greater conformity to Christ. Even though they experience the restoration of the moral image of God through entire sanctification, the natural and political images remain marred in believers. Sanctified Christians therefore require greater wisdom, knowledge, and understanding about themselves, their relationships, and the will of God in life. Doctrinal teaching and personal mentoring through discipleship help expose the problem of "seeing through a glass" darkly. While entire sanctification prepares Christians to see themselves more clearly and disposes them to amend their lives accordingly, they require greater knowledge and light to reach spiritual maturity in life—greater conformity to Christlikeness.

Wesleyan Discipleship and the Role of Discipline in Personal Holiness

John Wesley believed that sound teaching was not enough to experience personal holiness in its fullness. In his second "cause to the inefficacy of Christianity" he writes, "I conceive, thus: It was a common saying among the Christians in the primitive Church, 'The soul and the body make a man; the spirit and discipline make a

24. Dallas Willard, *The Divine Conspiracy: Rediscovering Our Hidden Life in God* (San Francisco: HarperCollins Publishers, 1998), 1-60.

Christian;' implying, that none could be real Christians, without the help of Christian discipline. But if this be so, is it any wonder that we find so few Christians; for where is Christian discipline? . . . Now, whatever doctrine is preached, where there is not discipline, it cannot have its full effect upon the hearers."[25] Because every aspect of personal holiness is dependent upon God's grace, even human acts of repentance, consecration and faith, Christians must avail themselves of the means of grace in disciplined and accountable discipleship.

Central to the Wesleyan tradition of discipleship is personal accountability for active participation in the "means of grace." While different Wesleyan traditions categorize the means of grace differently, they generally recognize John Wesley's "Works of Mercy" and "Works of Piety," both of which have individual and communal practices. Works of Mercy include individual disciplines like "doing good works, visiting the sick, visiting those in prison, feeding the hungry, and giving generously to the needs of others" and corporate practices like "seeking justice, ending oppression and discrimination, and resolving the needs of the poor." Works of Piety consist of traditional spiritual disciplines like "meditating and studying the scriptures, reading Christian literature, prayer, fasting, and regular worship attendance" and corporate practices like participation in the sacraments, Christian conferencing, Bible study and discipleship groups.[26]

The Wesleyan tradition believes these are the primary ways God works to preserve Christians in their faith and sanctify them. The necessity of ongoing grace is non-negotiable in the Christian life. Saving faith needs the fortification of active grace and personal holiness cannot happen without sanctifying grace. In the accountability formed in the relationships of Wesleyan discipleship, believers experience an immersion in the means of grace.

More specifically, Wesleyan discipleship holds people accountable to seek entire sanctification in the means of grace. If entire sanctification does not happen in the moment believers initially ask for it or even after a season of prayer, they need to seek persistently this experience and the faith that appropriates it in the means of grace, looking for the Holy Spirit to work through them to bring personal holiness into their lives. They are not to grow weary until God brings it to them. While God is not limited to bringing entire sanctification only to those who persistently seek it, Christians most likely will miss this divine gift without such diligence and hunger.

What does it mean to seek entire sanctification persistently until God brings it? Concretely, what does this look like? Although hardly exhaustive, here is a sketch of some of the ways Christians in the Wesleyan tradition diligently seek for personal holiness in the means of grace. They regularly set aside specific time in their lives to fast and pray for the experience of entire sanctification. They find people who have experienced entire sanctification in their lives, listen to their testimonies and

---

25. John Wesley, "Causes for the Inefficacy of Christianity," *The Works of John Wesley*, VII: 285.
26. John Wesley, "Minutes of Several Conversations," *The Works of John Wesley*, VIII: 322-24.

counsel, and ask for their intercession. They read and study holiness literature and biographies of Christians who lived lives of complete surrender to God. They seek out other Christians who believe in entire sanctification to "lay hands" on them and pray for this work of grace to be done in their lives. As they participate in Holy Communion, they ask God to sanctify them. When pastors invite Christians to come to the altar for entire sanctification, they go forward to pray.

They take opportunity to serve others through their local church, particularly the least, the last, and the lost, asking God to perfect their hearts in love as they serve. As they worship and hear the Scriptures read and the Word of God proclaimed, they listen attentively for the still small voice of the Spirit to say to them, "Today is the day of your deliverance." When they hear about God moving in power in a particular church or in a particular place, as they are able, they go to seek the Lord there. Through actively seeking the experience of entire sanctification by faith in these and other means of grace, they position themselves to receive God's sanctifying work when God by His grace brings it.

In the American holiness tradition, this active seeking is described often as "tarrying in Jerusalem until the Spirit comes," as adhering to the exhortation "do not grow weary" in seeking the fullness of the Spirit, and as "praying through" until victory has come. If Christians persist in seeking entire sanctification by faith in the means of grace, God will come and give this gift. After the experience of entire sanctification, Wesleyans recognize that only divine grace sustains personal holiness and enables it to intensify and grow. This occurs through the means of grace. Wesleyan discipleship works to hold Christians accountable for seeking personal holiness in the means of grace.

Wesleyan Discipleship and the Role of Self-Denial in Personal Holiness

Finally, John Wesley in "Causes for the Inefficacy of Christianity" mentions one last requirement for the Gospel to have full effect: the practice of self-denial. He states, "Why has Christianity done so little good, even among us? among the Methodists, -- among them that hear and receive the whole Christian doctrine, and that have Christian discipline added thereto, in the most essential parts of it? Plainly, because we have forgot, or at least not duly attended to, those solemn words of our Lord, 'If any man will come after me, let him deny himself, and take up his cross daily, and follow me.'"[27]

Wesley recognized that participation in the spiritual disciplines of Works of Mercy and Works of Piety are not a guarantee of people receiving grace from them.

27. John Wesley, "Causes for the Inefficacy of Christianity," *The Works of John Wesley*, VII: 288.

It is possible to practice them out of rote habit, done with no or little heart.[28] Just as there is dead orthodoxy, there is dead orthopraxy. This is the reason "heart attitude" is essential to Wesleyan discipleship.[29] Wesley understood the practice of "self-denial" and "taking up the cross" to be a process of self-examination of one's attitudes and motivation. Questions for personal reflection included: "Do you steadily watch against the world? The devil? Yourselves? Your besetting sin? . . . Do you deny yourself every useless pleasure of sense? ... Wherein do you 'take up your cross daily'? Do you cheerfully 'bear your cross' (whatever is grievous to nature) as a gift of God, and labour to profit thereby? ... Do you endeavour to set God always before you? To see his eye continually fixed upon you?"[30]

Wesleyan discipleship in personal holiness always asks questions that require personal reflection of the heart. It moves beyond knowledge, beyond practice, and focuses on the deepest motivations and intentions of the Christian. This knowledge of self is essential in seeking entire sanctification, having the witness of the Spirit to it, sustaining it once received, and growing progressively after its realization. Because the human heart remains mutable, subject to growth and development, as well as corruption and brokenness in present life, regular assessment is essential for ongoing health in personal holiness and progressive sanctification until glorification. This heart examination is a means of divine grace helping to insure that knowledge of sanctification and the practice of spiritual disciplines leads to deepening, living, dynamic orthodoxy and orthopraxy of personal holiness.

Conclusion

"Holiness unto the Lord" not only states what God requires of us, but points to a beautiful hope in present life – God can make us holy. This is especially true for those who are confronted continually with their own depth of sin and grow exhausted with the ongoing internal war between "flesh" and "Spirit"; for those who yearn to be fully devoted followers of Jesus Christ, yet lack the inner resources to be so; and for those who long for the full manifestation of the fruit of the Spirit in their lives. The Wesleyan tradition bears witness uniformly that Christ through the power of the Spirit can liberate the holiest longings of the human heart. In their witness, Wesleyans provide a clear vision of personal holiness, the means by which it occurs in human life, and the role discipleship plays in its realization.

---

28. One of the best discussions of the role of self-denial in early Methodism and the role it plays in relationship to Works of Mercy and Works of Piety in the larger framework of Wesleyan discipleship is Andrew Thompson's "The General Means of Grace," in *Methodist History* 51:4 (July 2013), 249-57.

29. John Wesley, "Self-Denial," *The Works of John Wesley*, VI:103-13.

30. John Wesley, "Large minutes," in *The Methodist Societies: The Minutes of Conference*, ed. Henry Rack, vol. 10 of *The Bicentennial Edition of the Works of John Wesley* (Nashville: Abingdon Press, 1986), 924.

Chapter 4
Discipleship and Self-Giving Love

M. William Ury, National Ambassador for Holiness, Salvation Army

Making your souls his loved abode,
the temples of indwelling God[1]

Tribute

For over four decades Al Coppedge has been to me a sterling example of what Scriptural holiness produces in the heart of one open to all that God has for His own. His radical desire for God's best has formed his marriage and family, his scholarship, and his generational mentoring. I was privileged to learn what it meant to be a disciple of Jesus in a small-group which Al led. That experience and the faithful, personal investment – up to the present – of a passion to follow Jesus have formed the contours of my walk with my Lord. He taught me the theology of holiness in the classroom, from the pulpit, on road trips, in many "interesting" accommodations, and at the kitchen table. I watched him respond to various crises with grace and a humble willingness to be personally changed by the Holy Spirit, no matter the cost to himself.

Not a day goes by without acknowledging Al's selfless bestowal of love and encouragement in my life. His sharing the transformed and disciplined life with me has translated into my desire to offer my life as a faint image of Al's single, obedient focus on 'making disciples' which is the best synopsis of his entire life. He has unreservedly taken Jesus at His word and thus, across the world, there are men and women who can testify to holiness of heart and life as more than a mere experience. Al's counter-cultural insistence on the power of the sanctifying Spirit of God has translated into a practical spirituality. He taught me that the holy love of God is formed and maintained in a community of mutually accountable persons who will pay any price to yield themselves to the God who is Love. For one who is honored to call Al my brother, I bear grateful witness to his unrelenting desire for all of the Life of God in all of his life. Few will leave an influence for good as fruitful, nor as pleasing to God, as Allan Coppedge.

1. From Sermon 74, "On the Church." Cf. Charles Wesley, 'Groaning for the Spirit of Adoption', in John and Charles Wesley, Hymns and Sacred Poems (1740), p. 132 (Poet. Wks., I.308).

Essay

The pan-Wesleyan tradition, like all traditions,. has a theological predisposition. There is something vital to be communicated. The loss of that message undoes the reason for our existence. The belief that the Holy One of Israel, the Triune God, can come to dwell in the human heart in all of His intended glory is at the center of what salvation means to us. But we are also taken into the heart of God. If personal participation, by grace, in the divine nature is a fundamental orientation, then the biblical metaphors of marriage, family, fatherhood and motherhood are important to note and then incorporate *into a systematic of sanctifying love.*[2]

Perspective as Dogma

Literally, dogma ought to be understood as that which gives ultimate meaning to what appears before us. I would like to use "dogma" here in a specific way. An example might help. After Peter's confession, which had been revealed to him by the Father (Mt 16:17), Jesus rebuked the disciple for a fundamental incomprehension of the suffering Messiah, which is the dogma of salvation. That perspective ran headlong against Peter's dogma. One was self-disposing, the other self-saving. Among the words Jesus chose in his rebuke, we find "*phroneo*" – a mindset or a way of thinking (Mk 8:33). There is only one dogma that results in salvation. That is the mind of God which Peter did not possess. A dogma that is connected to the Messiah is always self-giving. Wesley often used the concept of "disposition" in discussing the basic Christian stance on reality. He wrote in his sermon "On Perfection," reflecting on the *kenosis* passage

> Another view of this is given us in those words of the great Apostle, 'Let this mind be in you, which was also in Christ Jesus.' For although this immediately and directly refers to the humility of our Lord, yet it may be taken in a far more extensive sense, so as to include the whole disposition of his mind, all his affections, all his tempers, both toward God and man. Now it is certain that as there was no evil affection in him, so no good affection or temper was wanting. So that 'whatsoever things are holy, whatsoever things are lovely' are all included in 'the mind that was in Christ Jesus'.

There was an orientation, a disposition which all the disciples lacked and which had to be brought in from a supernatural source, that would transform reality as they had known it. It would fulfill, when present, what God intended for their needy hearts. Once that predisposing moment had come, the disciples never looked at reality in the same way again. This 'preoccupying perspective' is at the base of

---

2. As will be seen, 'Father' is different than other metaphors. It is metaphorical but is distinct from all others when applied to the First Person of the Trinity. It is a revealed term which indicates the Person co-equal to the Son and the Spirit.

what I mean by "dogma."[3]

Joseph Pieper, referring to one of Aquinas' discourses on the Trinity, claimed it shed "a penetrating light on the entire architecture of the world."[4] Speaking of metaphors, one philosopher wrote that they have the power to "cut at the sinews of reality." That's what proper dogma ought to do. If it is acceptable to tie ourselves to a particular tradition for the insights it can bear for the furtherance of the entire gospel, then we must see if Wesley and his theological progeny are drawing from the resources of the very highest and most personal Christian dogma.[5]

Encouraged by the renaissance of Trinitarian theology which marked the late twentieth century and still feeds the best theologies today, I posit there is a Trinitarian brilliance in the Wesleyan/Holiness tradition. It would behoove us to investigate the truest theological mooring for that which is the foundation of our lives. A perspective has incredible potential for reordering existence. A Trinitarian perspective transforms reality. It provides an intra-personal dogma. Holiness is nothing less than self-giving love. More than conceptual, this love is tangibly self-offering, self-dispensing, and self-emptying. It is the essence of biblical discipleship.

The Importance of a Wesleyan Trinitarian Perspective

The Trinitarian fullness in Wesleyan thought is much more than accidental. I discern that there is a need for us to re-orient ourselves along lines similar to Wesley's approach. When that prevailing perspective is recognized it serves to mitigate the descriptions of Wesleyan thought as an inadequate theological rendition because of its lack of a grandeur through a systematic or rationalistic structure.

It is becoming ever clearer to me that Wesley was concerned with Trinitarian dogma in a rich sense. Even though his hesitation as to speculation on the "manner" of Trinitarian existence is often underscored, the "matter" of that life permeates his view of real Christianity.[6] In large measure a Trinitarian worldview is what motivates the deepening Anglican categories of Wesley's own immediate theological background.[7] Thomas Oden has recognized that "triune reasoning is saturated throughout the entire (Wesleyan) enterprise." He sees it as "the pervasive principle of systematic cohesion of the whole corpus."[8] Wesley's 'perspective' is never merely

3. G. Kittel & G. Friedrich ed. *Theological Dictionary of the New Testament* trans. G. Bromiley (Grand Rapids, Eerdmans, 1974) vol. IX, 220-235, esp. 232-233. "On Perfection," *Works* III:I, 5.

4. Josef Pieper, *Living the Truth* (San Francisco: Ignatius, 1989), 80-81.

5. Geoffrey Wainwright refers to the creedal, Trinitarian, ecumenical, and homological consensual nature of Wesleyan thought in "Methodism and the Apostolic Faith." From *What Should Methodists Teach?* ed. M. Douglas Meeks (Nashville: Kingswood Books, 1990), 106-113.

6. For an example of this repeated emphasis, see *Letters* VI: 213, to Mary Bishop, April 17, 1776.

7. One thinks here of the term "*weltenschaaung*" or Hegel's "*Daseinsverständnis*." There have been a plethora of attempts to locate Wesley on the theological horizon, à la Outler, Piette, Schmidt.

8. Thomas Oden, *John Wesley's Scriptural Christianity: A Plain Exposition of His Teaching on Christian Doctrine* (Grand Rapids: Zondervan, 1994), 25; n. 23.

subjective. He is not just stitching things together; he is reconstructing, reshaping the dogma that had been passed on to him. He is always anchored in a broad view of Christian history and thought. But he was far too capable a thinker to allow any construct in tradition or history to circumvent the power of the Word of God itself.[9]

A Radically Different View of God

The Dogma of the God who is Holy and who is Love, Wesley would argue, militates against a preoccupation with sovereign antecedent and impersonal will that had resulted from centuries of Reformation theology. Rather the full personal implications of Trinitarian dogma are what motivate his use of the language of Fatherhood, familial intimacy, nuptial metaphors, and salvation as a recreation in the likeness and image of God this side of heaven. Though not as prominent as the preceding, there is a strain of Wesleyan thought which I would describe as nurturing or therapeutic. There is a satellite of terms or themes which indicate an awareness of the disposition of God's heart to bear His own in His heart in an intimate way. Though none of these terms, in my reading, stand out alone, together they offer a deeply personal dogma, Trinitarian in essence and salvifically self-bestowing.

In the effort not to force language to feed our perspective, it is intriguing to ask what symbol best informs and exemplifies holy love in a human heart. Besides the contrasting implications of a heart filled with perfect love and the litany of sins which accrue to self-love and self-will in every place in his corpus, Wesley uses a catena of positive terms such as born of God, begotten, bearing, tender love, wedding, filled with love, laying down one's life, and many more that together offer a picture that points us back to the image of God. Wesley was careful to not feed speculation or misinterpretation. The terms alluded to were never used in the way that mystics and Enthusiasts had used them and never misapplied like modern feminist interpretation. The overall rendition gives the reader the sense that the way of salvation issued from the Three-One God is a mutual relationship of ever-deepening implications where dying for the other is unquestionable. Self-love is replaced with social-love.[10] And that love is rooted in a fundamental death to oneself for the sake, the life, of another.

Far more expansive than the typical minimalist interpretation of Wesley as a "folk theologian," a comprehensive reading of the Wesleyan corpus reveals a thrilling Biblical worldview that propounds a consensual doctrine of the being of God,

9. Hence, his reservations about the usage of non-biblical terminology regarding the Trinity and his non-speculative approach to usage of Trinitarian verbiage. See his "On the Trinity," for just such an example, *Works* II:374-386.

10. "By experience he knows that social love, if it mean the love of our neighbor, is absolutely different from self-love." Letter to Dr. Conyers Middleton, 11:68.

as Father, Son and Holy Spirit. For him the Holy One is an eternal communion of Love. Where we may struggle to nuance the relationship between these two essence statements about God, Wesley offers no 'speculation.' But what he does see is a discernment of personhood which few had realized so clearly and have applied so expansively. There is an ontological starting point in Wesley's theology that enlarges the conception of the One who saves. It undergirds a doctrine of salvation that is able not only to meet every human need, but to make those persons who are saved to bear the Savior's own image by the transforming Holy Spirit, to be, as Charles Wesley so poignantly wrote, "transcriptions of the Trinity."[11]

One comes away from the origins of the Wesleyan tradition imbibing a fullness of Biblical reality, a Trinitarian theocentrism, with a concomitant infusion of the dynamic of divine life in actual human existence. Wesley's dogma did not see our need being merely a legal transaction regarding sin. Far more than that, he saw a gracious enablement to live in God and He in us, and thus the offer to live as He lives. Without this insight anything which calls itself Wesleyan is diminished in self-understanding or influence.

The Life of God in the Soul

The list of sources that led Wesley to Aldersgate—Law, Fenélon, à Kempis and Taylor—ought to also include that unique Scottish Reformed author, Henry Scougal, and his work *The Life of God in the Soul of Man.* Though predominantly practical in nature, Scougal's dominating themes of love for God and for others, purity, and humility are steeped in a sense of living within the nature of a holy God, and His mutual indwelling of the believer. Its uniqueness derives from the dogma to which it points. Scougal defines true religion as "divine life,"

> not only in regard of its fountain and original, having God for its author, and being wrought in the Souls of men by the power of his Holy Spirit; but also in regard of its nature, Religion being a resemblance of the divine perfections, the image of the Almighty shining in the soul of man: nay it is a real participation in his nature, it is a beam of the eternal light, a drop of that infinite ocean of goodness; and they who are endued with it, may be said to have *God dwelling in their Souls, and Christ formed within them* (italics mine).[12]

One cannot help but notice the Trinitarian cast to his definition. Each of the three persons is described as indwelling the image of God. Similar sentiments arise

11. OT *Notes*, I: 7-8.

12. Henry Scougal, (1650-1678) *The Life of God in the Soul of Man: or the Nature and Excellency of the Christian Religion* (London: J. Downing) 1726, 10-11. First published in 1677, this tome had remarkable effect on the leaders of the Oxford Holy Club. Whitefield's reading of it was directly tied to his conversion. The intriguing thing is that what for Wesley became an encouragement for the fullness of God in the life of a believer became for the Calvinistic Methodists a clear reference to the irresistible life of God predestinating the elect to salvation.

throughout the Wesleyan corpus. In the sermon "Awake, Thou That Sleepest," a Spirit-enabled responsiveness is only fulfilled when the believer moves into "a participation of the divine nature, the life of God in the soul of man."[13] In a letter, he describes true religion as did Scougal and Scoupoli and Lopez, as "not an external, but the life of God in the soul of man, the image of God stamped on the heart."[14] As Wesley stated in another place, "But in Christ dwelleth all the fullness of the Godhead; the most full Godhead; not only Divine powers, but the divine nature.... Christ is filled with God and ye are filled with Christ. And ye are filled by him.... He is originally full. We are filled by Him with wisdom and holiness."[15]

Where else in the history of hymnody do successive editions of a hymnbook begin with a theological and soteriological preface like the following? Speaking of an entire salvation, he writes, "He stamps upon them his own image and superscription; he createth them anew in Christ Jesus; he cometh unto them with his Son and his blessed Spirit, and, fixing his abode in their souls, bringeth them into the 'rest which remaineth for the people of God.'"[16] One will look far for a hymnbook to the Trinity comprised of over a hundred paeans of praise to the Three-One God that the Wesleys incorporated into their collection of hymns and poetry.

Fatherhood as the Foundation of Trinitarian Dogma

The origins of that truth in relation are emphasized in an unselfconscious way in Wesley. He is consistently overwhelmed by the love of God the Father. Holiness is viewed through this fundamental dogma. He is in complete agreement with the basic definitions of holiness, but the Otherness of God is always Personal. It is never a concept that is separable from the Father's shared love with the Son and Spirit. Whatever defines holiness starts first with the word "Father." Before creation, before the burning Bush, before Israel is called Son, there is an eternal Father who gives and receives love from the Son and the Spirit. Progressive revelation gives to us truth as we fallen creatures are able to receive it but that does not discount the fundamental relationship between the Triune Persons as foundational to the dogma of holiness. At the center of the being of God is self-giving Love.

Dogma is personal and it points us to ultimate truth. The Triune God who is

---

13. *Works* I:150.

14. *Letters* V:301, May 30, 1765 to Mr. James Knox. He says in "On Friendship with the World," "Yet are there very few subjects of so deep importance; few that so nearly concern the very essence of religion, the life of God in the soul, the continuance and increase, or the decay, yea, extinction of it." *Works,* Sermon 80 para. 3. Also Sermon 6, "Righteousness of Faith," *Works* Vol. 1. p. 209 para.11. Sermon 21, Ibid., p. 481 II:11. It appears twice in Sermon 24, Ibid., p. 541, III:1.

15. Comment on Col. 2:9-10. *Notes,* 520. A cursory review of terms like "fullness" or "filled" does not focus on the Holy Spirit as in common evangelical emphases; Wesley emphasizes a fullness of divine life, as here the "fullness of the life of God." He often quotes Eph. 3:19, 4:13 and 2 Pet 1:4.

16. Preface to *Hymns and Sacred Poems* 1740 edition. See *Works* XIV: 327

absolute Truth reveals Himself to us in both conversational and familial terms. Just as important as starting theology with creation prior to the Fall was for Wesley, so is his 'tacit and explicit' agreement that the Father's love is the best place for beginning a Christian view of reality. The progress of revelation climaxes in the incarnation of a Son by the Holy Spirit for the glory of the Father.

Wesley knew that when Jesus referred to himself as "from" his Father he did not mean as a physical, spatial, or temporal way.[17] When the East took the West to task on linguistic differences with regard to Trinitarian language it attributed to the Father the terms 'agennetos' (unbegotten) and 'arche' (origin, source) with no temporal or material essence in mind. The nature of thought of creation and salvation necessitated a personal 'origin' to enable (ensure) basic human comprehension of divine mysteries. The revelational concepts that fed that fundamental awareness of the transcendent One satellite around the term "Father."[18] But the 'logic of origin' was always perceived as Trinitarian dogma. The Father is eternally the Father to the Son and to the Spirit. He is Sovereign Creator, King, and Shepherd to us, but it would behoove us to connect those attributes to his eternal nature. This is surely the most illuminative term about the Holy One in the New Testament. No one expected the Holy One of Israel to be a faithful Father. That kind of intimacy was a redefining of Holiness that took Israel centuries to be able to comprehend.

The Western lawyer-theologian Tertullian gave to us the structure of Trinitarian 'economia' (divine actions) as inseparable from the 'monarchia' (the relationship within the Trinity). He did so in a way that was subtler than we in interpreting those insights with interpersonal love as the foundation of God's acts. He also gave us the first use of the word 'persona' to describe what Scripture pointed us to. The earlier trinitarians advocated the external actions of God as issuing from his internal reality. They were quick to redefine regal categories, so easily construed along human definitions of sovereignty, by positing for the first time a personal monarchy.[19] The dogma of the early church was summed up as 'A patre ad patrem' (from the Father and to the Father). The flow of holy love is summarized here in short form. When everything issues from and is returning to the heart of a Father, then dogma is radically different from other explanatory options.

Just as revelation is Trinitarian, love as a concept is an inter-trinitarian real-

---

17. Jn 1:14 states it explicitly but it is implied in numerous ways throughout the book.

18. John Zizioulas, *Being as Communion* (Crestwood: St. Vladimir's Press, 1985), 83-89 as an example of a consistent theme throughout this discussion. The opposite opinion is found in the uninformed criticism of Brian Leftow in "Anti Social Trinitarianism" from *The Trinity: An Interdisciplinary Symposium on the Trinity* (Oxford: Oxford Univ. Press, 1999), 236, 244-245. A recent discussion across the waterfront of criticisms, including terminological, monotheistic, Christological and feminist arguments, is done by John L. Gresham in "The Social Model of the Trinity and its Critics," *Scottish Journal of Theology* 46:325-343. While it is a profitable survey not very much time is given to constructive analysis.

19. S. Mark Heim, *The Depths of the Riches: A Trinitarian Theology of Religious Ends* (Grand Rapids: Eerdmans, 2001), 172-173.

ity. The Wesleyan tradition must maintain this emphasis first and foremost. If one starts where Scripture points rather than where the Reformation does, then a different perspective arises. It is very difficult to ground love in sovereignty alone. Otherness can begin and remain an impersonal category. The opposite is apparent. It sits closer to reality to base love in a divine Fatherhood, a divine person. Those who have believed that God could sanctify the human heart have, whether they know it or not, advanced a categorical shift in dogma.

Wesley had no qualms at all with that revealed metaphor of transcendent divine life. He did not debate it, probably more because of its acceptability in his day, but that did not mean he did not also let the origin of revelation, creation and salvation begin in time and space. He focused, without any apparent self-consciousness, on its deeper meaning: that at the heart of all that is, is a heart of love best expressed in non-politicized, non-pagan, non-coercive terminology.[20]

The dogma of which I speak might be seen in the usage of the scriptural term "Father" in Wesleyan thought. By contextual resonance it is never connected to an independent potentate or insensitive divine child-abuser.[21] Far from it. There was, for Wesley, no Father without a Son or Spirit. He was unknowable and indefinable without the other two persons. When He comes, He always does so through and in the other two persons.

The Fatherhood of God permeates the writings of the Wesleys.[22] The Apostle John's exclamation becomes Wesley's: "Oh what manner of love the Father has given unto us, that we should be called the children of God."[23] And when the Spirit comes in sanctifying power, the immediate response of the human heart is a cry which mirrors the intimacy of the divine Trinity: "Abba, Father." His Person suffuses not only the Wesleyan 'via salutis,' but there is also a strong focus on the continual personal providence of the Father, "the universal friend" and the One whom we shall be "conversing with 'face to face.'"[24]

20. A highly engaging book on this issue is *Speaking the Triune God* (Grand Rapids: Eerdmans, 1992), ed. Alvin F. Kimel.

21. Coppedge, *Portraits of God*, 244-260.

22. A search of the term "Father" on the Abingdon disk of Wesley's sermons and hymns elicits 558 occurrences. Of those 437 appear in 131 of 151 sermons. Only 20 sermons have no specific reference to the Father in some distinct way. Those that do not are sermons; 35,38,41,48,(note how seldom missing in the standard sermons) 58,78,93,101,104,116,124, 127,128,129,137,138,139,140 and 147.

23. Other 'Father' passages that re-occur often in the written sermons of Wesley are: Mt 5:16, 48; 6:4b; Jn 5:23; Rom 8:15,16; Gal 4:6; I Jn 1:3,9 and 3:1; I Pet 1:3-4. He loved the titles; "Father of spirits," (Heb 12:9, Num 16:22), "Father of All," "Father of light," (Ja 1:17). The title, "Abba" occurs 38 times.

24. Sermon #73 "Of Hell" III:3; Sermon #80 "On Friendship with the World" para. 9.

The Son as the Image of God

As with Trinitarian exegesis, Wesley does not force the Old Testament in specifying a christological interpretation, but he is not averse to mentioning that others have seen Christophanies in the text.[25]

The Son, True God, because of his incarnate life, became—as the Pastor of Hebrews affirms—the perfect expression of God, the exact impress of His Person. There is no clearer picture of holiness for us than Jesus. Both the Father and the Spirit are revealed and comprehended most fully through Jesus of Nazareth. His distinctiveness and particularity, as the Sent One, as the Son who shared eternal glory with his Father, is the One who reveals to us the mind, heart and life of God the most clearly. Wesley refers over and over to the expression of the initiating love of the Father in the actual sending and obedience of the Son. "Sending" is the implication of the mutual responsiveness of the Persons of the Trinity. Like the early Fathers, he does not view that move as ontological subordination but simply as the response of a co-equal Person to Another. At several points Jesus underscores his worthiness to be heard in the prior word of the Father and attestations of the Spirit as well as his divine works.[26] Genuine Truth comes from more than One Person at any given time. There is no truth that is not Trinitarian. Self-giving love that is holy is never self-seeking and never self-authenticating in an individual sense.

Conversely, we humans also are perfectly expressed in Jesus, as the Perfect Man, or True Man. Granted, Wesley heavily emphasizes the divinity of Jesus in response to an encroachment of a strain of Arianism in 18th century Anglicanism. But it is still mystifying to find him accused of a 'practical monophysitism' by some.[27] Is the reality of Christ's humanity really subsumed under divinity? While all must acknowledge the difficulty of balancing the mystery of God become Man, it does not seem to be accurate in terms of what Wesley believed was possible by grace in the life of believers. Jesus' humanity is never far from ours. The Word enfleshed explains who I am to be. Wesley's continued refrain is that He is The Image whom I am made to image. Myriad hymnic statements affirm what Wesleyans believe about the True Man in human nature. Take for instance this from Charles,

> Thy image, love, thy name impress, Thy nature on my heart.
> Bowels of mercy, hear! Into my soul come down!

---

25. OT *Notes*, I:73 note on Gen. 18:2ff. He is more attentive to the Trinitarian implications of verses like Gen. 19:24, OT *Notes*, I:76.

26. John 3:31-36; 5:19-23; 7:16-18; 16:13-14.

27. Ted Campbell alludes to the contemporary expressions of Arianism to which Wesley responded in *John Wesley and Christian Antiquity: Religious Vision and the Cultural Change* (Nashville: Kingswood, 1991), 79-81. On "practical monophysitism" see *Works*, I:470, Sermon 21, note f. One also wonders about the Docetism alluded to by Deschner, *Wesley's Christology* (Grand Rapids, Francis Asbury Press, 1988), 28. See also Ibid., n. 15 on p. 41.

Let it throughout my life appear That I have Christ put on.
O plant in me thy mind! O fix in me thy home!
So shall I cry to all mankind, Come, to the waters come!
Jesus is full of grace...
Behold in me, ye fallen race, That God is only love![28]

It is the relationship between the Father and the Son and the Son and the Spirit which illuminates both divine personhood as well as human. Independent self-will is absolutely impossible for the existence of Holy Love, as self-emptying (*kenosis*) is not something Jesus *did*; it is who he *is* in heaven and expressed in the flesh. Since it is impossible "to sound the depths of love divine" by human machinations, "He emptied himself of all but love," that we might see the love which precedes, informs, and continues in his incarnation.[29] And the one who is filled with his life, the Life He shares with the Father and the Spirit, can only do the same. Every element of our self-denial is encompassed in his prior self-abnegation. A Wesleyan dogma sees the meaning of humanity in imaging the life of God, making all that He offers possible before death. That life is best expressed in receiving and in self-giving, that is the Life of God. I am convinced that Wesley's Christology at every point arises out of the reality of the Father in the Spirit and that is why his dogma is so refreshingly engaging in the narrowing influences of eighteenth century reformed Anglicanism.

The Person of the Holy Spirit

Wesley was not bothered by the *filioque* debate; even though a Western Christian, Wesley does not deal with this issue specifically. It is clear that he does not merge the Holy Spirit with the other Persons, nor does he equate the Spirit with grace or its equivalent. He speaks as if the interrelationship between all three persons is crucial for our being fully restored to the image of the Trinity.

Wesley presents the Holy Spirit in active ministry,[30] but he does so in a way that is much more personal than most of his contemporaries. He does not appear to follow unthinkingly the Augustinian tradition of the Holy Spirit as the "bond of love" (vinculum). While we do not find the typical Western approach to pneumatology, neither do we find an overt understanding of the Eastern perspective on the personhood of the Spirit. But we do find the third Person as much more than a benefit bestower or executor; the Spirit is the Person who fills the soul with divine

28. *Works*. Hymn 147 Hymns on God's Everlasting Love (2nd Series), [1742], a continuation of Hymn 146, vv. 14-16 of the original. No. 134 in the 1778 draft.

29. From the hymn now known as "And Can It Be." HSP, 1739, pp. 117-19, entitled 'Free Grace'; vv. 1-4, 6 of six. No. 177 in the 1778 draft. Written immediately after Charles' conversion, May 21, 1738; in all probability either this hymn or Hymn 29 was sung when John came late in the evening of the 24th to announce his own conversion.

30. See for instance his comments on Gen. 18:13, OT *Notes*, I:74.

life. Apart from him there is no revelation or redemption or sanctification.

In one of his strongest statements in the Notes concerning Trinitarian salvation, Wesley says of the Spirit, He "is a co-equal partner in the amazing condescension that was needful to complete (salvation)."[31] We are to share in a personal communion with him like unto that of the Father and the Son.[32] He does not do so perfunctorily or merely objectively. As a triune Person, His work is radically personal, interrelated, selfless. He is not merely applying the benefits of another person. He comes to His own, and bears with Him all that the Trinity desires and is able to be in the human life. It is by him that we are enabled to be the image of God, to be what God intended us to be, and by Him we are enabled to walk as Christ walked.

Pneumato-centric soteriology is part of the consensual nature of Wesleyan thought.[33] Every aspect of the life of Jesus was accompanied by the Spirit. Likewise, for Wesley there is no dispensational reading of the Spirit's activity. He is personally present in every aspect of the "way of salvation." It is intriguing how often Wesley highlights that it is the ministry of the Spirit of adoption to enable our understanding of the Father as "Abba" and thereby to be welcomed into the fullness of divine life. "Because ye are sons, God hath sent forth the Spirit of his Son into your hearts, crying Abba, Father." "Amen, Lord Jesus! May everyone who prepareth his heart yet again to seek thy face receive again that Spirit of adoption, and cry out, Abba, Father!"[34] This, he explains, "is that religion which our Lord has established upon earth, ever since the descent of the Holy Ghost on the day of Pentecost. This is the entire, connected system of Christianity."[35]

The Expansive Self-Giving Nature of Redeeming Grace

The enduement of divine life, neither as a mystical experience nor as an imagined projection of the divine, but the actual life and nature of God dwelling in the total life of the believer, is what motivates the Wesleyan heritage. Wesley sees the image of God, much like Luther and Calvin, as "knowledge, righteousness and true holiness."[36] Even though far gone, Wesley envisions a restoration of that image brought about by "sanctifying grace."[37] All descriptions of this biblical promise are centered

31. *Notes* , 581 on Heb 9:14. This is also one of his strongest statements in the Notes concerning Trinitarian salvation.

32. *Works*, "On Spiritual Worship," Sermon 77 para. 4. Speaking on the structure of I John, Wesley writes, "First, severally, of communion with the Father, chapter one, verses 5-10; of communion with the Son, chapters two and three; of communion with the Spirit, chapter four."

33. The phrase occurs in the introduction to the Sermons in *Works* Vol. I:81.

34. On the New Birth, *Works* Vol. 1, Sermon 18 IV:6, p. 430. "Abba" occurs no less than 30 times in the Sermons and Hymns. "Spirit of Adoption" occurs 35 times in the same sources.

35. Sermon 92 " On Zeal, " II:6.

36. OT *Notes*. I:7 on Gen 26-28.

37. OT *Notes*. I:8 on Gen 26-28. See also his reading of the blessing given to Abraham after the near sacrifice of Isaac. He writes the blessing includes the promise of the Gift of the Holy Spirit. Ibid I:87 on Gen 22:17.

on a self-denial that issues in life for another. Nurturing life begins by the willingness to die completely to one's own way.

There is no doubt that a second definite work of grace is the clearest expression of what is unique in Wesleyan synthesis and the tradition which followed him. The tendency to overemphasize one facet of this marvelous doctrine has led to confusion and, sadly, to actual rejection of its inherent truth. To separate faith from grace, crises from process, experience from the means of grace, purity from maturity, cleansing from power, love from righteousness, substance from relation, is, at the least, to be non-Wesleyan. But might I add that to separate the inter-personal life of the Trinity from sanctification is also not Wesleyan dogma.

It is the self-bestowal of the heart of the Father that gives ontological meaning to the sending of the Son in incarnate redemptive love. It is the Son who became who we are ontologically "in every respect," so that by taking humanity into himself he could "recapitulate" fallen humanity and begin the *anabasis* (or ascent) to that City whose founder and maker is God.[38] It is the work of the Holy Spirit to make us as selfless as He himself is revealed to be. If Jesus was full of the Spirit, then His life must be the self-same Spirit in us. If the example of a Spirit-filled person is Jesus Christ then surely that experience is much more intimate that most of us have ever dreamed.

Perfect love is self-emptying love. Truly other-oriented love is non-grasping love. The model for that love is not human originally, it is divine. We are the copy, the Three-in-One are the original. True personhood is not defined exclusively by reason, or volition, but by a fundamental disposition toward an other. Wesley builds on Scougal, and I might add also Irenaeus, Athanasius, Aquinas, et al. If one is to claim the life of God in the soul, that life is no less than Trinitarian. I think that is what the Wesleys meant by being "transcripts of holiness," "transcripts of the divine nature," and they would add transcripts of "his own nature," "of divine purity."[39] They also spoke of being "stamped with the Triune character."[40]

Some refer to this aspect of Wesley's thought as mystical; and it is unusual. De Renty's call to experience the presence of the ever blessed Trinity influenced Wesley and several near him.[41] The testimony of Charles Perronet, a figure similar to De Renty, who expressed an experience of communion with each person of the Trinity, was received with initial reservation. However, his quote indicates an application of Trinitarian reality that most Christians live without even considering as possible.

---

38. *Works*, Jackson ed. Vol. VII: 513. The newest edition notes that this is a sermon by John Gambold, not John Wesley, but its inclusion is resonant with all that Wesley taught.

39. *Works* Hymn 517, Hymn 253 v.2, Vol. II. Sermon 34, II:6. Ibid., II:10, Sermon 20, I:2.

40. *Works* Hymn 253 verse 2 and Hymn 7, I:1 respectively.

41. *Works*, IV: 37, "On the Discoveries of Faith," dated 1788. Though the actual words that Wesley records here differ from his original version in the "Extract of the Life of Monsieur De Renty," nothing is lost. This sermon concludes with a paragraph on the intimate relationship only known to the most faithful.

> After some years my communion was with Christ only, though at times with the Father, and not wholly without the Spirit. Of late I have found the same access to the Triune God. When I approach Jesus, the Father and the Spirit commune with me.[42]

Although he did not deem it requisite for sanctification, as a heart of perfect love would be, nonetheless Wesley, one of the foremost critics of quietistic enthusiasm, was open to encouraging a deep awareness of the Trinity in those seeking to go on to perfection.[43] It also appears to be the case that this sense of the three Persons became of more interest to him in the last decade or so of his ministry. What follows is an example of a Trinitarian view of the deeper life which arose in the correspondence:

1. "Do you still (as Mr. de Renty says) 'carry about with you an experimental verity and a fullness of the presence of the ever-blessed Trinity'?" *Letters* VI: 270, Aug.2, 1777.
2. "(You have) experienced more of the life of faith and deeper communion with the Father and the Son that ever she did in her life." *Letters* VII: 67, June 10, 1781.
3. "...Of having had such a manifestation of the several Persons in the ever-blessed Trinity." *Letters* VII: 392, July 4, 1787.
4. "... we persuade men not to be almost but altogether Christians; to maintain a constant 'fellowship with the Father and his Son Jesus Christ'...." *Letters* VII: 391, June 18, 1787.
5. "Do you always find a clear sense of the presence of the ever-blessed Trinity?" *Letters* VII: 27, Dec. 17, 1787 (also Oct. 6, 1787).
6. "And tell me, on the other hand, whatever manifestations of the ever-blessed Trinity you find...." *Letters* VIII: 160, Aug 3, 1789.
7. "Do you still find deep and uninterrupted communion with God, with the Three-One God, with the Father and the Son through the Spirit?" *Letters* VIII: 183, Nov. 3, 1789.
8. "I trust you still enjoy communion with God the Father and His Son Jesus Christ. I hope you are still sensible wherever you go of the presence of the ever-blessed Trinity, and that you continually enjoy that loving-kindness which is better than life itself." *Letters* VIII: 248, Nov. 9, 1740.

42. *Letters* VI: 253, Feb. 11, 1777 to Hester Ann Roe. De Renty's experience was also found in Perronet. Letters VII: 83. He says later that he heard of this experience first in his close associates in Hester Ann Roe and then Elizabeth Ritchie and then the members of the London Select Society. *Letters* VII: 392, July 4, 1787. On August 8, 1788 he says Ritchie was the first and then Roe, however.

43. *Letters*, to Hannah Ball, June 11, 1777. See his correspondence with Elizabeth Ritchie, June 16, 1777, "do you never lose your consciousness of the presence of the Three-One God?" Ibid., April 26, 1777 to Miss March. He does say that he at one time thought this experience was for all perfected in love but after researching the experience he changed his mind. *Letters* VIII:83, Aug. 8, 1788.

The reality of entire sanctification is the life of the Triune God. It is more concerned with a "magnificent obsession" of the Love of God than it is about emotion or perfect performance. Wesley saw this life as an in-breathing, a perichoretic mutuality of the very life of God in the life of a believer. In the famous "respiration" passage of his sermon, "The New Birth," Wesley describes this life in Trinitarian terms as he states that when regeneration occurs,

> God having quickened him by his Spirit, he is alive to God through Jesus Christ. He lives a life which the world knoweth not of, a 'life' which 'is hid with Christ in God'. God is continually breathing, as it were, upon his soul, and his soul is breathing unto God. Grace is descending into his heart, and prayer and praise ascending to heaven. And by this intercourse between God and man, this fellowship with the Father and the Son, as by a kind of spiritual respiration, the life of God in the soul is sustained: and the child of God grows up, till he comes to 'the full measure of the stature of Christ'.[44]

Is a fundamental aspect of holiness obfuscated when we attempt to consider it or remove it at all from the inner nature of God? Transcendence is crucial, revelation irreplaceable, but the Father showed Himself to us in the Son. He came in power and brilliance, but the Holy One is seen most clearly at the basin and on the Cross. One of the Persons is so self-effacing we have difficulty even naming him. Scougal refers to perfect love as a type of "self-dereliction."[45]

In more recent terminology, egocentricity is only redeemed by a preceding and personal "exocentricity." Sin for Wesley is often defined by the twins, pride and self-will.[46] Redemption is only fulfilled when that which is self-curved is turned toward another. Is that what this verse points to?

> And when we rise in love renewed,
> Our souls resemble thee,
> An image of the Triune God
> To all eternity.[47]

"Social holiness" is a key component in the Wesleyan order of salvation. Grace and gifts for ecclesial *koinonia* can become independent grasping and grafting. The glory we often hear about veils the true nature of God. We are like Moses when

---

44. Wesley continues: From hence it manifestly appears what is the nature of the new birth. It is that great change which God works in the soul when he brings it into life: when he raises it from the death of sin to the life of righteousness. It is the change wrought in the whole soul by the almighty Spirit of God when it is 'created anew in Christ Jesus', when it is 'renewed after the image of God', 'in righteousness and true holiness', when the love of the world is changed into the love of God, pride into humility, passion into meekness; hatred, envy, malice, into a sincere, tender, disinterested love for all mankind. In a word, it is that change whereby the 'earthly, sensual, devilish' mind is turned into 'the mind which was in Christ'. This is the nature of the new birth. 'So is everyone that is born of the Spirit.' *Works* Sermon 45 "The New Birth " II:4, p.193-194.

45. Scougal, *The Life of God in the Soul of Man,* 41.

46. *Works*, Sermon 128, "The Deceitfulness of the Human Heart" I:1

47. Hymn 248, Section I of *Works* Hymns

he asked for 'glory' and God lovingly offered him what he most needed: goodness. Glory, for Wesley, was unveiled holiness.[48] Expressions of power must reveal the glory of Spirit who enabled the glory of the Cross for the glory of the Father.

There is for the Wesleyan an irreplaceable element to our theological perspective that is an embattled position and augurs to continue as one. Without the Holy Father, the Holy Son and Holy Spirit are foundationless as Persons. Once removed from the life of the Father, it is quite common to reduce the Son to a functional and adopted replacement for the guilt of sin while the Spirit becomes merely an encouraging presence in the midst of problems. They both quickly become pawns of atoning grace and sanctifying power. But worse, they become agents in our own definitions of power; dictated, as it were, to assist us in our self-assurance that we are manifesting our descriptions of God's presence. As a result our view of salvation becomes anthropocentric. Deschner asks a poignant question for our tradition, "Does perfection serve Christ or Christ perfection?"[49]

Conclusion

The dogma one finds in the Wesleyan tradition is one of deep underlying truth, undeniably construed from a variety of sources, but constructed with consensual inclusivity, vibrant orthodoxy, radically personal spirituality, pastoral clarity, and evangelistic fervor – all of which are exceedingly helpful to the discipleship task of the Church. The Wesleyan tradition must orient itself in a Trinitarian way if there is going to be a re-engagement with other evangelicals who have misunderstood many points of our theology, and if there is going to be a Wesleyan gospel that can feed into the movements of God's Spirit around the world and more adequately make disciples of the nations.

Wesley for the most part was very grateful for preceding thinkers. But he did not feel that the Reformed categories alone were sufficient in themselves to express the fullness of God. He saw more than Luther's *simul iustus,* more than Calvin's sovereign decrees, more than the Westminster Confession's displacing the being of God and placing Scripture to its doctrinal forefront; more than Beza, who removed predestination as a pastoral discussion and moved it into the very nature of God; and more than the ephemerality of the "signs and wonders movement" of his day. Justification and holiness were viewed as inseparable counterparts, not as divorced items in the order of salvation. But he placed them within the nature of a self-giving God, The Holy One who is Love, first.

What the Wesleyan tradition cannot afford to do is to retreat into either a non-thinking trinitarianism or a functional soteriology. Even well-meaning evangelical minds have brought into the mix an historically recurring "distancing" when

48. Deschner, *Wesley's Christology*, regarding Wesley's comment on Rev. 4:8, p. 61.
49. Deschner, *Wesley's Christology*, 184.

it comes to a nuanced social trinitarianism. The argument goes, if we follow this love stuff too far we have a Trinity that is more like a committee or a family comprised of individuals, and we all know that is ludicrous. Granted, tri-theism is heretically ludicrous. However, the theological offerings that follow the criticism also appear less than cogent. We are left with the panoply of impersonal terms for God and for His salvation. Or worse, we are given impersonal terms for God's life (i.e., three dimensions, modes, aspects, faces *et al.*) and then we are called to become persons, as if we could be something that God in Himself is not originally.[50]

I am convinced that if we appropriate these insights and construct a philosophy of life and salvation from them we will advance the gospel in a more complete way – with fewer gaps. If one could simplify the tendency in theology to first objectify truth and then to swing in the opposite direction to 'subjectify,' we could say that evangelicals are clearly tending toward the latter in this period of our existence. We, like Wesley, need to read our future out of a rich past. Our perspective is not our own. We must share in the clarifying vision of centuries of Trinitarian wisdom and worship. Rather than reifying narratives or deifying subjective experiences, maybe a theological launching pad could be rediscovered and redeployed for the ensuing call to minister to the world as it is.

Only True Persons can offer true personhood and Christ-like discipleship. But that offering is self-divesting and the metaphors for that personal dispensation must be lived out in self-giving ways. The dogma of the Trinity permeated the reasoned discourses of Wesley. Eternal life was to know the heavenly Persons as one's own.[51] To use a Trinitarian concept, mutual co-indwelling was for him the only way to truly comprehend who God is and what God does. It is Christian dogma, intimate, personal, and Trinitarian, that filled Wesley's veins. May it be that we may equally affirm in our understanding of reality and in our communication of it this benediction along with Wesley,

> Unto God the Father, who first loved us, and made us accepted in the Beloved; unto God the Son, who loved us, and washed us from our sins in his own blood; unto God the Holy Ghost, who sheddeth the love of God abroad in our hearts, be all love and all glory for time and for eternity!

50. One recent example of this sort of argumentation is found in Donald Bloesch's *The Holy Spirit: Works and Gifts* (Downers Grove: InterVarsity, 2000), 269-271. Bloesch's section on the Trinity is appalling. He prefers the metaphor of "one sun and three dimensions–fire, light, and heat." Beside the traditional critique of this type of metaphor, his ensuing argument amounts to a manifest modalism in the middle of a bold rejection of personhood.

51. *Works*, Hymns Part 4 For Believers, Section 1,Rejoicing, Hymn 249.

Abbreviations used in the notes

- *Notes.* Wesley, John. *Explanatory Notes upon the New Testament.* rep. Salem: Schmul Publishers, 1975.
- *Journal.* Wesley, John. *The Journal of the Rev. John Wesley.* Edited by Nehemiah Curnock. 8 volumes. London: Epworth Press, 1909.
- *Letters.* Wesley, John. *The Letters of the Rev. John Wesley.* Edited by John Telford. Standard Edition. 6 volumes. London: Epworth Press, 1931.
- *Works, Jackson ed.* Wesley, John. *The Works of John Wesley.* Edited by Thomas Jackson. Authorized Edition. 14 volumes. London: Wesleyan Conference Office; reprint ed., Grand Rapids: Zondervan Publishing House.
- *Works.* Wesley, John. *The Works of John Wesley.* [editors vary]. Bicentennial Edition. 32 volumes. Oxford: Clarendon Press, 1979.

Discipleship and the Church

Chapter 5
Discipleship and the Growing Church

Rurel and Lisa Ausley, Crosspoint United Methodist Church
Niceville, Florida

Tribute

Rurel: Allan Coppedge has impacted many lives. Ours are two of them. My earliest contact with Dr. Coppedge was my first semester, which was also his first semester, at Asbury Theological Seminary. While wrestling with "Basic Christian Theology" I learned why students advise unsuspecting classmates never to take a professor the first year after he receives a PhD. He was a bear! January term brought on "Theology of John Wesley," challenging my academic prowess even more. But surviving both classes paid off! Al Coppedge approached me about being in a Bible study, or at least that's what I thought the invitation involved. The more I learned about the opportunity, the more I wrestled with the time commitment.

My girlfriend (and now wife), Lisa, was looking for a discipleship group, with no success. (She began meeting with Beth Coppedge, Al's wife, the next semester, though.) Lisa clued me in to the fact that this wasn't a haphazard invitation but was probably the result of much prayer and strategic thought and was possibly the opportunity of a lifetime. "You'd be crazy to turn down that offer!" she said. I'm glad I listened!

I quickly began to comprehend that I was embarking on an adventure far greater than I had realized. I had no concept of how this would shape my life and ministry, but joining Al's first Barnabas discipleship group had profound results. Sitting under his tutelage, learning from the Word and from his example cultivated in me a lifelong commitment to the Great Commission. The personal discipline he practiced and his pursuit of holiness were inspiring to observe. The spiritual formation and the value of being under his leadership were as important as any of the academic classes I had in seminary. Much of the practice in my 37 years in ministry has flowed from the leadership and discipleship I learned. I am eternally grateful for Al's investment in my life, an investment that is still making a difference in the Kingdom of God today through the men and their families into whom he poured himself.

Essay

Culture Shift

Leaving the warm, nurturing cocoon of seminary was exciting. We were sure any church we were appointed to would appreciate our brand of discipleship leadership and explode because of it! The first little hiccup occurred the morning my district superintendent called to tell me I'd been appointed to a three-point charge at Silas, Alabama. I'd lived an Alabama boy most of my life and had never heard of Silas. So I grabbed a state road map, and panic began to rise when it was nowhere on the map. No wonder! When I moved there it had one blinking light. Maybe you had to have at least two to make the map.

Nevertheless, among our tiny country churches, Lisa and I began praying about whom to begin investing in first. We had grown together as a couple while being in separate men's and women's discipleship circles and also by investing in other students ourselves. We wanted to continue the model, knowing it would aid our personal spiritual growth, benefit our members' and our church's growth, and also help our new marriage blossom.

We had three churches in our charge, so we wanted to begin working with someone from each fellowship. A young couple not much older than we were had just married and were starting out their journey. They were open to things of God, so we began meeting individually with Sarah and Jimbo. Sarah was an English major and teacher, like Lisa, and their discipleship relationship took off! They were scholars, studying the Word and reading Dostoyevsky on the side. Jimbo was a kind-hearted, hard-working man who was open to things of God, but we had a hard time connecting and making it work. He floundered to complete his commitments of Bible reading and it wasn't long before I found out why. He had never read an entire book of any genre and sitting down to read wasn't his gig. He was more comfortable in the woods, hunting, or in the garden, planting. No instruction in seminary helped me to know how to handle this!

When I realized this was the case for many of the men in our three little country churches, I realized the discipleship model we had learned would have to be tweaked. Well, maybe totally redesigned! I began hunting a lot (hey, every appointment has its perks!) and I planted a garden in the back yard of the parsonage even though I had zero interest in horticulture. Of course, since I knew nothing about gardening (skipped that class in seminary, too!) I began inviting men over to my house to train me. The first guy I reached out to, James Lewis, accepted Christ on my back doorstep during one of his visits. Related to Daniel Boone and famous in those parts for his hunting prowess, he already had the respect of the community. When he began coming to church and bringing his young family of four, it made headlines! The churches began to grow.

Still, how do you disciple men who don't read? Since they travel hours every day to lumber yards and distant jobs, the sensible thing was to begin a Bible reading program in our churches and purchase the Bible on CD for those with long commutes. James Lewis listened to the whole Bible in 3 months and began participating more and more with spiritual things, as did my other disciple, Jimbo.

The Aquilla church had a Wednesday night "prayer meeting" which, we were told, was a Bible study. Another discipleship opportunity! But the largest crowd was on those dusky evenings we had three sweet little women who spent most of the time talking about what a shame it was that no one ever came to "prayer meeting." Patsy attended and she seemed to be the neighborhood people magnet (when she wasn't at church). She was gregarious, kind-hearted and could she cook! With not even a store or gas station in that community, most of the action seemed to be at Patsy's and George's house. Patsy was the likely person for Lisa to begin meeting with, but with Patsy being 20 years her senior, Lisa was hesitant. This didn't seem to be a problem to Patsy.

Lisa: *Yes, I was so overwhelmed by the fact that Rurel and I were supposed to be in spiritual leadership but, at 26, we were the youngest couple in any of the three churches. They called him "our little preacher" and that wasn't a reference to his size! I couldn't think or pray myself out of this intimidation factor, until one day Rurel told me, "Lisa, you only have to be one step ahead of someone to lead them." I could humbly admit that if I prayed, ran hard, and stayed humble I might be able to stay one step ahead!*

So I kept meeting with Sarah weekly and our hearts were nourished together. She became my intellectual community which I missed so from our seminary world. I also began meeting with Patsy. She was so excited that she began inviting the community (a little country road with a cluster of homes on both sides) to join us. I kept trying to force the discipleship model I knew (men with men, women with women) and she kept reaching out to every adult and even boys and girls in the community. I threw my hands up and gave in. Rurel joined us and we began a Bible study group out of her home. We had older elementary children, teenagers, couples, widows, and divorcees. Our Bible memory whiz was Mrs. Smith, at age 80. The population of the home group rivaled church attendance on Sunday mornings! Several came to the home group who wouldn't consider taking a step into the church doors. Ever. Until they found Jesus. Then, He drew them. The Aquilla Church started growing, too. All I wanted to do was disciple Patsy, but she wanted the joy to be shared with everyone up and down their little country road. I realized we had to get in sync with what God was doing rather than try to cram Him into our own discipleship box.

We felt a little unsettled that the exact discipleship model we had learned and loved in seminary didn't quite fit in the real world. Well, we weren't quite sure this was the real world. But it was *our* world. We were teaching and baptizing as referenced in the Great Commission (Matthew 28:18-19). We were helping lots of different people take steps towards Jesus, trying to meet them where they were, not expecting them to meet us where we were so we could launch something. If we had, we would have stood alone on a little island for way too long. By the time we left the Silas charge after two years, all three churches had shown significant percentage growth. We realized this was fruit born out of discipleship. We looked for any who were leaning into Jesus; we met individually with people, which birthed small groups while using whatever measure seemed to fit their unique personalities and needs.

Growing Forward

In every church we've served in the last decades, small groups were key components of helping the local church grow. The names change but small groups, home groups, more formal classes, covenant groups, accountability groups and care groups all point to the model Jesus implemented of pouring his life into a group of followers and teaching them in his "doing life together" model.

For the last 19 years, we've served a fellowship of believers that has grown into a mega-church and a multi-site church. The original campus resides in a small town, Niceville, in the Florida panhandle. As we've grown, we've been able to launch into nearby communities. So Crosspoint United Methodist Church currently has four campuses with the vision that each campus grows to the point that it will plant another campus every five years or so. Our vision statement communicates that: "Crosspoint is a movement connecting communities in northwest Florida to Christ by starting multiplying campuses."

In order to maintain healthiness and not become scattered and unfocused, we have to clearly focus on five "big rocks": worship, children's ministry, student ministry, group life and missions. Many other fun ministry opportunities and ideas vie for our attention weekly, but by limiting our emphasis to these five areas we have the financial resources, people resources and talent/gifting resources to continue growing without getting bogged down in non-essentials. What we refer to as *Group Life* embraces a wide variety of opportunities for seekers to find Christ and for followers to grow. In fact, the *Group Life* ministry has outgrown space availability on our campuses and the majority of the groups meet in homes. Children's needs are prioritized and they "own" almost all the space on campuses on a Sunday morning. So these groups which focus on discipleship have to meet in homes during the week. The flavor is warm and intimate, allowing participants to become very close. Size of homes limits the size of groups and as groups grow, they naturally have to split and multiply. Sounds a little like the early church, doesn't it?

Discipleship is accomplished by much more than Bible studies together. Each individual is encouraged to find a place to serve at Crosspoint, and the natural next step is for small groups to participate in serving opportunities together. Each group is expected to be a missional group and look for ministry opportunities within the community to touch lives for Jesus. The social component is important as well and the life group becomes a community for "doing life together." Just as John Wesley's, the father of Methodism, original groups went to prisons, tutored children and served those in poverty, our life groups serve. They regularly have made visits and purchased necessities for the residents of indigent nursing homes, helped stock the local crisis pregnancy center with baby goods, gathered food for the local food pantries, fed and befriended the homeless on "cold shelter nights" on our campus, reroofed the home of a retired pastor or purchased and packed care bags for victims of cancer in our community. Some groups have gone on international mission trips together. Teams have worked to deliver supper to 1,300 underserved persons in our community every Saturday afternoon and have engaged in a Transformations Ministry that helps individuals escape from the cycle of poverty. Transformations is a one-on-one mentorship program and is discipleship with incredible results as the bonds of poverty are broken. Two of our campuses host a Celebrate Recovery program that involves step studies for men and for women. Perhaps recovery from addictions and life-long hurts and habits is the boldest and bravest form of discipleship.

Care ministry is practiced within each group. When a young mother is pregnant, group participants rally to keep their children while the parents race off to the hospital and then bring a string of meals to the home in the weeks following the baby's arrival. When a group member is having surgery, it's not unusual for the care pastor to find him at the hospital surrounded by a half dozen members of his small group. When divorce, death, or tragedy occurs, the little spiritual family is there to comfort, encourage and practice the ministry of presence in a way that no staff person at the local church could.

A local church that does not embrace discipleship and a variety of small groups does not have the potential to be a healthy church at all. Without group life, the church may enjoy an initial season of growth but it won't sustain the long-term season of vitality, depth and continuous growth. This is why discipleship must be a "big rock" in local church ministry. Can discipleship flourish without the support of a healthy growing church? Can a church be vital without the support of a robust discipleship ministry? The healthy church/discipleship relationship is a symbiotic one.

Ingredients of Healthy Discipleship

I have been in an accountability group for 19 years now with the same Christian brother. At times, the group has embraced two other men, but Mike and I have been together from the beginning of my ministry at Crosspoint and he has walked with me through the twists and turns of church life and personal discipleship. Mike is a Christian psychologist who uniquely comprehends the mental and emotional stresses of ministry. God could not have selected a better small group for me. He also understands the unique influence of spiritual warfare on any who engage in leadership roles in the Kingdom of God. *Accountability* and *authenticity* are very key components for my own spiritual health and the health of any small group. Having an ongoing relationship with men who desire the same openness and emotional depth that these long-term relationships have offered is primary to my own well-being and survival as a pastor, husband and dad. My thoughts and concerns are bared and there is no one else with whom I share the same level of safety with vulnerability than I do with these men. They pour so much more into me than I do into them, and the relationships born out of this particular discipleship group have sustained me during years of challenging ministry and heavy life trials. Lisa has had unique discipleship relationships, too.

Lisa: *I have been part of many different types of groups. Presently, I'm in an eclectic neighborhood group made up of an atheist, two Baptists and a burnt out Methodist. Uh, it's interesting.*

But my prayer partners and a women's prayer team have made the most dramatic difference in my life as a pastor, wife and mom. The safety *and* confidentiality *I have experienced with these women bring me into a circle of trust and support that is indescribable! I would drop anything at any time to serve any of these ladies and they have done the same for me, many times.* Prayer *and* communion *(the Lord's Supper) are key ingredients in this group. The robust hours I spend with them are full of much laughter, agonizing tears and long seasons of prayer. Knowing I have a team of women who have my back no matter what the circumstance has sustained Rurel's and my ministry many times.*

A new disciple must wade in slowly regarding the matters of accountability, authenticity, safety and confidentiality. But as the importance of these ingredients is validated and impressed on a small group, the security and safety of those relationships grow. There's nothing on this side of heaven that can equal the power, sense of community, love and care that is tangible when all these ingredients are interwoven in a group.

Goals of discipleship

When discipleship is done well in the local church, it connects new people to Jesus (evangelism), helps believers grow into Christian maturity (spiritual formation), and develops and nurtures leadership. As our church grows in worship attendance by 200-300 each year, it is evident that weekend worship is not always the first connection for a guest. Many people come into the church through a back door or a side door. Our Korean-speaking small group members easily find others to invite. There is an immediate connection when one Korean woman meets another out in the community. It's only natural to invite to their discipleship group, which is conducted in Korean.

In a community with a strong military presence where deployments are easily 6-9 months out of every year, our military wives' group is a first connection to our local church for many military families. Also, people find us through Celebrate

Recovery in their search for solutions to their "hurts, habits and hang-ups." Home groups meet in neighborhoods across our towns and it's easy for neighbors to invite another neighbor into their home to engage in Bible study or a sermon discussion event. In these venues, people find Christ and become more deeply connected to the church and begin to grow spiritually. The numeric growth within small discipleship groups pushes the need to multiply, which pushes the need for new leadership to step up to lead more groups.

Lisa: *One of my life goals has been for God to call fifty people into the mission field through my influence and ministry. As I have watched Him at work for over thirty-seven years, I look back and realize that most of this has been accomplished by mentorship/discipleship relationships. As I prayed carefully about each one-on-one discipleship opportunity with women in the six church appointments, He selected many to invest my life into who later went to seminary and into ministry or who went directly to a foreign mission field. Others became key leaders in local church ministries.*

Of course, God wants all of us to reach our spiritual potential, a potential which often embraces leadership. In the Scriptures, Jethro mentored Moses, who mentored Joshua. Eli mentored Samuel, who grew up and mentored Saul and David, the greatest king of Israel. David went on to mentor his son, Solomon, who also became King, and Solomon mentored the Queen of Sheba who took his wisdom back to her people. Mordecai mentored Esther, his young cousin, who followed his advice to risk her own life to save God's people from total destruction. Elijah mentored Elisha, who mentored King Jehoash. Jesus mentored his twelve disciples as well as a handful of women like Mary Magdalene, Martha and her sister, Mary. Paul mentored Timothy and Titus and many others. All of these became leaders in the movement of God, but the leadership was birthed in a relationship, a mentorship. This discipleship process which is woven through the Old and New Testaments became a relationship model that God used to raise up Kingdom-shaking leaders. He did it then and he is still doing it today.

In our church model of planting multiplying campuses (currently each of the four campuses is working to plant another campus in five years), this discipleship model of raising up leaders needs to become an even more serious effort in our church. Every campus will need a campus pastor, a starter staff and lay volunteers who will be leaders to direct areas represented by the five "big rocks": worship, children's ministry, student ministry, group life and missions. Each launching campus will be given 100-200 volunteers to seed the work of ministry. We've found that when leadership is pulled from our present circle of ministry, our DNA is already planted in new leaders and the transition is seamless.

Beyond authenticity, vulnerability, intimacy and the safety that is born out of confidentiality, people simply crave mentors. They crave relationships that offer answers, support, and encouragement—*life transference*. I realized this early on when my first discipleship group leader, Dr. Al Coppedge, invited me to accompany him on a revival. He was going to speak, over a weekend, to a group of men and invited me to go along. I was rather confused about why he needed me to go with him, but I went. Enroute home during the 2-hour car trip, it dawned on me: he didn't need me to do anything! He was practicing "life transference." Doing life together, shoulder to shoulder. As we debriefed and discussed the meeting, conversation turned to more personal matters. In the safety and vulnerability of that moving car, I shared my heart over my seminary girlfriend. I couldn't decide if I should ask her to marry me or not. He asked me one question which clarified everything: "Does she have a heart for the Lord?" Because I really hadn't known anyone who had loved Him more, it became clear that this was the most important matter in our relationship. His question was a turning point in my life. I asked her *THE* question and we've been a wonderful team in ministry ever since. In that moment, I understood why he had invited me. I understood the life transference issue of discipleship. I understood that people crave relationships and that I should spend the rest of my life doing something about that.

As was true for me, today's millennials have strong desires to connect with others outside of their age demographic. Churched and unchurched young adults desire to connect with others to find answers for life's questions, build stability into their lives, and cultivate meaningful relationships. This is the stuff great relationships are made of. This is the stuff that is foundational in bringing people to Christ. Young adults, middle-aged parents, empty nesters, and retirees will find groups to bring meaning to their lives. We, the church, must be better than anyone else in society at offering people exciting and meaningful opportunities to connect with others and to connect with Christ.

Let's facilitate relationships

Lisa: *So, in the growing church situation, Rurel and I and our awesome team work hard at being creative so we can facilitate great relationships. Group life and great mentorships take some strategic thinking and planning. There are hundreds of ways to support the development of discipleship relationships. But the best place to start is to look around and ask: OK, whom do we have? Recently a team from Asbury Seminary/Orlando campus came to our church. Rurel and I took them to lunch and before their departure asked the usual question we pose to all our guests: As a first-time casual observer, tell us something we're doing right and tell us something we could improve. Jose shared he had observed quite a few Hispanics on our campus. He had a number of delightful chats in Spanish as he manned his ATS promotional table. He asked us: "Do you have any Spanish-speaking small groups?" The idea had never occurred to us! On the campus where I serve we also have a sizeable group of worshiping Korean women who are married to American husbands. A lightbulb went off in my head! We can gather people around their heart languages.*

Presently, we have a small group in Korean and one in Spanish and dream about having others. We have other groups for homogenous communities: homeschool parent groups, groups for parents of teenagers, a group for parents of special-needs kids and groups for those recovering from various addictions. We have a group for mothers of preschoolers, one for single mothers, one for people who are divorced and another for people who are grieving. Our young professionals group has multiplied several times and spread to several towns in our county. We have groups of empty-nesters and groups of retirees, and we are currently discussing the launch of a group for grandparents raising grandchildren. So, in our Group Life ministry world, we often ask ourselves the question: Where is there a felt need? Where is there a hunger for a unique community? We pray and we launch a new group. A new discipleship opportunity!

The most creative group I enjoyed was one I led for three years. It was an intergenerational group. To participate, a family had to have a middle-schooler. The middle-schooler was allowed to bring his or her mom and dad, as well as big and little brothers and sisters. God bound our hearts together and family friendships were forged which have lasted over a decade and a half. Children were mentored; parents were mentored. We prayed for one another, memorized scriptures, reenacted Biblical stories, role played together, and then went on to lend emotional support through the rest of the teenage years. We became family.

One of the successful models we use to get people connected to life groups is what we call Group Link Events. It's like speed dating, but with groups. At the beginning of Spring and Fall semesters (mid-January and early September), we throw all our weight into an exciting Wednesday night event. We set up a large space to look like six or eight living room venues. Each smaller circle is hosted by a group life leader and a hospitality person, the warmest and most gregarious people we can find. The groups have already been loosely defined based on the needs we have observed among our church family. Over the course of 90 minutes, heavy *hors d'oeuvres* are served and people can float from group to group, checking out the demographic of each group, the facilitator, the topic of study and the chemistry of each circle. There's even a group built for people who don't fit anywhere else. Not all groups "make," not all needs are met, but most people take the plunge to try a group which will become a home group. Plans are made for the care of children, either on campus or at the host home or a different host home especially for the kids.

Every semester we launch dozens and dozens of new groups across the campuses of Crosspoint. We as pastors have the opportunity to lead a new group, serve as a guest facilitator in a number of different groups, continue with a group we are currently in or work at mentoring someone one on one. We often give ourselves to the mentorship of those who are feeling a call to ministry, enrolled in seminary or going through the ordination process. Every pastor and every one of our over 200+ staff people have agreed in Crosspoint's staff covenant to be part of a small group, either as a participant or leader. No one needs community more than those who are on the front lines serving in ministry. Nevertheless, most of the dozens of groups are led by lay people. Often, our leaders don't feel qualified to disciple or lead or teach. We remind them that feeling qualified is NOT a qualification. They must only stay one step ahead of those they are leading. When a leader is placed with a group, we try to put an apprentice alongside him or her. The apprentice's job is to assist, learn, grow and be prepared to launch their own group when the opportunity comes (as it likely will the next semester).

Forget a 100% success rate!

Jesus had Judas. Not every discipleship relationship has a happy ending. Some mentees fall away from the faith. Some see too many chinks in their mentors' armor and grow disillusioned because they haven't kept their eyes on Jesus. Others just get caught up in the whirlwind of life and forget Whose they are or don't guard their margins well and become burnt out and fed up. Some get connected to a group that is not a good fit for them and they give up on the process. When these sad circumstances occur, we learn. Our personal leadership skills grow as we assess the problems and risks, tweak our style and systems, and sometimes just look hard at our own hearts. We pray a lot. We admit that Jesus is still discipling us. And we pray. We pray that not one single sheep is lost. We go after them and keep trying and never give up.

Lisa: *I had a very precious relationship with a woman my age and stage in life. We both had three adorable boys who all became close friends, too. People in the church had warned me about her but I found her warm and easy to talk with and every time I prayed about whom to invest in, she seemed like the perfect fit. She was hungry for a prayer partner and we enjoyed walking three mornings a week. I called on Joan when family emergencies occurred and the friendship was honey to my heart. She was growing spiritually but one day something changed or snapped and I never understood it. She made accusations against church staff members which turned out to be unfounded, threatened to sue the church and did sue her own mother. She wouldn't answer my calls and refused to meet with me.*

I never understood what happened. Others whispered that she had struggled with mental illness for years. I kept my door open but she never walked through it again. My heart was broken and I guess hers was too, and I may never know why. I moved on but not until I practiced the profound ministry of prayer for my friend and disciple.

We never know what God will do with our investments. Maybe we'll get a clear picture of that in heaven or maybe we'll be so overwhelmed worshiping at the feet of Jesus that we won't care. We have to go back to the Scripture and ask: "What does God call me to do?" Then do it! The results are His. He told us to go into all the world and make disciples (Matthew 28:19) and that mandate will keep the church busy for a long, long time. Until Jesus comes, actually!

It's been a thrilling ride. We've forged deep friendships, laid our hands on many ordinands, enjoyed a wide and diverse assortment of small groups, and had the support of unique groups that were our lifelines through traumatic chapters in our lives. We've launched missionaries to foreign fields, discipled our own children and their friends within the nurturing atmosphere of the church and have watched dozens of people come back and serve him full-time or half-time as staff or brave, bold volunteers in the church. No doubt, discipleship ministry has been the lifeblood of our growing churches and we're absolutely certain the best is yet to come!

Chapter 6
Discipleship and Multiplication

Wes and Joy Griffin, International Leadership Institute, Carrollton, GA

Tribute

We arrived on the campus of Asbury Theological Seminary in our early twenties, hungry to grow spiritually and to further prepare for ministry. We wanted rigorous academics, deep spiritual formation, and a community of faith where we could establish deep relationships that might last a lifetime.

I (Joy) had met Dr. Allan and Beth Coppedge in August 1982 at Indian Springs Holiness Camp Meeting in Georgia, after being miraculously healed. I had suffered a tragic injury playing softball, while attending another graduate school and was left paralyzed from the waist down at age 22. Eventually doctors told me to accept the fact that I would never walk again and would never have children. God sent Howell and Velma Hearn, Asbury graduates, to serve our small rural church. Over many months, they shared with me, as I lay on the floor, about heart holiness. Finally, on July 16, I asked Howell Hearn to pray with me, and he led me into the experience of full surrender and entire sanctification. Two weeks later, at Union Camp Meeting, Dr. Tom Barrett prayed with me and I was instantly healed and stood to my feet. I had not walked in eighteen months but ran a 10k race a week later. I then went to Indian Springs Camp Meeting to tell the Hearns that I was healed. They introduced me to the Coppedges, who gave me an application to study at Asbury Theological Seminary. Al would become my academic advisor.

Wes was not raised in church, but came to Christ at age fifteen and was called into full-time Christian service before departing for the University of Colorado where he would earn a tennis scholarship. After college, he attended a year of graduate school, but desiring deeper theological and biblical training, he transferred to Asbury Theological Seminary where he begged Dr. Dennis Kinlaw, Al's father-in-law, to allow him to attend his Christian theology class. Wes also studied under Dr. Robert Coleman for evangelism and Dr. Allan Coppedge for Wesleyan theology.

Desiring to be deeply discipled, we learned about the Barnabas Foundation and attended a weekend retreat led by the Coppedges. The Scriptures were unpacked and we committed ourselves to a lifetime of discipleship and disciple-making based on the Great Commandment and the Great Commission. We joined Barnabas Foundation discipleship groups and became grounded in a lifestyle of spiritual disciplines, life-to-life transference, accountability, community, and multiplication.

For more than thirty years, we have taken seriously the challenge to discipleship and multiplication. First in the local church, then as missionaries, and now through the ministry of the International Leadership Institute (ILI), we have applied the lessons learned from Al and Beth on a global scale. There are now over 200,000 men and women in more than 120 nations equipped with the biblical principles of discipleship and multiplication that the Coppedges invested in our lives.

Essay

> *Go and make disciples of all nations, baptizing them in the name of the Father and of the Son and of the Holy Spirit, and teaching them to obey everything I have commanded you. And surely I am with you always, to the very end of the age.*
>
> \- Jesus

> *And the things you have heard me say in the presence of many witnesses entrust to faithful people who will also be qualified to teach others.*
>
> \- Paul

In the Middle Ages, God spoke to a young man in the Italian city of Assisi about "repairing My church." Francis of Assisi went on to become a leader of one of the most significant monastic orders in the Catholic Church. The impact of Francis' words and life echo through the centuries and influence people today. In the sixteenth century, the world was changed by the Protestant Reformation started by Martin Luther, an ordinary priest in a small corner of Germany. A couple of centuries later, England was spared from a bloody peasant revolution by the evangelical revival ushered in by John and Charles Wesley.

In the last century, a preacher from the Southern region of the United States, Dr. Martin Luther King, Jr., "had a dream" and started a movement that helped change the face of a nation and shape the thinking of the modern world. Also in the last century, a small Albanian woman known as Mother Teresa touched the lives of countless poor men, women, and children, launching a movement that serves those in need by alleviating suffering and sharing the Gospel.

God used each of these people to change history. The common factor among all of them was a desire to live a life of true discipleship and fulfill Christ's command to "go and make disciples."

God's Passionate Heart for the Harvest

The Bible tells the story of God's passionate love for people. His actions reveal his passion for those he has created. When he becomes flesh and takes center stage in Jesus, we see a man relentless in the pursuit of the Heavenly Father and others, including those who have been discounted, rejected, and despised.

One simple touch and the leper is healed. While others push lepers away, Jesus reaches out in love. A blind beggar cries out loudly as Jesus nears. The crowd tries to silence him, but Jesus stops to give him full attention and heals him, also. Nicodemus, a religious leader with sincere questions, approaches Jesus at night. Jesus speaks straight to his heart, letting him know there is something more he needs – he needs to be born again. After Jesus' death, Nicodemus asks for the Savior's body and buries him.

Then there is the day when Jesus enters the temple courtyard, which is filled with money-grubbing marketers taking up all the space and displacing those who came to the temple to seek God. Jesus' passion rises to the surface. His love wants seekers to have access to God. He takes a whip, turns over tables, clears the courtyard and proclaims, "It is written, 'My house will be called a house of prayer,' but you are making it a 'den of robbers.'"

Of course, God's ultimate heroic moment comes when Jesus allows himself to be betrayed into the hands of those who wanted him dead. After putting him through a show-trial, he is handed over to the brutal power of Rome to be hung on a cross until dead – the price to be paid for our sins. "Like a lamb led to the slaughter," he goes to his death, taking the sins of the world upon himself. Scripture reveals that God longs for people. Jesus gave his life so all people would know God's love. Now he invites us to share his passion and be his instrument of love to others.

Passion is a force burning in you, which seizes you and provides a power that moves you beyond ordinary human activity. Passion will not let you go until God's goals are reached. Passion is the fire and urgency that vision needs to remain alive and active. The root word of passion in Latin means 'to suffer for.' Passion is what you hunger for so much that you will sacrifice anything to have it.

Biblical Foundations for Passion

The Bible is full of individuals who embody God's passionate heart for others. Moses responded to God's call to lead his people out of slavery in Egypt. A young shepherd boy named David stood against a giant named Goliath who threatened God's people. A fisherman left his nets and extended God's offer of forgiveness to the very people who crucified Jesus. A Jewish nationalist changed his name to Paul and spent his life offering God's love to the nations he once despised.

Jeremiah was a young man, perhaps a teenager, when God filled him with his passion. To Jeremiah, passion was a fire that came from God and could not be extinguished.

> But if I say, "I will not mention him or speak any more in his name," his word is in my heart like a fire, a fire shut up in my bones. I am weary of holding it in; indeed, I cannot. (Jeremiah 20:9)

For Peter and John, passion is a compelling conviction that demands radical obedience, even in the face of persecution.

> Then they . . . commanded them not to speak or teach at all in the name of Jesus. But Peter and John replied, "Which is right in God's eyes: to listen to you, or to Him? You be the judges! As for us, we cannot help speaking about what we have seen and heard." (Acts 4:18-20)

For the apostle Paul, passion is a crucified life lived by faith in Christ.

> I have been crucified with Christ and I no longer live, but Christ lives in me. The life I live in the body, I live by faith in the Son of God, who loved me and gave Himself for me. (Galatians 2:20)

Historical Examples of Passion

Throughout history, God has filled men and women with his passion and used them greatly. God used John Wesley to bring revival and transform England. Today, 60 million people all over the world owe their spiritual heritage to this movement. Wesley exhorted his preachers, "Let us all be of one business. We live only for this, to save our own souls and the souls of those who hear us."[1]

William Booth started the Salvation Army when his church turned a deaf ear to his plea to help the desperately poor in nineteenth-century London. The King of England asked Booth what the ruling force of his life was. Booth replied, "Sir, some men's passion is for gold, other men's passion is for fame, but my passion is for souls."[2]

Much of the world knows Billy Graham as the greatest evangelist of the twentieth century. As a young man preaching to America's youth he wrote, "We are kindling a fire in this cold old world full of hatred and selfishness. Our little blaze may seem to be unavailing, but we must keep our fire burning."[3]

Mother Theresa, founder of the Missionaries of Charity and winner of the Nobel Peace Prize, expressed deep passion for the lost when she said, "If I ever become a Saint—I will surely be one of 'darkness.' I will continually be absent

1. Wesley Duewel, *Ablaze for God* (Grand Rapids: Zondervan, 1989), 107
2. Ibid.
3. Billy Graham, *Calling Youth to Christ* (Grand Rapids: Zondervan, 1947), 45.

from Heaven—to light the light of those in darkness on earth."[4]

Each of these examples was at one time a simple individual who sought to simply be a faithful disciple. Because of their faithfulness with a little, God entrusted each of these disciples with greater influence as a disciple-maker.

Passion for the Harvest

As a disciple grows deeper in his or her relationship with God, the disciple will seek to be filled with more of God's passion for others. In Luke 19:10, Jesus proclaims that he came to "seek and to save that which was lost." God desires for everyone to be reached with the life-transforming power of the Gospel. Just as Jesus sought lost people when he walked on earth, still today he seeks the lost, and we are his messengers. Jesus' passion becomes our passion. He referred to those living without a relationship with God as "the harvest," ready to be gathered into the passionate love of the Father.

The Global Challenge

We are living in one of the most exciting and yet challenging periods in God's salvation history. During the twentieth century, the world population multiplied 3.7 times. Yet in Asia there are 15 times more Christians than 100 years ago, and in Africa, there are 38 times more Christians. However, the percentage of Christians in North America has remained about the same, while the number of Christians in Europe has not kept pace with the population, growing only 1.5 times. In Latin America, thousands are coming to Christ every day.

In Matthew 28:19, Jesus commanded all Christians to "go and make disciples." He instructed us to carry the Good News to every person in every culture, beginning across the street and going to the ends of the earth.

The population of planet earth is over seven billion people. The Church has been in existence and sharing the Good News of Christ for two thousand years. Yet two thirds of the global population has yet to make a decision about the claims of the Gospel. Currently, the global challenge looks like this:

The Challenge to "Seek and Save the Lost"[5]

More than two billion people are followers of Christ. This figure includes all the different Christian denominations and groups. These people are saying, "Thank you, Jesus." They have a Bible in their language, a local church to attend, and a commitment to Jesus.

---

4. Mother Teresa, Brian Kolodiejchuk (ed), *Mother Teresa: Come Be My Light — The Private Writings of the Saint of Calcutta* (Doubleday Religion, 2007), 416.

5. Luke 19:9-10.

More than two billion people are non-Christians who have access to the Gospel. They live where they can hear, learn, and respond to the Gospel, but they are not yet following Christ. These people are saying, "No, thank you, Jesus."

Almost two billion people remain unreached. They have little or no access to the Gospel. They have no Christian influence in their lives, no churches in their areas, and usually no Bibles in their languages. These people are asking, "Who is Jesus?"

Nothing has changed in God's heart, and Jesus invites his followers to join him in his mission to seek and save that which is lost.

The Challenge to Meet Practical Human Needs

In Matthew 25:31-46, Jesus calls his followers to action through his command to passionately meet the needs of others. In this powerful passage, the Lord comes to judge the nations by separating the sheep, or the faithful, from the goats, who are those found faithless. The faithful respond to the needs of people and are gathered up into glory. The faithless ignore the needs and experience some of the strongest language of judgment in the Bible. We live in a world of pressing need. God expresses his passion for those in need through the actions of those willing to respond in the name of Christ.

> Then the King will say to those on his right, "Come, you who are blessed of My Father, inherit the Kingdom prepared for you from the foundation of the world. For I was hungry, and you gave me something to eat; I was thirsty, and you gave me something to drink; I was a stranger, and you invited me in; naked, and you clothed me; I was sick, and you visited me; I was in prison, and you came to me." (Matthew 25:34-36)

I Was Hungry and Thirsty

Approximately 850 million people across the world are hungry. Every five seconds, one child dies from hunger-related causes. Approximately one in every eight people lack access to safe water supplies, resulting in easily preventable diseases.[6]

I Was Naked

Approximately 2.7 billion people in the world live on less than $2 a day. More than 385 million human beings have to survive on less than $1 a day.[7]

6. "U.S. Food Aid Reducing World Hunger." Posted September 2007. U.S. Department of State, Vol. 12, No. 9. www.america.gov/publications/ejournalusa/0907.html. Accessed August 9, 2010.

7. "Poverty Reduction and Equity." Posted 2010. The World Bank Group. Permanent URL for this page is http://go.worldbank.org/RQBDCTUXW0. Accessed August 9, 2010.

I Was in Prison

More than 9.8 million people around the world are in prison, where they struggle with loneliness, rejection, and the cost of their crimes. In addition, many Christians have been unjustly imprisoned for their faith. In one nation, more than 3,000 Christians have been jailed during the last decade. In addition to imprisonment, more Christians were martyred in the twentieth century than in the previous nineteen.[8]

I Was Sick

Malaria is the leading cause of death and illness worldwide. Dysentery, which is easily preventable by simple sanitation, continues to kill 1.4 million children every year. More than 30.8 million adults and 2 million children live with HIV. In the year 2009, more than 2.7 million people became infected with this virus.[9]

The Spiritual Challenge in the United States[10]

The American Church faces significant spiritual challenges. Most mainline denominations are declining, and the nation is increasingly secular. There are outstanding churches and ministries in the USA who are effectively making disciples; however, the following facts must be faced:

- Half of all American churches failed to add one new member in the last two years. Every year, more than 4,000 churches close their doors, and just over 1,000 new churches open.[11]
- One out of four people in the USA have never been invited to attend a church.[12]
- On any given Sunday, roughly 15% of adults in the USA will attend a small group, and attendance is declining. Less than one in five adults (19%) volunteer their time to serve at a church in a typical week.[12]

In a poll, a total of 5,200 participants (1,300 persons in each of four generational groups) responded to the simple Evangelism Explosion question, "Have you come to the place in your spiritual life where you know for certain that if you were to die

---

8. Roy Walmsley, "World Prison Population List (Eighth Edition)," International Centre for Prison Studies. January 26, 2009. King's College London—School of Law: http://www.kcl.ac.uk/depsta/law/research/icps/downloads/wppl-8th_41. pdf (accessed July 11, 2011).

9. "AIDS Epidemic Update." November, 2009. UNAIDS: 2009 Aids Epidemic Update. http://data.unaids.org/pub/Report/2009/JC1700_Epi_Update_2009_en.pdf. Accessed August 9, 2010.

10. George Barna, *Grow Your Church from the Outside* (Venture: Regal, 2003), 82-85.

11. Ibid.

12. George Barna, *Futurecast* (Wheaton: Tyndale House Publishers, 2011).

today you would go to heaven?"[13]

- For those born before 1946........ 65% professed Christ
- For those born between 1946 and 1964...35% professed Christ
- For those born between 1965 and 1976...15% professed Christ

Do you detect a trend? Here comes the reality check.

- For those born between 1976 and 1994...4% professed Christ[14]

How God's Passion Becomes Our Passion

Although the challenges are great, we know that all things are possible through him who strengthens us (Philippians 4:13). Our intimate walk with God leads to his heart and passion for the lost. God's passion becomes our passion. Consider the following three key facts about passion:

Passion is the direct result of our love for Christ and our commitment to Him

> For Christ's love compels us, because we are convinced that one died for all, and therefore all died. And he died for all that those who live should no longer live for themselves, but for him who died for them and was raised again. (2 Corinthians 5:14-15)

In his devotional *My Utmost for His Highest,* Oswald Chambers states, "The passion of Christianity comes from deliberately signing away our rights and becoming a bondservant of Jesus Christ."[15]

Passion Must Be Nurtured

As God feeds and nurtures our soul through spiritual disciplines and his presence, our passion increases and sustains our vision. Passion must be nurtured and maintained like a fire. Just as our intimacy must be continually rekindled, so must our passion. Vision relates directly to passion. When passion decreases, vision also becomes more distant and dim.

---

13. Adapted with permission from the globally recognized Evangelism Explosion International's training materials on personal testimony.

14. Frank Newport, "Questions and Answers About Americans' Religion" Posted December 24, 2007. Gallup, Inc. www.gallup.com/poll/103459/Questions-Answers-About-Americans-Religion.aspx#1. Accessed July 25, 2011.

15. Chambers, Oswald, *My Utmost for His Highest: Daily Devotionals by Oswald Chambers.* November 3. (New York: Dodd, Mead & Company, 1935).

Passion Comes from God

Wesley Duewel writes in *Ablaze for God:*

> *We cannot light this fire. In ourselves we cannot produce it.*
> *No man can kindle in himself that celestial fire;*
> *it must come from the coal from the altar above.*[16]

Personally Experiencing God's Passion

God looks for men and women who share a passion for those without Christ. God desires for everyone to be reached with the life-transforming power of the Gospel.

Being a disciple means that you share God's love in word, deed and sign. The needs of the world can seem overwhelming; however, as God's love and passion for others fills your heart, you will be empowered to share God's love with lost and hurting people so they, too, can be transformed by God's love through Jesus Christ.

To be filled with God's passionate love for others, Jesus calls us to ask, to seek, and to knock. His passion comes only with a persistent pursuit of his heart. Too many people drift in the easy currents of self-satisfaction and comfort, while yearning for a life filled with passion. Ask for his fullness. Seek his presence. Knock until he opens to you his most precious possession: his passion for the lost. Consider this prayer as you seek to experience God's passion for his harvest field

> "God, I want the passion that you have for the lost to become my passion. I ask that from on high you send fire into my bones just as you did to Jeremiah. Let this fire burn away anything that is keeping me from experiencing your divine passion. Following the example of your passionate Son, I want to "seek the lost" and help others become followers of Christ. In Jesus's name I pray. Amen."

Fulfilling the Great Commission

True discipleship and multiplication are impossible without God's passion filling a disciple's heart, mind and soul, but with God's passion a person is properly prepared to fulfill Christ's command to "go and make disciples."

A farmer plants a seed in the ground, expecting it to grow into a fully mature plant that will produce fruit and develop seeds for other plants. When you became a follower of Christ, God sowed a seed of godliness and abundant life in your heart. However, godly character does not happen randomly. It is developed over time through intentional effort as you inwardly come to know Christ and outwardly live in love and obedience to him.

With spiritual growth comes the challenge to multiply yourself in others, shar-

---

16. Duewel, *Ablaze for God*, 107–108.

ing what God is doing in your life and helping others grow to maturity in Christ. We are commanded by Jesus to "go and make disciples" so others can grow in their relationship with Jesus.

Definition of a Disciple and Discipleship

A disciple is someone who is living out the decision to follow Christ in everyday life. He or she is a person who knows Christ inwardly and is committed outwardly to living in love and obedience to him. Discipleship is the relational process of helping someone grow spiritually by:

- Deepening the other individual's intimacy with God through prayer.
- Building the principles of God's Word into that person's life.
- Equipping him or her to understand and follow the promptings of the Holy Spirit.
- Responding in obedience to any situation with Christ-like attitudes and actions.

Jesus Christ: The Master Disciple-Maker

Jesus is the supreme example of how to make disciples. He selected key individuals and invested his life in them over a period of time. These men and women changed the course of human history by following his example. Jesus' secret is illustrated by a series of circles. The outermost circle in Jesus' life represents his ministry to the world. The remaining circles can be followed to the core of his ministry and influence.

While Jesus had a large public ministry, his ministry of discipleship focused on investing in a few lives and helping them grow to spiritual maturity until they, too, were disciple-makers.

Jesus' Circles of Influence

- **The Crowd** — Large crowds followed Jesus. He preached and served by healing the sick and miraculously feeding thousands of people; however, the large crowds were not the main focus of Jesus' ministry. (Matthew 4:25, Luke 9:11)
- **The One Hundred and Twenty** — When the Holy Spirit came, there were one hundred and twenty believers in Jerusalem. They were faithful followers of Jesus Christ. (Acts 1:15)
- **The Seventy** — Jesus entrusted seventy disciples with a special task of traveling in groups of two to the villages where he was about to go preach. (Luke 10)
- **The Twelve Apostles** — Jesus invested personally for three years in twelve of his followers; they are known as the Apostles. (Mark 3:14)

- **The Three** — Jesus invested further in three of his closest disciples: Peter, James, and John. He took them when he raised the daughter of Jairus from the dead (Mark 5:37). They were present when Jesus was transfigured (Matthew 17:1-9), and Jesus met privately with them in the garden of Gethsemane the night before he was killed (Matthew 26:37). These three became the key leaders in the early Church.

Our lives also involve a series of relationship circles. It is important for us to identify our different circles and determine those we can influence.

Jesus' Command to Make Disciples

Jesus modeled disciple-making, and he gave a specific command to his followers in what is called the Great Commission (Matthew 28:19-20). In the original Greek, the main verb is "make disciples" of all nations – "Go," "baptizing" and "teaching" are the participles whereby we accomplish the task given by Jesus.

Paul and Disciple-Making

Paul made disciples wherever he went. In his letter to a young man named Timothy, he encourages his disciple to multiply the principles of discipleship to others: "And the things you have heard me say in the presence of many witnesses entrust to reliable people who will also be qualified to teach others." (2 Timothy 2:2)

Paul expects Timothy to reproduce the discipleship process in others. In another New Testament passage, Paul writes to the Philippians with the following instructions: "Keep putting into practice all you learned from me and heard from me and saw me doing." (Philippians 4:9).

Discipleship is practical and focuses on real-life application. Paul's instruction to Timothy and the Philippians outlines a process of multiplication and guarantees the growth of the Church. We are followers of Christ today because of this multiplication process that has been producing faithful disciples for almost 2,000 years. This process began with Jesus and has continued to our generation.

Characteristics of a Faithful Disciple

The following are four key characteristics of a faithful disciple. In the beginning of the discipleship process, these characteristics are seeds that need to be cultivated. As the disciple grows, these characteristics become more evident in his or her attitudes and actions. This is called the HAFT principle.

Heart for God

A true disciple of Jesus will hunger for God's presence. They will look for opportunities to experience God and be in fellowship with him. David expressed his longing for God, "As the deer pants for streams of water, so my soul pants for you, O God" (Psalm 42:1).

Seekers and new followers of Christ often hunger for more of God in their lives. As understanding grows, their desire to continually experience God's presence and intimate fellowship in their lives only increases.

Available for God

God will bless and use those who are available to him. From the early stages, disciples need to open their hearts to God's voice. The prophet Isaiah exemplifies this characteristic when he describes his experience: "Then I heard the voice of the Lord saying, 'Whom shall I send? And who will go for Us?' And I said, "Here am I. Send me!'" (Isaiah 6:8).

Availability requires faith and a willingness to go where God sends. It may be tentative at first, but in time, the new disciple's faith will strengthen as he or she takes steps in the direction of God's purpose and will.

Faithful to God and Others

God is looking for those who will be faithful followers. Paul instructs Timothy to entrust the message to those who are reliable and faithful: 'And the things you have heard me say . . . entrust to reliable people who will also be faithful to teach others." (2 Timothy 2:2).

Faithfulness does not mean the disciple is absolutely perfect but that he or she is willing to let God lead his or her life. A faithful disciple desires to walk sincerely with God in the discipleship process.

Teachable Spirit

Invest in those who are willing to learn. In Matthew 13, Jesus compares those who hear God's teaching to different soils. The teachable person is compared to the fertile soil where the seed of God's Word grows and bears fruit.

> But the one who received the seed that fell on good soil is the man who hears the word and understands it. He produces a crop, yielding a hundred, sixty or thirty times what was sown. (Matthew 13:23)

The first letter of each principle forms the word "HAFT." A haft is the handle, grip and guard of a sword. It is what allows a soldier to hold and use the sword. In the same way, when these qualities are in the life of a disciple, God is able to get a strong hold on that disciple's life. God is looking for these characteristics in your life and the lives of those whom you disciple. If these qualities are present and increasing, then a person will be growing toward spiritual maturity.

Spiritual Disciplines – God's Path for Discipleship

Spiritual disciplines are tools that God uses in our lives to help us grow deeper in an intimate relationship with him. The word "discipline" is defined as "training that is expected to produce a specific character or pattern of behavior."[17]

Spiritual disciplines are a primary path that God uses to build godliness in our lives. There are many spiritual disciplines, including worship, meditation, fasting, and tithing. Three primary ones for a disciple are prayer, Scripture, and obedience.

A disciple is one who longs to follow Christ and grow in these areas. A clothes hanger is a good illustration of an intimate life with God and how disciplines are essential for a disciple's development. The disciple "hangs" on God through a relationship of intimacy. Just as all three sides of the hanger are essential for its usefulness, the three spiritual disciplines of prayer, Scripture, and obedience are essential in our lives. If a side is missing, the hanger will be off balance and will not be useful.

Prayer

Our depth of intimacy with God is directly related to the time we spend with him in the discipline of prayer. In Psalm 27, God tells us to seek his face. Prayer is growing deeper in our communication with him. Both we and those we disciple will be amazed at God's faithfulness as we pray. When meeting with those we disciple, it is crucial to always include significant time for prayer and covenant to pray over specific areas of our lives.

Scripture

Growing deeper in God's Word is the mark of a disciple. In his letter to Timothy, Paul advises his disciples,

> Study to present yourself to God as one approved, a worker who does not need to be ashamed and who correctly handles the word of truth. (2 Timothy 2.15)

Paul's advice is a good illustration of the need to deepen our knowledge of God's Word. The human hand has five fingers. To properly grasp an object, every finger is required, and they all work together. There are five specific disciplines regarding God's Word that we need to develop in order to properly handle the Word of God: hearing, reading, studying, memorizing and meditating. God's Word is a key resource for understanding His purpose and plans.

---

17. American Heritage Dictionary. Entry: Discipline. "American Heritage Dictionary." Posted Online 11 April 2012. http://ahdictionary.com/word/search.html?q=discipline (accessed February 11, 2013).

Obedience

God's Word tells us that if we obey God's voice and Word, we will be blessed and anointed,

> You have declared today that the Lord is your God. You have promised to obey his laws, commands, and regulations by walking in his ways and doing everything he tells you. The Lord has declared today that you are his people, his own special treasure, just as he promised, and that you must obey all his command. And if you do, he will make you greater than any other nation. Then you will receive praise, honor, and renown. You will be a nation that is holy to the Lord your God, just as he promised (Deuteronomy 26:17–19, NLT)

Obedience is putting our faith to work in practical day-to-day life. Through obedience, our faith is proven; without practical obedience, our faith is dead (James 2:17).

Spiritual Reproduction

God looks for men and women who disciple others, who in turn become effective disciple-makers. Spiritual reproduction is the goal. It is important for us to pray for clear direction from God as to whom we should disciple. We must ask God to lead us to one or more people in whom we could make a life-to-life investment. It takes consistency and effort in our Christian life to inspire others to grow in their spiritual lives; yet, the result is one of the most satisfying experiences we will know as a follower of Christ. God will use us, and at the same time, we will become a deeper disciple who is faithfully fulfilling Jesus' words in the Great Commission to "go and make disciples." The words of the Apostle John in his third letter powerfully express the joy of making disciples: "I have no greater joy than to know that my [spiritual] children are walking in truth" (3 John 1:4).

The Prayer of a Disciple Maker

Thirty-plus years ago, Al and Beth Coppedge led those of us who were on that Barnabas Foundation retreat in a profound prayer. We prayed that prayer and we have shared it around the world in the hopes of creating a global movement of disciple-makers. It has been shared in nations where the Christian faith is spreading rapidly, and we have shared it in nations where the Christian faith is greatly persecuted. The prayer of a disciple-maker simply says,

> *Lord, lead me to the people whom I should disciple to be fully committed followers of you. Give me spiritual children, those in whom I will multiply myself through discipleship, who will walk in your truth and give glory to you.* Amen.

Chapter 7
Discipleship and Conflict

Stan Key, President, Francis Asbury Society
Wilmore, Kentucky

Tribute

My connection with Al Coppedge is primarily through the fact that we married sisters. Because Al is ten years older and because he was my professor in seminary, his influence in my life has been like that of a big brother. He was always out in front, up ahead, setting the pace, and raising the standard. I have always wanted to be like him when I grow up.

Forty years ago, Al invited me to be in a discipleship group he was leading. To be honest, I didn't even pray about it. It was a no-brainer. Immediately, I said yes. We met every Thursday night in Al's living room, and what transpired in that circle of men has influenced my life in profound ways. The friendships made in that group have lasted a lifetime. Until then, my daily time in the Word and prayer was sporadic and unfocused, but, with encouragement from Al, daily spiritual disciplines became a life-defining part of my existence. The weekly rhythm of meeting with a small group of like-minded men for accountability, study, and prayer set a standard that has remained with me.

When I try to imagine how my life would have been different if Al had not stepped into my life so many years ago, I tremble. Would I have developed the discipline of a daily quiet time? Would I have made small group fellowship a vital ingredient of each week? Would I have understood the importance of Christian friendships and accountability? Would I have recognized the Gospel imperative of investing in the lives of other men? Thanks Al, for what you did, but thanks especially for who you are. From you, I learned that discipleship is so much more than a method of spiritual growth or a strategy of evangelization. It is a life to be lived so that it can be shared with others.

Essay

A pastor was walking through the lobby of his church when he saw a young boy staring at the large marble plaque on the wall. Entitled "In Remembrance," the plaque had two columns of names with a small American flag next to each one. "Who are these people?" the boy asked his pastor. "Johnny, these are the names of the men and women who died in the service," the pastor replied with an air of solemnity. Swallowing hard and almost whispering, Johnny asked, "Was it the 9:00 or the 11:00 service?"

Church can be a dangerous place![1] Though the fellowship of the saints is supposed to be a safe environment, the family of God all too often is the scene of ugly conflicts where brother fights against brother. The wounds inflicted in such confrontations are often deep and sometimes require years to heal. Building relationships with other Christians is a bit like dancing with porcupines. You have to be careful or you just might get pricked!

> *And if one asks him, "What are these wounds on your back?"*
> *he will say, "The wounds I received in the house of my friends."*
> *(Zech. 13:6)*

As Christians, we are taught to expect conflict with the world, the flesh, and the devil. We should not be surprised when we receive wounds while engaged in hand-to-hand combat with the enemy. But how should we respond when we are stabbed in the back "in the house of [our] friends"?

> *To dwell above with saints we love,*
> *That will be purest glory.*
> *To live below with saints we know;*
> *Now, that's another story!*

The fact that Christians experience conflict, however, really should not be a surprise. In one sense, Christians are no different than other groups of people. *Any* close relationship between persons is, by nature, potentially conflictual. Take marriage, for example. Although no human relationship has the ability to be the source of greater joy, it is equally true to say that no human relationship has the ability to be the source of greater pain. The two realities go together. To be in authentic relationship with someone else is to take the risk of being hurt. C.S. Lewis understood this well:

> To love at all is to be vulnerable. Love anything, and your heart will certainly be wrung and possibly be broken. If you want to make sure of keeping it intact, you must give your heart to no one, not even to an animal. Wrap it carefully round with hobbies and little luxuries; avoid all entanglements; lock it up safe in the casket or coffin of your selfishness. But in that casket – safe, dark, motionless, airless – it will change. It will not be broken; it will become unbreakable, impenetrable, irredeemable. The alternative to tragedy, or at least to the risk of tragedy, is damnation. The only place outside Heaven where you can be perfectly safe from all the dangers and perturbations of love is Hell. (The Four Loves, p. 169).

---

1. Having been a missionary for 10 years, a pastor for 25 years, and on the staff of a parachurch ministry for 4 years, I have had numerous personal encounters with conflict among Christians. Sometimes, I was on the receiving end. Sometimes, I was the cause!

But what lessons should we learn from this truth and how does it relate to discipleship? It is the purpose of this chapter to explore this question.

Defining Terms

Dictionaries define "conflict" as a struggle or a disagreement; a clash of desires; a collision of wills. The word describes the confrontation that results when two persons seek to achieve different purposes. Such a definition implies that conflict is inherent in all human relationships. Because personhood consists, at least in part, in having desires and intentions, two persons in relationship inevitably will experience conflict. Because no two persons are identical, a clash of desires is unavoidable. If one person in the relationship has no will of his own, then conflict can be averted. But to have no will is to cease being a person! This explains why cemeteries are places of quiet serenity. The persons there are all dead!

Such a perspective on conflict helps us to realize that the strength of a relationship is *not* measured by the absence of conflict. Married couples who never argue may be envied by those looking in from the outside. However, on closer inspection, such marital serenity may indicate that one of the partners has no will of his or her own: "Whatever you say, dear." Like a cemetery, the tranquility may be a sign of death, not life. When Ruth Graham was asked if she and Billy always agreed, she replied by saying; "Heavens no! If two people agree on everything, one of them is unnecessary!"

Healthy relationships are not measured by the absence of conflict but rather by how such conflict is managed. Whether in a marriage, a friendship, a church, or a discipleship group, when relationships are healthy, differences of opinion are welcomed and other perspectives valued. The presence of disagreement is actually a sign of strength in a relationship, not a sign of weakness.

The reason this truth is so difficult for many Christians to grasp is that they have never seen a model of healthy conflict. Life experiences in their families, churches, and workplaces have convinced them that disagreements always are sinful and the outcome is inevitably negative: someone wins and someone loses. To think that conflict could be a good thing is incomprehensible for such people.

The Bible gives us a dramatic picture of one conflict that we know is sinless: when God the Son prays to God the Father in the Garden of Gethsemane. "My Father, let this cup pass from me" (see Luke 22:39–46). We can be sure that no sinful self-interest provoked this collision of wills. The Father's desire was for the Son to give his life on a cross for the sins of the world. The Son hesitated. This was not what he wanted to do! He asked if he could somehow *not* drink the cup the Father had placed before him. Two persons of the blessed Trinity were in disagreement! Though it sounds almost blasphemous to say it, the will of the Son was contrary to the will of the Father. Though some may prefer to find a word other than "conflict" to describe this disagreement within the Godhead, the turmoil it generated in Jesus' heart was so intense his "sweat became like great drops of blood falling down to the ground" (v. 44). The disagreement was resolved and the unity of the Trinity preserved when Jesus submitted his will to that of his Father: "Not my will, but yours, be done" (v. 42).

The prayer in Gethsemane alerts us to the fact that not all conflict is bad. Not all disagreements are motivated by sin. The submission of the Son to the Father helps us to understand that resolving conflict is not always a matter of winners and losers. Gethsemane gives us a model of unity that values differences of opinion and welcomes their free expression. "Love does not insist on its own way" (I Cor. 13:5). The "disagreement" between the Father and the Son was resolved when both parties absorbed the other's perspective in love. We can be sure that when Jesus died on the cross, the Father's pain was just as great, if not greater, than that of the Son.

The Right Fist of Fellowship

Although the example of how God the Father and God the Son resolved their "conflict" in the Garden of Gethsemane gives us a model to which we can aspire, our disagreements with one another are notably different. The many examples of interpersonal conflict in the Bible all are tainted by some degree of human frailty and sin. It is not always easy to discern who is right and who is wrong. The complexities and nuances of human behavior are such that sometimes we must await Judgment Day to know the truth. Yet each Biblical example is not only incredibly interesting to study but also pregnant with valuable lessons to be learned for those who seek healthy relationships with others. The list of stories below is certainly not exhaustive and the Scriptures alluded to are examined only cursorily. The intent is to show how conflict consistently defines human relationships in the Biblical narrative and to introduce us to the wealth of wisdom in these stories for helping followers of Christ discover principles for dealing with conflict and building healthy interpersonal relationships.

The first human conflict in history occurred between *Adam and Eve*. When sin entered the picture, their ideal marriage in paradise quickly turned sour. A simplistic reading of the story seems to indicate that Eve was to blame for the problems in the home. After all, *she* was the one who struck up a conversation with the serpent and *she* was the one who took the first bite of the forbidden fruit (see Genesis 3:1–6). But the Bible recognizes that Adam was standing right next to her as she was tempted and lured into sin. As the head of his home, why didn't he say something? Why didn't he intervene to protect his wife from Satan's deception? Indeed, Adam's passive silence is just as culpable as Eve's active disobedience—maybe more. The consequences of this tragic situation can be seen when God asked Adam to give an account of what happened. "The woman whom you gave to be with me"—*she* is the one who caused this mess, Adam lamely answers (Gen. 3:12). Refusing to take responsibility and playing the blame game have characterized human conflict ever since. Where once the relationship was defined by transparency and trust ("naked and not ashamed," Gen. 2:25), now it is marked by fear, distrust, and competition.

The next conflict recorded in the Bible comes in Genesis 4:1–8; the story of *Cain and Abel.* Occurring at the dawn of history, it is almost as if the author of Genesis records this event to prepare us for the way conflict is going to be such an integral part of the human drama. Motivated by jealousy over the way God seems to show preference for his brother, Cain kills Abel. Everything about this incident is evil, diabolically evil. For one thing, the text emphasizes how Cain's act is premeditated and coldly calculated. The first murder in history is not something done in a fit of uncontrollable rage. In fact, God himself stepped in and tried to talk Cain out of it! The plot thickens when we realize that Cain didn't kill an enemy, but a brother. It was cold-blooded fratricide! Finally, the serious nature of this treacherous act is underscored by the scene of the crime: a worship service. Abel may have been the first person killed in church but he certainly wasn't the last.

The conflict between *Abraham and Lot* (Genesis 13:5–13) was resolved when Abraham gave up his rights as the elder leader of the team so that his younger nephew could have his own way: to choose the land he preferred to inhabit. Abraham's initiative and quick action prevented a simmering conflict from breaking out into open hostility. His willingness to let Lot make the decision shows that he valued maintaining the relationship more than winning the argument. It is Abraham's faith in the overarching purposes of God that enabled him to take his hands off the situation and trust God with the results.

The conflict between the twin brothers *Jacob and Esau* began even before they were born; they fought one another in their mother's womb (Gen. 25:22). The conflict was provoked primarily by Jacob's devious character and dishonest behavior. On two separate occasions, Jacob cheated his older brother: first by taking his birthright (Gen. 25:29–34) and then by stealing his father's blessing (Gen. 27). The conflict turned to hatred and Esau wanted revenge. Only a miracle of divine grace brought about reconciliation between these rascals (see Genesis 32–33).

Numbers 16 tells the story of *Korah's rebellion.* In what is clearly an effort to depose Moses and bring in a new leadership team, Korah led a revolt against the man whom God himself had appointed to lead the nation. Speaking to both Moses and Aaron, the conspirators went public with their complaint: "You have gone too far! For all in the congregation are holy, every one of them, and the Lord is among them. Why then do you exalt yourselves above the assembly of the Lord?" (v. 3). Korah wanted his boss's job. He was convinced he could do it better. Moses recognized that the rebellion was spreading so rapidly and growing so intense that he had no recourse but to turn the situation over to the Lord. Speaking to the conspirators, he said, "In the morning the Lord will show you who is his, and who is holy...." (v. 5). This conflict was resolved when God himself showed up and declared who was right and who was wrong in a manner that no one could misunderstand.

> And as soon as (Moses) had finished speaking all these words, the ground under them split apart. And the earth opened its mouth and swallowed them up, with their households and all the people who belonged to Korah and all their goods. So they and all that belonged to them went down alive into Sheol, and the earth closed over them, and they perished from the midst of the assembly. And all Israel who were around them fled at their cry, for they said, "Lest the earth swallow us up!" And fire came out from the Lord and consumed the 250 men offering the incense. (Numbers 16:31–35)

The relationship between *King Saul and David* should have been a beautiful illustration of discipleship in action, an older mentor training a younger man for a glorious future in leadership. However, David's gifts and popularity caused Saul to be jealous and insecure. How difficult it must have been for David to relate to the one who was discipling him! Three times Saul threw his spear at David, seeking to kill him. (I Sam. 18:10–11; 19:9–10). Learning the art of spear-dodging was vital to David's survival and integral to his spiritual formation. God was preparing David for leadership, and one of the best ways to learn how to be a good leader is to have the privilege of serving a bad one!

David's family is full of conflict. When his oldest son, Amnon, raped his half-sister, Tamar, David did nothing to address the flagrant injustice committed against his own daughter (II Sam. 13:21–22). When Tamar's brother, Absalom, murdered Amnon to avenge his sister's rape, again David was passive (II Sam. 14:33). Apparently David hoped the problems in his family would just go away. Finally, when Adonijah wanted to take David's concubine, Abishag, as a wife and then formed a conspiracy to take the throne, David again did nothing (I Kings 1:5–6). David's consistent response to conflict in these situations was to deny the truth and avoid the conflict. His inaction only made things worse.

The conflict between *Mary and Martha* is not violent or ugly, but it is no less real. The sisters illustrate the tension that often exists between those who are more contemplative and those who are more practical. When Jesus and a large group of friends visited the home of these sisters, the conflict bubbled to the surface (see Luke 10:38–42). While practical Martha was frantically working in the kitchen, contemplative Mary was sitting at Jesus' feet, listening as he talked. The heat coming out of the kitchen wasn't coming only from the oven! Martha blurted, "Lord, do you not care that my sister has left me to serve alone? Tell her then to help me" (v. 40). Jesus' tender response was loving, but at the same time spoke clearly of the importance of getting one's priorities straight. "Martha, Martha, you are anxious and troubled about many things, but one thing is necessary. Mary has chosen the good portion, which will not be taken away from her" (v. 41–42).

One of the most interesting conflicts recorded in Scripture is the one between *Paul and Barnabas* over whether or not John Mark should remain a part of the team (Acts 15:36–41). "Paul thought best not to take with them one who had withdrawn from them in Pamphylia and had not gone with them to the work" (v. 38). In other words, Paul sought to pull rank and imposed his will on Barnabas.

Paul intended to *win* this argument! The result was a rupture in the relationship of one of the most effective church-planting missionary teams in history. Though some commentators believe they can discern who was right and who was wrong, the text simply does not give a clear answer. Paul certainly had valid reasons for not wanting John Mark on the team. But Barnabas also had valid reasons for wanting to take him along. Could it be that Luke, under the inspiration of the Holy Spirit, recorded this incident to teach us that sometimes the ambiguities and nuances are so great when saints disagree that we will have to wait until heaven to have a final verdict on the matter?

We have a clear picture of *healthy* conflict resolution in Acts 6:1–7. The story tells of a dispute that erupted in the Jerusalem church over how the budget was being distributed. The Greek-speaking widows were apparently being neglected in the daily food distribution. For many, it seemed that the church leaders were guilty of showing partiality, playing favorites. The conflict was resolved when both sides worked together on a solution. The result was that everyone felt satisfied and, most importantly, "the word of God continued to increase and the number of the disciples multiplied greatly" (v. 7).

Though many other examples of conflict in the Bible could be mentioned, these illustrations suffice to show the complexities involved in human relationships. These stories remind us that conflict is inevitable. The only way to avoid conflict is to live alone. There is no single formula for resolving conflict, because each situation has its own unique ingredients. Discerning where sin influences conflict is of vital importance, but it may be harder than you think. God is very interested in human relationships, and he is very interested in conflict and how it is managed. Through his Word and his Spirit, God is ready to offer wisdom, grace, and strength to those who seek his assistance in dealing with a difficult relationship. Learning to handle conflict in a biblical manner should be a primary goal in the spiritual formation occurring in the discipleship process. The best teaching on this subject will occur not through Bible studies on the topic but through personal experiences of dealing with the conflict that arises in the context of discipleship relationships.

The Cause and Cure of Conflict

It would be difficult to find a passage of Scripture more helpful in dealing with conflict than James 4:1–10. These verses provide guidance for a wide range of situations that characterize the lives of many Christians.

> What causes quarrels and what causes fights among you? Is it not this, that your passions are at war within you? You desire and do not have, so you murder. You covet and cannot obtain, so you fight and quarrel. You do not have, because you do not ask. You ask and do not receive, because you ask wrongly, to spend it on your passions. You adulterous people! Do you not know that friendship with the world is enmity with God? Therefore whoever wishes to be a friend of the world makes himself an enemy of God.

> Or do you suppose it is to no purpose that the Scripture says, "He yearns jealously over the spirit that he has made to dwell in us"? But he gives more grace. Therefore it says, "God opposes the proud but gives grace to the humble." Submit yourselves therefore to God. Resist the devil, and he will flee from you. Draw near to God, and he will draw near to you. Cleanse your hands, you sinners, and purify your hearts, you double-minded. Be wretched and mourn and weep. Let your laughter be turned to mourning and your joy to gloom. Humble yourselves before the Lord, and he will exalt you. (James 4:1–10, ESV)

Like a skilled doctor looking beyond the symptoms of a disease to find its root cause, James digs deep, searching for the definitive explanation for why we fight and hurt one another. Like peeling layers of skin off the proverbial onion, James uncovers one layer after another to expose the root issue that explains why human relationships, even among Christians, are so often adversarial and contentious.

First-level Cause: Unmet Desires

What causes quarrels and fights? James begins to answer his question by looking at the most obvious answer; the one that lies on the surface: "Is it not this, that your passions are at war within you?" (v. 1). We are at war on the outside because there is a war going on inside! The word translated "passions" comes from the Greek word *hedone* (the root of our word "hedonism"). The term refers to the self-indulgent pursuit of pleasure. We *want* something that we believe will give us pleasure and make us happy. And when that desire is unmet, we suddenly want to pick a fight with whoever is perceived to be standing in the way. It may be as innocent as a husband wanting the covers on *his* side of the bed during the night or as brazenly hostile as Hitler's invasion of Poland. At a surface level, the cause of conflict is crystal clear: unmet desires. "You desire and do not have, so you murder. You covet and cannot obtain, so you fight and quarrel" (v. 2). When we can't have what we want, we declare war.

Second-level Cause: Prayerlessness

James takes us a level deeper when he analyzes *why* our desires are unmet. The answer may surprise you. Our desires are unmet because we haven't prayed! "You do not have, because you do not ask" (v. 2). Jesus explained that our Father in heaven is eager to grant our requests and so he urged his disciples to pray, pray, pray. God cares about our needs and wants to be involved in meeting them. But he wants to be asked. Charles Spurgeon expressed the matter succinctly: "Whether we like it or not, asking is the rule of the Kingdom." Notice the progression of James' thought. The reason we fight is because our desires are not met. The reason are desires are not met is because we do not pray. This line of thinking leads logically to a third level of reflection. But what if I *do* pray and ask God to give me what I want but he doesn't answer? What then?

Third-level Cause: Selfish Ambition

The reason God doesn't answer our prayers is because we pray wrongly. When our motives are impure, our prayers are not in sync with God's will. And prayers not aligned with God's purposes will not rise higher than the ceiling. "You ask and do not receive, because you ask wrongly, to spend it on your passions. You adulterous people! Do you not know that friendship with the world is enmity with God? Therefore whoever wishes to be a friend of the world makes himself an enemy of God" (vv. 3–4). In James' logic, why would God answer the prayers of his enemies? Why should we be surprised when God doesn't answer prayers motivated by worldliness and selfish ambition? "For where jealousy and selfish ambition exist, there will be disorder and every vile practice" (James 3:16).

James' logic is irrefutable. If I have worldliness and selfish ambition in my heart, then I pray wrongly. If I pray wrongly, God will not answer my prayers. If God doesn't answer my prayers, then my desires remain unmet. And if my desires are unmet, then I find myself frustrated, looking for a fight. But this leaves us with one final question: *Why, oh, why* is my heart filled with worldliness and selfish ambition? I now see that all my interpersonal conflicts are caused by the state of my ego-centric heart. So *why* am I like this?

Fourth-level Cause: Double-mindedness and Pride

Following the logic of James' descending levels of diagnostic analysis prepares us to hear the explanation for the root cause of fighting and quarreling: we are proud and double-minded (vv. 6, 8). The reason we love this world and are consumed with selfish ambition is because we are proud. Like Lucifer's rebellious attempt to dethrone God, and like Adam and Eve's arrogance in eating forbidden fruit, our proud hearts put us in conflict with God. "God opposes the proud" (v. 6). To be proud is to be God's enemy. Coupled with the inner cancer of pride is double-mindedness (v. 8). The word describes a type of spiritual bipolar disorder that makes a person "unstable in all his ways" (James 1:8). Will I obey God or will I follow the voice of selfish ambition? Will I live for the kingdom of God or for the kingdom of this world? Will I say yes or will I say no? We fight one another on the outside because on the inside we are a seething cauldron of competing desires; we are a walking civil war!

Is There a Cure?

Can the heart be healed so that our desires become pure, so that we pray rightly, so that our prayers are answered, so that our needs are met, and so that we no longer fight and quarrel with those around us? Let's let James speak for himself.

> But he gives more grace. Therefore it says, "God opposes the proud but gives grace to the humble." Submit yourselves therefore to God. Resist the devil, and he will flee from you. Draw near to God, and he will draw near to you. Cleanse your hands, you sinners, and purify your hearts, you double-minded. Be wretched and mourn and weep. Let your laughter be turned to mourning and your joy to gloom. Humble yourselves before the Lord, and he will exalt you. (James 4:6–10)

James tells us that the cure for quarreling and fighting is entire sanctification! God gives more grace, enough grace to enable a man who is worldly and proud to humble himself before the Lord, thus making possible the healing of his divided heart and the purifying of his worldly desires.

A century ago, President Woodrow Wilson led our nation into the First World War, promising that it would be a war to end all wars. He was mistaken. Rather than ending human conflict, the First World War laid the foundation for future wars. Although Woodrow Wilson was mistaken, James is not. When God's sanctifying grace enables us to win the victory over the passions that churn within us, then the war to end all wars has been fought—and won! When sanctifying grace purifies the heart, our desires become aligned with God's will, which enables us to pray rightly. When we pray rightly, God will answer our prayers so that our desires will be fully satisfied, bringing an end to all conflict and bringing peace on earth. A world full of disciples where this inner work of heart purity is a reality will be the glorious fulfillment of that promised day when "the kingdoms of this world become the kingdom of our Lord and of his Christ, and he shall reign forever and ever" (Rev. 11:15).

Discipleship and Mission

Chapter 8
Discipleship and Compassionate Ministry

Matt Friedeman, Professor of Evangelism and Discipleship,
Wesley Biblical Seminary, Jackson, Mississippi

Tribute

"Jesus is more important than the discus." Those were the first words I remember Al Coppedge saying to me. I had just met him and proceeded to tell him that I was red-shirting my senior year on the track and field team at the University of Kansas and would attend Asbury Seminary in a couple of years. He was unimpressed that I was second in the nation in the discus throw, a Big Eight champion and coming off participation in the Olympic Trials. He thought Jesus should take precedence over athletic ambitions. In his estimation, I ought to get to seminary as soon as possible.

He got my attention.

When I finally did arrive at Asbury, my first stop was his office. I wanted to be in his discipleship group. And that eventually happened, also. He and a band of other students that he had gathered ate together regularly in the cafeteria, held Bible studies in his home, and ministered together from time to time. It made an enormous difference. And it was a regular pattern of his life during his entire tenure at ATS.

A few years later, Al was a special entry on my dissertation committee at the University of Kansas. Actually, he was one of the people I had interviewed for that dissertation on discipleship in higher education. As a result of his recommendation, my first teaching position was a summer stint as adjunct professor at Nairobi Evangelical School of Theology; that fall, I began what has become a thirty-year career at Wesley Biblical Seminary.

In the midst of those interactions, he bestowed on this disciple life-transforming principles: the import of the spiritual disciplines and of small group discipleship, premarital counseling, a living example of how to raise extraordinary children, perseverance through hardship and disappointment, the priority of and prayer for the local church and its leadership, and the impact of classroom excellence.

A word on the latter dynamic: I attended a conference with a group of Asbury graduates who had studied at ATS from the late seventies through the early nineties. Recognizing our shared educational background, I posed a question: "What seminary professor had the most impact on your life?" In light of all the outstanding educators present at the seminary during those years, there was surprising unanimity in the answers. Multiple professors were mentioned, but everyone finally agreed that the professor and the course that had made the most impact was Al Coppedge and his class on John Wesley. "Once you were through with that semester you knew John Wesley–really knew him." This result was due to the combination of excellent lectures, accountability for time-on-task outside the classroom, and the requirement of reading and outlining a significant number of John Wesley's 52 Sermons. But it was all grounded in an extraordinary professor.

Throughout his career, Al has done what exceptional professors do – wrote significant volumes, counseled students, lectured with great effectiveness and set a holy example. What set him apart from many theological minds in ivory towers was that he made a radical decision – that it was more important to spend time with students and, by God's grace, form them into Great Commission disciples, than to simply further his own career within the academy.

Essay

Life is simpler if you know what the outcomes are supposed to be.

My systematic theology professor in seminary[1] taught a Bible study in his living room that was designed to convey to the discipleship group gathered there God's objectives for His people. He used Exodus 19:3-6, and what he said gave me a paradigm of practical theology that has carried me throughout my life in ministry. Here are the words contained in those verses:

> Then Moses went up to God, and the Lord called to him from the mountain and said, "This is what you are to say to the descendants of Jacob and what you are to tell the people of Israel: 'You yourselves have seen what I did to Egypt, and how I carried you on eagles' wings and brought you to myself. Now if you obey me fully and keep my covenant, then out of all nations you will be my treasured possession. Although the whole earth is mine, you will be for me a *kingdom of priests and a holy nation.*' These are the words you are to speak to the Israelites."[2]

Verse 6 of that passage was especially pregnant with meaning: "…a kingdom of priests and a holy nation." Embedded in those eight words are three objectives for the people of God.

- "Kingdom...nation" seem to imply a *community* of people, not merely individuals blazing a future for themselves.
- "Priests" indicates *service*, equipping the community to be all that God wants them to be in giving of themselves.

1. Dr. Allan Coppedge. I have taken liberties with his original study and stated conclusions a bit differently.

2. Exodus 19:3-6, New International Version (NIV). Emphasis mine.

- "Holy" implies a certain *character*, as other studies of the Text adequately prove, to reflect God's character in their own lives.

When the gospel of Matthew describes the inauguration of Jesus' public ministry, we shouldn't be surprised that these Judaic emphases are highlighted. After the temptation of Jesus, the gospel records that He began:

- Gathering a *community* of disciples who soon begin… (4:18-22)
- *Serving* people via preaching and outreach to the margins of culture (4:23-25). He then begins…
- Teaching His disciples about *holy character* (5:3-16)

Community. Service. Character. These emphases in the Exodus account are reiterated rather forcefully in Matthew. It is hard to find an aspect of Christian discipleship that doesn't fit well into one of these scriptural categories that describe our destiny. And the emphases are complementary, indeed, are necessary to each other. Through community we begin to emulate the God Who is Community – Father, Son and Holy Spirit, who are three distinct but not separate Persons. John Wesley famously declared that there is no holiness without *social* holiness and certainly no Christian solitaries. In a more recent era, Eugene Peterson proposes that

> There can be no maturity in the spiritual life, no obedience in following Jesus, no wholeness in the Christian life, apart from an immersion in, and embrace of, community. I am not myself by myself.[3]

Through service we connect with people who are in desperate need and find ourselves transformed through that contact. Nothing changes a person like touching the needy in humility and love. Wesley, in his notable sermon "On Visiting the Sick," maintained that we all ought to reach out to the afflicted because it is an oft-neglected – but necessary – means of grace. Further, he said, such service increases thankfulness to God, increases our sympathy, our benevolence and our "social affections." And it wasn't a tangential issue for Wesley; it was a heaven and hell issue.

> What then will be the consequence? Instead of hearing that word, "Come, ye blessed! – For I was sick, and ye visited me;" you must hear that awful sentence, "Depart, ye cursed! – For I was sick, and ye visited me not!"[4]

The English word "character" is derived from the Greek for "engrave." As we live and serve in community led by Jesus, by grace He begins the engraving process of making us like Himself. We experience increasing maturity in our soul life – thinking more like Him, acting more like Him, feeling more like Him about the matters prioritized in His Kingdom.

---

3. Eugene Peterson, *A Generous Savior* (Tyler, TX: The Gathering, 2012), p. 32.
4. John Wesley, Sermon #98, "On Visiting the Sick."

E. Stanley Jones called the Sermon on the Mount the self-portrait of Jesus,[5] and that can certainly be said more particularly of the beatitudes. As "iron sharpens iron" in community and we serve others, He marks us with poverty of spirit, meekness, purity of heart, and a passion for peacemaking. In other words, we become like Jesus, "holy as He is holy." For Wesley's part, the beatitudes were "the sum of all true religion"[6] and the model of what we are all to become.

Discipleship and "the missing link"

The premier method of making disciples in America seems to be gathering a group of erstwhile disciples in order to study the Scriptures and articulate practical applications. What seems to be missing in the typical mix of evangelicalism is service to the poor, the needy, the "margins" of culture. The aforementioned paragraph out of Matthew that speaks to service is here highlighted. After Christ begins gathering His community of disciples together,

> Jesus went throughout Galilee, teaching in their synagogues, proclaiming the good news of the kingdom, and healing every disease and sickness among the people. News about him spread all over Syria, and people brought to him all who were ill with various diseases, those suffering severe pain, the demon-possessed, those having seizures, and the paralyzed; and he healed them. Large crowds from Galilee, the Decapolis, Jerusalem, Judea and the region across the Jordan followed him.[7]

In Matthew's introductory paragraph concerning the ministry of Jesus, he mentions disease, sickness, pain, the demon-possessed, those with seizures and the paralyzed. While many rabbis and priests were stepping around or avoiding altogether the outcasts of Palestine, Jesus with disciples in tow met them, talked with them, touched them, healed them. Throughout the gospels, this seems to frame Jesus' primary conception of "the priesthood": they were to be doers of the Word, not speakers, readers or hearers only.

Can we have real community and expressed Christlikeness without such service to the "untouchables"? Regrettably, the vast majority of modern discipleship groups, and even the vast majority of churches, try. And therein lies the *biggest problem* with Western discipleship. Would-be disciple-makers need to remind themselves that if they make disciples by sitting around and talking, their disciples will – in all likelihood – sit around and talk. Movement is integral to the disciple-making process.

---

5. E. Stanley Jones, *The Christ of the Mount: A Living Exposition of Jesus' Words as the Only Practical Way of Life* (Nashville: Abingdon, 1931), 27.

6. John Wesley, Sermon #16, "Upon Our Lord's Sermon on the Mount, Discourse 1."

7. Matthew 4:23-25, NIV.

Cor Incurvatus

A Latin phrase used by Martin Luther perfectly describes this discipleship deficit: *cor incurvatus ad se.*[8] *Cor* is the word for heart. *Incurvatus* means "curved in." *Ad se* means "on itself." So...a heart curved in on itself. Luther was thinking of individual hearts, of course, and that certainly hits the nail on the head. But in a collective sense, *cor incurvatus ad se* accurately describes a considerable number of local churches. More to the point, most churches exist for themselves. Years ago, evangelical Tom Skinner remarked that most modern tithers tithed to themselves. When they gave their weekly or monthly offerings to the church, those funds were going to support the best preacher they could afford (for the best listening experience), the best worship service their money could hope to achieve, the best youth and children's pastors the collected monies could attract, and the best possible facilities. But at the end of the day, those are things designed to bless the *already gathered* community.

A shoe factory makes shoes for those outside the shoe factory. An oil refinery prepares oil to supply businesses beyond itself. Entertainers practice diligently so that audiences outside those rehearsals can enjoy their talent. And, by common-sense extension, churches do church in order to exercise their gifts for the Great Commission[9] and the Great Commandments[10] – basically, for those outside the church.

Even so, most churches, if they recognize this calling in theory, dismiss it in actual practice. And many, truthfully, don't know it even in theory. Chuck Lawless, Professor of Evangelism and Missions and Dean of Graduate Studies at Southeastern Seminary, explains that, in his consulting work, no church leader has ever said to him, "Our church really doesn't want to do the Great Commission." But he did have some hunches why churches talked about Great Commission priorities yet never actually got around to doing anything about them:

- Church leaders talk the language without letting the biblical texts "sink in."
- Pastors are themselves not committed to this task.
- Churches see the Great Commission as a task for full-time ministers or missionaries.
- Churches do not really believe nonbelievers are lost.
- Churches tell members to do the Great Commission without teaching them how.
- Church members fail to see the world around them.
- Church members don't know missionaries.

---

8. Dennis F. Kinlaw, *Let's Start with Jesus: A New Way of Doing Theology* (Grand Rapids, MI: Zondervan, 2005), 112.

9. "Go...and make disciples of the nations..." (Mt. 29:19).

10. Love God and neighbor (Mt. 22:37-40).

- Churches confuse "sheep swapping" with the Great Commission.[11]
- Some leaders settle with partial obedience to the Great Commission.[12]

In years of teaching and consulting with churches on compassionate ministries, I can report a similar list of why the vast majority of congregations have no regular and significant ministries in their local communities:

1. They use a different operational definition for disciple than Jesus apparently embraced.
2. Most congregations have virtually no exposure to radically needy people in the community.[13]
3. There is little honest application of the sermons and lessons when preaching, for instance, through the gospel narratives.
4. Pastors don't lead by serving those outside their own faith community.
5. Leaders in the church beyond the pastor don't lead by serving those outside their own faith community.
6. What you count matters (money, attendance), and service to the poor isn't counted.
7. There is a false bifurcation of compassionate ministry and evangelization.
8. Churches confuse giving money to a cause with actual participation in a cause.
9. Churches do not believe the entire biblical emphasis on the poor and the needy is as serious a discipleship teaching as it really is.

Is a disciple "made" in the Great Commission sense if he doesn't engage the poor and needy in his community? If such service is as central to the life of Jesus as the gospel accounts portray and the call of a disciple is "Follow Me," one is forced to admit that a disciple without compassionate ministry is no disciple at all.

---

11. Ibid.

12. Chuck Lawless, "Why Churches Talk the Great Commission But Don't Do It," http://thomrainer.com/ 2014/06/churches-talk-great-commission-dont/: "The Great Commission passages resound with proclaiming the Word, making disciples, teaching obedience, reaching the nations, and relying on the Spirit. Some churches focus, though, on evangelism while failing to teach believers. Others emphasize discipleship but do not evangelize. Some influence their community but never touch the nations; others focus on global needs but miss their local community. These congregations may be partially obedient to the Great Commission – but partial obedience is also disobedience at some level.

13. John Wesley, Sermon #98: "One great reason why the rich, in general, have so little sympathy for the poor, is, because they so seldom visit them. Hence it is, that, according to the common observation, one part of the world does not know what the other suffers. Many of them do not know, because they do not care to know: they keep out of the way of knowing it; and then plead their voluntary ignorances an excuse for their hardness of heart. 'Indeed, Sir,' said person of large substance, 'I am a very compassionate man. But, to tell you the truth, I do not know anybody in the world that is in want.' How did this come to pass? Why, he took good care to keep out of their way; and if he fell upon any of them unawares 'he passed over on the other side.'"

In the Early Church

Some moderns like to think that concern for the poor and inclusion of the destitute in certain cutting-edge churches is a new thing God is doing, a fresh wind across our frequently "curved in" landscape. Thomas Oden debunks such a conception:

> The churches of ancient Christianity were practically engaged in organized and regular ministries to the alienated, disabled, and addicted long before modern transformations of these concerns. These ministries to lepers, outcasts, pariahs, and rejects had been proceeding for two millennia prior to the advent of modern inclusion ideologies that claimed to humanize them. We are surprised then these ministries are found to have persisted for two millennia. It is a fantasy of the modern imagination that the ancient sources had no clear understanding of the importance of inclusion of the outcasts.[14]

In Acts there are many examples of compassionate concern, the first of which came in the chapter just after the Spirit-filling of Acts 2. Phineas Bresee, primary founder of the Church of the Nazarene, recognized the significance of this: "It means that the first service of a Holy Ghost-baptized church is to the poor; that its ministry is to those who are lowest down; that its gifts are for those who need them the most. As the Spirit was upon Jesus to preach the gospel to the poor, so His Spirit is upon His servants for the same purpose."[15]

In Acts 2:45 we read, "They sold property and possessions to give to anyone who had need." In Acts 4, "there were no needy persons among them" for lands and houses were sold and the money given to the apostles that they might distribute it "to anyone who had need." (Acts 4:34-35) From there, in quick succession, people are healed, widows are fed, unbelievers are evangelized and the gospel shows its great cultural versatility by winning over the rich, the poor, the pagans, the disenfranchised. When Paul makes his way across multiple Roman provinces, he establishes house churches that teach the believers these compassionate precepts handed down from one generation of Christians to another.

Around 125 A.D., the philosopher Aristides described Christians to the Emperor Hadrian:

> ...they love one another, and from widows they do not turn away their esteem; and

14. Thomas C. Oden, *The Good Works Reader* (Grand Rapids, MI: Eerdmans Publishing, 2007), 198.

15. In the September 1901 *Nazarene Messenger*, Dr. Bresee wrote, "The evidence of the presence of Jesus in our midst is that we bear the gospel, primarily to the poor." In a January 1902 issue of the *Messenger*, he wrote, "We can get along without rich people, but not without preaching the gospel to the poor." And in an October 1898 *Messenger* article he exhorted, "The gospel comes to a multitude without money and without price, and the poorest of the poor are entitled to a front seat at the Church of the Nazarene, the only condition being that they come early enough to get there." These and other similar quotes can be found in "A Church For All People," by Ron Benefiel, October 1995 *Herald of Holiness*, pg. 12ff.

> they deliver the orphan from him who treats him harshly. And he, who has, gives to him who has not, without boasting. And when they see a stranger, they take him in to their homes and rejoice over him as a very brother; for they do not call them brethren after the flesh, but brethren after the spirit and in God. And whenever one of their poor passes from the world, each one of them according to his ability gives heed to him and carefully sees to his burial. And if they hear that one of their number is imprisoned or afflicted on account of the name of their Messiah, all of them anxiously minister to his necessity, and if it is possible to redeem him they set him free. And if there is among them any that is poor and needy, and if they have no spare food, they fast two or three days in order to supply to the needy their lack of food. They observe the precepts of their Messiah with much care, living justly and soberly as the Lord their God commanded them.[16]

Rodney Starks writes in *The Rise of Christianity* what it was that made the early church such an evangelistic force. He describes how they "outlived the pagans" in numerous ways. During plagues, Christians ran to the diseased with water and food as the godless were running away. When women cast their female babies out onto the road (because, alas, they weren't boys), Christians picked them up and raised them as if they were their own. In urban areas, Christians provided sanctuary for the poor and the alien. The emperor Julian grumbled, "The impious Galileans support not only their poor, but ours as well." Tertullian wrote that while pagan temples spent their donations "on feasts and drinking bouts," Christians spent theirs "to support and bury poor people, to supply the wants of boys and girls destitute of means and parents, and of old persons confined to the house."[17]

In Wesley/Asbury

When Wesley began his ministry, he was already well-practiced in compassionate service; he and other members of the Oxford Holy Club regularly visited the sick and the imprisoned as part of their agreed-upon discipline. He was an evangelist in a nation rife with drinking and gambling addictions, child neglect, horrific prison conditions, slavery, deficient medical care and widespread moral malaise among both clergy and laity. Therefore, evangelism for Wesley meant calling people away from moral turpitude and into societies, classes and bands that could, by God's grace, transform their hearts and habits. He described the Methodist way to his preachers and those who followed them:

> Let us be employed, not in the highest, but in the meanest, and not in the easiest but the hottest, service – ease and plenty we leave to those that want them. Let us go on in

16. *The Apology of Aristides the Philosopher*, translated from the Syriac version by D.M. Kay. Earlychristianwritings.com

17. Rodney Starks, *The Rise of Christianity: How the Obscure, Marginal Jesus Movement Became the Dominant Religious Force in the Western World in a Few Centuries* (Harper: San Francisco, 1997), 84, 189.

> toil, in weariness, in painfulness, in cold or hunger, so we may but testify the gospel of the grace of God. (Acts 20:24) The rich, the honourable, the great, we are thoroughly willing (if it be the will of our Lord) to leave to you. Only let us alone with the poor, the vulgar, the base, the outcasts of men. Take also to yourselves 'the saints of the world': but suffer us 'to call sinners to repentance'; even the most vile, the most ignorant, the most abandoned, the most fierce and savage of whom we can hear. To these we will go forth in the name of our Lord, desiring nothing, receiving nothing of any man (save the bread we eat while we are under his roof), and let it be seen whether God has sent us.[18]

In one of his engravings, "The Idle Prentice," 18th-century artist William Hogarth satirized the excited pleadings of a Methodist preacher as he tried to convince a condemned man on the way to execution to abandon his life to the Lord. A closer perusal of the image also reveals an official Anglican clergyman sitting idly by in comfort. The contrast is clear: be a fool for Christ or rest contentedly. Wesley, with a holistic Scriptural foundation, chose the former and thus cultivated in his British disciples "a desire to flee from the wrath to come" along with a willingness to run towards the sound of their nation's pain. That combination proved to be overwhelmingly powerful.

In 1771 Wesley sent Francis Asbury to America. After the Revolutionary War, Asbury became the leader of American Methodism. His journal entries on the Methodist penchant towards the needy are instructive:

> O, what happiness do they lose who never visit the poor in their cottages! (February 11, 1786)

> Religion is reviving here among the Africans; several are joined in society: these are the poor; these are the people we are more immediately called to preach to. (March 5, 1797)

> To begin at the right end of the work, is to go first to the poor; these will, the right may possibly, hear the truth: there are among us who have blundered here. (June 19, 1789)

> The Baptists have built an elegant church, planned for a steeple and organ: they take the right; and the commonality and the slaves fall to us: this is well. We have about twenty whites, and between three and four hundred backs in society here. (January 27, 1804)

> [Letter to Nelson Reed] My dear I feel! I feel! for the Baltimore Road prisoners. Oh that some local brother would consent to preach to them every Sabbath, one that could gain their confidence, they are degraded far below domestic slavery, but their rights as they respect the Gospel, they ought not, no State should dare to rob them of this. Oh help those outcastes, those dregs of human nature, precious, perishing souls....do, do

18. John Wesley, "A Farther Appeal to Men of Reason and Religion, Part III" *Works* [BE], 11, 315-316.

> my dear do something for them if possible, save these from utter destruction and sweeten the bitters of their affliction (March 22, 1810)[19]

Asbury and early Methodism in America had an inclination towards the poor and an impulse to address both their physical and spiritual need. That a wealthier and unfeeling Methodism might undermine that proclivity was Asbury's nightmare, for he knew full well that prosperity would tempt believers from their obligations to the impoverished.

In the Modern Church

The typical denomination in North America has precious few churches involved in any significant way in the margins of their communities. We have discipled our congregations in worship services, Sunday school classes and small groups that prefer to sit, listen, and then return to their abundant technologies that woo them from personal involvement, let alone the uncomfortable inclusion in their lives of the poor and the oppressed.

Decades ago Martin Marty of the University of Chicago wrote a column in the *Wall Street Journal* lamenting the state of contemporary evangelicalism.[20] He said "If you're part of the evangelical subculture it's your whole life....you go to church, you buy religious books, you watch the television programs. But if you're not part of the subculture, you never know it exists." The subtitles of the Journal article reflected the author's findings:

An Evangelical Revival Is Sweeping the Nation But with Little Effect

Shunning the Sinful World

Effect Has Been Small

Shying from Involvement

It should encourage the reader that the situation we find ourselves in has existed in the past. Indeed, to a greater or lesser degree this was the situation in which Jesus, the early church, John Wesley and Francis Asbury found themselves (and many more besides in Christian history). And yet they were able to start movements that prompted evangelism, disciple-making, and compassionate ministry that reverberated around the globe.

---

19. All quotes from *The Journal of Rev. Francis Asbury: Bishop of the Methodist Episcopal Church.* 3 volumes, (New York: Eaton & Mains, Cincinnati: Jennings & Pye, 1821).

20. Jonathan Kaufman, "Old-Time Religion", The Wall Street Journal, July 11, 1980, 1. Quoted in Jim Peterson, *Evangelism as a Lifestyle* (Colorado Springs, CO: NavPress, 1980), 84.

Confusion between Evangelism and Social Action

I spent my youth in a United Methodist family that regularly bemoaned – as did the evangelical renewal movements of which they were a part – the social action proclivities of their denomination at the expense of soul-winning and evangelical concerns. It seemed as if social action became equated with bad theology and evangelism, with good. I have since joined a denomination which, perhaps sensitive to the controversy, has largely expunged the words "social action" and instead now uses "compassionate ministry."[21] Robert Coleman tries to clarify the issue:

> There is often confusion among churchmen today. Some contend that evangelism involves only the gospel declaration, while others identify it essentially with establishing a caring presence in society or seeking to rectify injustice. It should be clear that both are necessary. One without the other leaves a distorted impression of the good news.[22]

E. Stanley Jones, missionary to India, warned,

> Evangelism without social action is like a body without a soul. Social action without evangelism is like a soul without a body. One is a ghost; the other a corpse. We don't want either one.[23]

Still, many in the *evangelism-prioritized* camp don't want there to be confusion between compassion and the sharing of the gospel. My local church has decided that the best time for evangelism is in the midst of our compassionate outreach. We lead people to the Lord through our prison ministries. We share the gospel at a public school Bible club. We invite people to know Him at the nursing home, or at the half-way house, or at the abortion clinic, or at the strip clubs. Our consistent, weekly presence in these places affords opportunity to invite people into a relationship with Jesus.

Historically, church growth movements indicate that those who are in stress or times of displacement and transition are typically more open to the gospel. The Holmes-Rahe stress chart is sometimes used to measure stress by calculating the number of "Life Change Units" that apply to events in any given year an of individual's life. According to this methodology, the final score provides a rough estimate of how stress affects health.

---

21. Church of the Nazarene.

22. Robert Coleman, *The Heartbeat of Evangelism* (Colorado Springs, CO: NavPress, 1985), 9.

23. E. Stanley Jones, attributed. I once asked J.T. and Ruth Seamands (friends and missionary colleagues of Stanley Jones) if Jones actually said this and in what book I could find it. They replied, "Don't know about which book, but he said it all the time." A bit different form: "An individual gospel without a social gospel is a soul without a body and social action without an individual gospel is a body without a soul. One is a ghost and the other a corpse" in *The Unshakable Kingdom and the Unchanging Person* (Nashville: Abingdon Press, 1972), 40.

Life event	Life change units
Death of a spouse	100
Divorce	73
Marital separation	65
Imprisonment	63
Death of a close family member	63
Personal injury or illness	53
Marriage	50
Dismissal from work	47
Marital reconciliation	45
Retirement	45
Change in health of family member	44
Pregnancy	40
Sexual difficulties	39
Gain a new family member	39
Business readjustment	39
Change in financial state	38
Death of a close friend	37
Change to different line of work	36
Change in frequency of arguments	35
Major mortgage	32
Foreclosure of mortgage or loan	30
Change in responsibilities at work	29
Child leaving home	29
Trouble with in-laws	29
Outstanding personal achievement	28
Spouse starts or stops work	26
Beginning or end school	26
Change in living conditions	25
Revision of personal habits	24
Trouble with boss	23
Change in working hours/conditions	20
Change in residence	20
Change in schools	20
Change in recreation	19
Change in church activities	19
Change in social activities	18
Minor mortgage or loan	17
Change in sleeping habits	16
Change in number of family reunions	15
Change in eating habits	15
Vacation	13
Major Holiday	12
Minor violation of law	11

Score of 300+: At risk of illness.
Score of 150-299: Risk of illness is moderate
Score <150: Only have a slight risk of illness.

A modified scale for non-adults has also been developed. Like the previous chart, it assigns points for various life events; the higher the final tally, the more significant the level of stress.

Life event	Life change units
Death of parent	100
Unplanned pregnancy/abortion	100
Getting married	95
Divorce of parents	90
Acquiring a visible deformity	80
Fathering a child	70
Jail sentence of parent for over one year	70
Marital separation of parents	69
Death of a brother or sister	68
Change in acceptance by peers	67
Unplanned pregnancy of sister	64
Discovery of being an adopted child	63
Marriage of parent to stepparent	63
Death of a close friend	63
Having a visible congenital deformity	62
Serious illness requiring hospitalization	58
Failure of a grade in school	56
Not making an extracurricular activity	55
Hospitalization of a parent	55
Jail sentence of parent for over 30 days	53
Breaking up with boyfriend or girlfriend	53
Beginning to date	51
Suspension from school	50
Becoming involved with drugs or alcohol	50
Birth of a brother or sister	50
Increase in arguments between parents	47
Loss of job by parent	46
Outstanding personal achievement	46
Change in parent's financial status	45
Accepted at college of choice	43
Being a senior in high school	42
Hospitalization of a sibling	41
Increased absence of parent from home	38
Brother or sister leaving home	37
Addition of third adult to family	34
Becoming a full-fledged member of a church	31
Decrease in arguments between parents	27
Decrease in arguments with parents	26
Mother or father beginning work	26

Score of 300+: At risk of illness.
Score of 150-299: Risk of illness is moderate
Score <150: Only have a slight risk of illness.

Apart from the basic health issue, groups such as Church Growth, Inc., suggest that people are much more receptive to assistance and likely to respond to the gospel when experiencing these transitions, especially when more than one is occurring simultaneously. To adjust ministry emphasis toward people in need is wise. Strategies that combine compassion and gospel declaration are most effective with people that have a lifestyle reflective of a high score on the Holmes-Rahe stress test.[24] Our local church has found that working with prisoners and ex-offenders (among others) is an extremely fruitful endeavor because of the cumulative stress in their lives. They frequently not only need, but want, the aid a congregation of compassionate believers can bring.

George Hunter notes that John Wesley practiced this receptivity principle in his ministry. As he interviewed people, analyzed history, took notes on the numbers and made theoretical conclusions, he was able to determine where responsiveness most likely lay within England. He thus

> shifted his time and energy toward those thought to be responsive – the new urban working classes, mining peoples, Bristol, Cornwall, the North of England. In Ireland, Wesley found soldiers to be receptive; he preached in the barracks and many soldiers became Methodist Christians. Indeed, many of the Irish people were open, so Wesley went to Ireland twenty times in forty-three years.[25]

Hunter contends that this was not a mathematically precise strategy, for receptivity could wax and wane; even speaking boldly to unreceptive people, however, could sow seeds for future receptivity. Still, the fields were not "white to harvest" everywhere, and special attention needed to be concentrated where souls were positively responding to the message. Had the Holmes-Rahe charts been available in the eighteenth century, they would have undoubtedly underscored Wesley's effectiveness with those whose situations were characterized by stressful life events. Not surprisingly, Wesley's efforts combined compassionate ministry with gospel proclamation as impressively as just about any major voice in Christendom through two millennia.

The Story of One Church

Two experiences were both dreaded and formative in my seminary student tenure. Dr. Robert Coleman would take his evangelism class to the Lexington, Kentucky, bus station to preach the gospel to what could only be described as a very challenging, frequently inebriated, sometimes drug-influenced group. Although I was not enrolled in that course, friends who were invited me to come along on one of those

---

24. Win Arn, *The Pastor's Manual for Effective Ministry* (Pasadena, CA: Church Growth, Inc., 1992), 38-43.

25. George G. Hunter III, *To Spread the Power: Church Growth in the Wesleyan Spirit* (Nashville: Abingdon Press, 1987), 67.

forays. I cowered in the back of the student pack, hoping that Coleman wouldn't call on one of us to preach or otherwise minister to the crowd.

The second experience was a supervised ministry at an approved institution. Some buddies and I opted to go to a prison on Sundays and minister to the inmates by preaching to them and then hanging around with them in a minimum security facility. It was not a very enjoyable experience; the prisoners didn't really want to be with us and, truthfully, we weren't particularly keen on being with them. We were all grateful when the semester came to an end.

But those two experiences lodged deep in my soul and lingered there until the Lord brought them to the forefront of my life with a vengeance. When I became a graduate school professor, I presumed that I should teach about the responsibility of earnest and faithful Christians to engage those on the margins of culture through evangelism and compassionate ministry. I had experienced such ministry – somewhat reluctantly and to a very limited degree – in seminary and had read voraciously along these lines. In succeeding years, I became increasingly aware of this emphasis in the pages of Scripture. Not only that, it was at the core of the Wesleyan theological tradition to which I subscribe. Thus I emphasized from the class lectern the necessity of compassionate and evangelistic involvement to the least of these. Appealing to Matthew 25:31-46, I reminded students of Jesus' disquieting warning to those who neglect them.

It gradually became obvious that, while being quite exercised about the topic of the poor and the needy, I wasn't myself actually involved with the poor, or the prisoner, or the men and women in crisis in my community. I lacked the integrity of being an exemplar of what I taught.

One of my acquaintances in the community was the sheriff. At the time I was a radio talk show host and a newspaper columnist in addition to being a professor, and through those media I had articulated an opinion about criminality that caught his attention. He offered to give me a tour of the county Penal Farm. At the end of that eye-opening tour, I was compelled to ask him if a place like "the Farm" could use a minister like me. Before long I had a badge and was informing students at Wesley Biblical Seminary that if they wanted to be in my discipleship group (or wanted an "A" in whatever class they were taking from me), they needed to follow me to the jail. For the first time in my life, I felt like I had a real discipleship group – a group on the move like Jesus' band of twelve. Traveling together in a large van, we would sing and pray on the way to the prison, minister and teach there together, then report on our experiences and engage in a discussion-based Bible study on the way back.

From those experiences arose the dream for a church as active in evangelism and compassionate ministry as were my seminary discipleship groups. I had ceased to believe in a legitimate discipleship without substantial movement towards human need. So we planted a church, DaySpring Community, with a focus on taking the gospel beyond the four walls. Our first external ministry was to the men's detention center, but that was quickly followed by an abortion clinic ministry and outreach at a local nursing home. In subsequent years, additional opportunities arose: a food ministry, a public school Bible club, outreach to ex-offenders, a women's prison ministry, etc.

Former Superintendent of the Mississippi District Church of the Nazarene Dr. Greg Mason has remarked, "DaySpring, as much as any church I have ever known, believes completely they are a released people and practices that in multiple ways." Members and now missionaries in Swaziland Matt and Sara Marshall say that "DaySpring's emphasis on vital discipleship revolutionized our family and its mission. We received our call to serve in southern Africa in a DaySpring service, but we learned how to fulfill that call on the streets of the Jackson Metro area."

One of the ways that DaySpring keeps the outward mission of the church in front of its members is by reciting weekly a mission statement that is evangelistic and missional in emphasis[26] and by displaying every Sunday the number of people engaged in and impacted by the church's outreach. For instance, in a recent week...

Ministry	# DaySpringers Involved	# of People Reached
FestiFall	55	1,500
Celebrate Recov @ Penal Farm	2	15x2 groups
New Way Bible Study	2	20
John Hopkins Bible Club	12	100
Women prison	2	60
Women jail	6	18
Strip Club Outreach	4	35
Abortion Clinic	8	60
Prison PodStudies	3	20
Penal Farm Bible Study	3	20
Nursing Home	6	21
Foster Family	5	1
Full-time Missionaries	10	South Africa, Senegal, Ecuador

26. "DaySpring exists to excite men and women, boys and girls about a life-changing relationship with Jesus and to release these disciples for ministry in this community and around the world for the glory of God."

The adage is true: "what we measure, matters." Numbers like those above both celebrate the involvement of those who engage in ministry and help to recruit others in the church to serve in similar – and perhaps new – ways.

DaySpringers are reminded regularly of the church motto derived from Catherine Booth: "We do not exist for ourselves. We exist for others. The world is waiting for us." Michael Thomas, who was reached by the church while housed in the county detention center and is today a member and former church board member, has testified, "Prison ministry changed my life...DaySpring comes to the darkest places to change lives...people don't find DaySpring, DaySpring finds people."

And it all started in the living room of an Asbury Seminary professor's home with a Bible study on Exodus 19:6. Three divine objectives for the life of the believer – character, service and community – are braided together through both Old and New Testaments, culminating in Jesus' ministry with His disciples and expanding through the testimony of the early Church.

Conclusion

Discipleship after the model of Jesus requires priestly service to the poor and the needy. It is rather surprising that more discipleship programs and strategies haven't recognized this central transformational scriptural directive. "If you make disciples by sitting around and talking, don't be surprised if your disciples sit around and talk." Talking at and with people is the premier model for Western discipleship. But it lacks compassionate ministry to the least and the lost, and anything with that deficiency can hardly be deemed Christlike. There is a better way, and it is the way of Exodus 19:6; the pattern of Jesus and of the early church; and the way of historical exemplars like Wesley and Asbury, the Booths and Mother Teresa. It is also the way of Spirit-filled, outward-bound disciple-makers today who desire to not merely convey content, but to develop followers of Jesus whose heads, hearts, and hands are actively engaged for the Great Commission and the Great Commandments.

Chapter 9

Discipleship and Preaching in a Global Context

Timothy C. Tennent, President, Asbury Theological Seminary
Wilmore, Kentucky

Tribute

I officially began my Presidency of Asbury Theological Seminary on July 1, 2009. I was anxious to get started, so I arrived in June and began to unpack my boxes and get my office organized. While boxes were still all around me, I received my first visitor. It was Al Coppedge. He came by to greet me and to pray for me and the ministry I was about to undertake. That was the first of many visits by Al Coppedge to encourage me and to pray with me.

From my first day I learned of his heart for discipleship and his earnest prayers for the ministry of Asbury. I also learned from that very first visit of his love for Indian Springs Campmeeting. It was such a joy to join him for ten days in July 2016 at Indian Springs. Al was the Bible teacher and I was the preacher. It was there at Indian Springs that I got to know Al even better and to see his heart for the world. Therefore, this essay seeks to weave together two great themes which are prominent in the life of Al Coppedge: his heart for the world and his heart for discipleship.

Essay

One of the most neglected aspects of discipleship is the need to raise up and nurture preachers of the gospel. This is a global need for the church around the world. One of the fundamental principles of preaching is that it does not occur in a vacuum. Indeed, authentic preaching is, by definition, a *contextual* event which must always bear the marks of universality and particularity. On the one hand, the preacher is one who is the bearer of the universal, unchanging message of the gospel. On the other hand, that gospel must be delivered in a very particular, local context. It has been said that "the strength of Christianity lies in its interweaving of the warp of world Christianity with the woof of local contexts."[1] Learning to faithfully honor the 'universal' and the 'particular' realities of the preaching task is one of the great challenges around the world which preachers face every week of the year. As pastors, we are always aware that the spiritual flock under our care has very real concerns, needs, burdens, doubts and questions which they bring with them as they gather as the church. As preachers, we are also aware that we are stewards of a very ancient message which is properly rooted in specific historical acts of God in human history and which was delivered to us by eye-witnesses and which has been preserved through the Scriptures and the creedal confessions of the church. To neglect the local context is to forfeit one of the great channels through which the Holy Spirit ministers grace, comfort, teaching and guidance to His people in real time. To neglect the universality of the gospel is to forget that we are not the source of the message, but we are seeking to faithfully deliver the gospel which we received. The Apostle Paul summarizes this well when he says,

> Now, brothers, I want to remind you of the gospel I preached to you, which you *received* and on which you have taken your stand. By this gospel you are saved, if you hold firmly to the word I preached to you. Otherwise, you have believed in vain. *For what I received I passed on to you* as of first importance: that Christ died for our sins according to the Scriptures, that he was buried, that he was raised on the third day according to the Scriptures.[2]

The believers in Corinth had very real concerns about their bodily resurrection at the end of time. Paul addresses that concern, but roots his response in the unchanging gospel which transcends all time and all cultures. Paul reminds the believers in Corinth of the "received" gospel which he, in turn, "passed on" to them. The text powerfully reminds us that we are stewards of a "received" message which we, in turn, "pass on" even when addressing the most pressing issues which our congregation faces. This, in seed form, is the challenge of the preaching task and is central to what it means to be an evangelical preacher. This chapter will seek to address how this process is understood in a global context as an integral part of the discipleship process.

The Global Context of Preaching Today

Christianity Shifting Southward

The church which closed out the 20th century looks vastly different from what it did even 100 hundred years earlier. Indeed, to borrow a phrase from William Temple, the globalization of Christianity is "one of the great facts of our time." When

1. Dana L. Robert, "Shifting Southward: Global Christianity Since 1945," *International Bulletin of Missionary Research* (vol. 24, No. 2, April, 2000), 56.

2. I Corinthians 15:1-4, New International Version, emphasis mine.

William Carey, the father of the modern Protestant missionary movement, went to India at the turn of the 19th Century only 1% of the entire world's Protestants lived in all of Asia, Africa and Latin America *combined*! 99% of all Protestants lived in the Western world. One hundred years later at the turn of the 20th century, only 10% of the world's Protestants were located in the non-Western world. Yet, even though the overall percentage of people in the world who call themselves Christians remained roughly even at about 33% through the entire 20th century, the ethnic identity of Christianity was experiencing the most radical shift in modern history.[3] Today the majority of Protestants live outside the Western world. In fact, 67% of Protestants now live in Asia, Africa, and Latin America. The visible Church of Jesus Christ is predominantly non-white and non-European in its cultural, ethnic heritage. The gospel is rapidly spreading in the Southern continents even while it is waning in the Northern continents. What are the implications of this for the preaching task? I will explore three major implications this has for preaching today.

Multiple Centers of Universality

The first implication of this global shift is that for the first time since the very origins of the Protestant movement in the 16th century we no longer have a single cultural locus which dominates the movement. Christianity is flourishing among thousands of people groups who do not share the cultural, ethnic heritage of the Western world. This is, of course, a cause for great rejoicing and is a powerful testimony to the translatability of the Christian gospel. Nevertheless, this new reality should cause us to think more profoundly about the implications this has for the preaching task. We have long been aware of the presence of Christians in countries from all over the world. For example, many of us can undoubtedly attest that we have personally met Christians from Korea or India or Kenya. The difference is that even while we acknowledged the presence of Christians around the world, the Western world still exemplified *normative* Christianity.

In other words, by virtue of the fact that Christians of European heritage living primarily in Western Europe and North America vastly outnumbered all other Christians and because the West remained the locus of theological writing and reflection, it was hard to imagine a world where European Christianity was not *representative* Christianity. In short, the Western Church has been the de facto guardian of 'universality' since the dawn of the Reformation. We set the standard for what normative Christianity looked like. Even with the happy emergence of non-Western theological institutions, they, for the most part, doggedly follow Western theological curriculums. Their students dutifully learn the history of the

3. David B. Barrett and Todd M. Johnson, "Annual Statistical Table on Global Mission: 2003," *International Bulletin of Missionary Research* (vol. 27, No. 1, January, 2003), 24, 25.

Western church. If one of their more gifted students wants to gain a higher theological degree many of them still come West and sit in our classrooms and learn our systems of thought, our theological analysis and our preaching methodology. In the West, the history of the non-Western church is largely regarded as ancillary to the main thrust of Western church history. Thus, the growth and expansion of the non-Western church is all too often merely tacked on in an ancillary fashion to the normative, representative experience of the Western world.

Today, with the rise of the non-Western church, this entire paradigm needs to be re-examined and with it we need to reflect on how this impacts evangelical preaching in this new global context. Rather than a single center of universality, we are seeing the emergence of what African theologian John Mbiti called "multiple centers of universality."[4] That is, churches from around the world are starting to celebrate their own histories and grapple with how, in their context, the great, unchanging truths of the Christian faith can be preached, passed on and safe-guarded within their own cultural context. In the 21st century, African Christianity is far more likely to exemplify normative Christianity than Western Christianity. African Christianity will be more typical, more representative, of the world-Christian movement than the traditional Western churches.

As preachers of the gospel, we ignore this shift to our peril. We can no longer afford to preach in a way which assumes that the Western church represents normative Christianity and everything else is the "mission field." Today, we must allow our preaching to become more globally minded and to regularly acknowledge the global context in which we now live. Up to this point, the only time we talked about the African or Asian church was at our missions conferences or on a "missions Sunday." This approach effectively creates a "calendar isolation" whereby the only time we expose our church to the realities of an increasingly globalized Christianity is one or two Sundays per year. The result can be a painful loss of our own perspective on universality. In short, we need the voice of the non-Western church throughout the year to best maintain Biblical fidelity here in the West.

The most profound example of this took place at the well-known Lambeth conference which brings together every bishop in the entire, global Anglican communion every ten years to share ideas and to discuss church policy. For a number of years, the Anglican church in the West has been struggling with how to best respond to pressures by homosexuals to legitimize homosexual behavior within the church, even to the extent of granting full ordination to openly practicing homosexuals. As the 13th decennial meeting was convened in 1998, many (not all) of the Western Anglican churches were prepared to sacrifice Biblical standards of sexual fidelity in order to accommodate pressures from these special interest groups. However, when the actual debate began several Anglican bishops from Africa and

4. Kwame Bediako, *Christianity in Africa,* (Edinburgh University Press, Orbis Books, 1995), 157.

Asia stood and rebuked the Western bishops for their faithlessness to the gospel and challenged them to reclaim a Biblical standard of conjugal purity which defined marriage as the union between one man and one woman for life.

Archbishop Donald Mtetemela of Tanzania placed an amendment on the floor which rejected homosexual practice as "incompatible with scripture". A wide range of Bishops from the non-Western world rose to support the amendment. For example, Bishop Wilson Mutebi of the Diocene of Mitiyana (Uganda) declared that in his diocese the Bible is the foundation for faith. He noted that he was fully aware of the Western scientific and philosophical debates concerning homosexuality but he concluded, "for us the Bible and the apostolic tradition have authority through all of our church."[5] Bishop Michael Lugor of the Diocense of Rejaf in the Sudan added that "we only know the Gospel and we proclaim it." Bishop Eustace Kamanyire of the Dicese of Ruwenzori in Uganda argued that homosexual activity is condemned as immoral in both the Old and New Testaments. Pastoral care towards homosexuals is important, but, he noted, should emphasize repentance. He went on to criticize liberal bishops in the West for continuing to ordain non-celibate gay men and lesbians and to bless same sex unions which he declared, "is causing serious damage and scandal to Christ and his church." The Christian faith, he noted, "is not only under attack by nonbelievers but is actually being undermined by some of the same people who are supposed to be its defenders." The Western bishops were taken off guard by the out-spoken boldness of the African and Asian bishops. After an emotional three hour debate on August 5, 1998, the homosexual initiative was defeated and the amendment passed 389 to 190 in large part because of the bold stand taken by these non-Western bishops.[6]

From my perspective this was a powerful reminder that Christians which were once regarded as only "the mission field" were now standing shoulder to shoulder, face to face with their western brothers and sisters as full partners in the gospel. By demanding their right to be heard they were testifying that they had every bit as much of a claim on the Christian faith as did anyone in the Western world. The African bishops not only felt that they could equally and ably defend the universality of the gospel, but that they might have insights which were being neglected or ignored by the Western church.

By listening to the voices of the non-Western church, today's preachers in the West can better overcome many of our own blind spots. For example, Western preaching and theologizing can sometimes drift into a static state whereby we teach truths without engaging in the missional context of the church. This is not true of African preaching. Johannes Verkuyl has noted that "African theology does all the things which theology in general does, but in African theology all these other func-

---

5. David Skidmore, "Lambeth struggles over homosexuality in emotional plenary session", *Anglican Communion News Service*; www.anglicancommunion.org/acns/lambeth/lc098.html, 2.

6. Ibid, 3.

tions are embraced in a missionary or communicative function. It is not primarily an inter-ecclesiastical exercise, but a discipline driven by...active evangelization."[7]

Thus, the emergence of new centers of universality will continue to be a great strength in helping the global church maintain its fidelity to the Apostolic message. When the church in one particular culture dominates the locus of theological discussion, the church is vulnerable to the latest cultural winds which seek to blow the church off course. With multiple centers of universality, the preacher who is attentive can best stay the course and be faithful even in the midst of the most difficult challenges.

The Church in Space and Time

Stephen Neill, the late well-known bishop of the church of S. India, insightfully defined the church as the "community of the redeemed which exists in space and time."[8] This is one of the most helpful insights which is widely ignored by today's preachers. We often see ourselves as "voices crying out in the wilderness" in the midst of a culture which has largely rejected the claims of the gospel. Bishop Neill's insight reminds us that we not only have the insights and encouragement of the church around the world (as noted in the previous point), but also the witness of the redeemed all through *time*. Embracing the global context for evangelical preaching involves not only an increased sensitivity to Christian voices located in "space" around the world, but also listening to the voice of the historic church "in time" from the origin of the world Christian movement. This means a more intentional appreciation of church history in our preaching and our church leadership.

Some evangelical Christians think that as long as we have the Bible we can faithfully defend the apostolic message. While there is much truth to this, it can easily cause us to forget that the gospel is not only rooted in the witness of the Apostles who were the original eye and ear witnesses of Jesus Christ and His resurrection, but it is also expressed all through time in a living community of faith who have proclaimed that message in a multitude of varying cultural contexts and in literally thousands of languages. The Christian faith is, therefore, not only located in propositional truths (e.g. Jesus Christ rose from the dead), but it is an organic expression of real people who held a living faith in the resurrected Christ. Ultimately the written Scripture must sit in judgment against any historical expression of the church which is not faithful to the original apostolic witness. Nevertheless, the many faithful expressions of Christianity throughout history provide a powerful ally and support as we engage in preaching in our own context. It increases the

---

7. As quoted by Wilbert Shenk, "Recasting Theology of Missions: Impulses from the Non-Western World," *International Bulletin of Missionary Research*, July 2001, p. 98.

8. Kwame Bediako, *Christianity in Africa*, 205. Kwame Bediako is quoting from Stephen Neill's *The Christian Society*, (London: Collins, 1952).

importance of the stewardship aspect of our preaching. As noted at the outset of this chapter, Paul intentionally acknowledges that he "passed on" what he "received." That is primarily referring to living witnesses of the gospel. Even though we are removed in time from the actual events of the death and resurrection of Christ, we acknowledge that the living Christ who "walks among His church" (Rev. 2) continues to walk among the lamp stands of His church throughout history.

G. K. Chesterton once noted that "tradition is the greatest expression of democracy." In other words, we must preach in a way which allows other voices from the past who have not been unduly influenced by the vagaries of this generation to help guide us through the challenges we face. Undoubtedly, we will have insights which they will have been blind to. However, we also can continue to learn that most of the issues which we face in our day have been faced in various ways by the church throughout the ages. We often find ourselves preaching in an historic vacuum. Our preaching becomes more and more functional and less and less prophetic.

One example of this is the influence of the church growth movement on Western churches. On the one hand, we must gratefully appreciate the insights and help we have received from the sociological analysis of unsaved people and practical tips into how churches might better grow. On the other hand, if we are honest, we have to acknowledge that sometimes the church's prophetic voice has been diminished for the sake of church growth. We have, at times, allowed the painful call to repentance and new life to be drowned out by the unconditional acceptance of sinners which is inherent in the gospel. When we sing, "Just as I am without one plea" we sometimes forget that even though the gospel accepts us just the way we are, we are not called to stay "just the way we are." Instead, we must be continually transformed into the likeness of Christ. That sanctifying work of the gospel can be painful. Our word to the surrounding culture must, at times, be painfully prophetic as we call people out of darkness into his marvelous light.

Partners in the Gospel

A dearth in global awareness among Western preachers has caused us in the Western world to either be ignorant of our role or to overly inflate our role in reaching the world for Christ. Among the more evangelical churches which actually thought about the many thousands of people groups with no knowledge of Christ, the often unspoken pre-supposition behind much of our preaching was the assumption that missions is about Western Europeans relocating to the non-Western world to bring the gospel to those who have not heard. While this is still (and should continue to be) an important part of the missionary thrust, we are no longer the only ones who are the bearers of this message.

In the 19th century the almost singular role of the Western missionaries to the non-Western world was commonly known as "the white man's burden." Today that burden is no longer being carried by Western Christians. Today we are experiencing a dramatic rise in missions from the non-Western world. Our preaching should reflect this new attitude of partnership which has dawned on the church. Today, Korea represents the second largest mission-sending force in the world with over 10,000 cross-cultural missionaries in the field.[9] At least 25,000 Indians from the Southern (more Christianized) part of India have relocated to North India with the gospel. For many outside of India this may not seem like a true missionary outreach, but there are profound social, cultural and linguistic differences between North and South India. For an Indian to relocate to North India he or she must learn a new language, learn to eat different foods and be regarded as a 'foreigner' by those who immediately recognize that this newcomer is not from North India. Not only is Asia now sending out missionaries, but it is also happening in Latin America and Eastern Europe. Hundreds of Brazilians, for example, are now being mobilized to reach the Islamic world with the gospel. Likewise, Russian Christians are bringing the gospel into the former Eastern bloc countries. These are exciting new initiatives which challenge our existing understanding of the role of the Western world around the world.

This poses a unique two-fold challenge for preachers today. The first challenge is that we must recognize that sharing the gospel cross-culturally is no longer a role which we undertake alone or in isolation from our brothers and sisters around the world. This has important implications for the preaching task. As preachers we are called to engage in creative and authentic partnerships with other pastors and church leaders from around the world. Despite the popularity of the terms 'partnership' and 'networking' in our churches today, the actual reality of it eludes many of our churches and church-based initiatives. Sometimes the word partnership is reduced to mean "we pay and you obey," i.e. we provide the funds and you faithfully do what we have already decided needs to be done. Networking can be reduced to mean, "we have decided to do something and we are going to include a few non-Westerners on the initiative to give it a global flavor." However, true partnership must involve an authentic two-way 'give and take' and honest exchange of ideas, vision and initiative. If the Western church is providing the bulk of the funds for an initiative, it is all too tempting to seek to control the ministry and severely limit the input and direction of our non-Western brothers and sisters. Instead, insist on authentic partnerships. Invite visiting pastors and church leaders from the non-Western church to speak from our pulpits. Furthermore, when we are making decisions which reflect our giving and/or involvement in the mission field, consult with national, indigenous leaders and elicit their opinion and advice.

The second challenge which preachers face in this regard is to accept the notion that the only contribution we can make is financial. A well-known Asian missionary organization has spread this notion by its constant refrain that Westerners

9. Steve S. C. Moon, "The Recent Korean Missionary Movement: A Record of Growth, and More Growth Needed," *International Bulletin of Missionary Research* (vol. 27, No. 1, January, 2003), 11.

should just "stay home" and let the indigenous evangelists do the work. However, nothing would be more disastrous than for the Western church to retreat from the field and accept our role as merely 'writing checks' to support the work of the non-Western church. There will be even more leanness in the soul of the American church if we send our checks and dollars but are not willing to also send our sons and daughters. It would further insulate us from the world Christian movement and essentially say to the non-Western church that we are not willing to allow our children to die or suffer on the mission field. It would send the message that we are going to stay home, earn the money, write the checks and continue living in our comfortable homes. As preachers, we must constantly remind our congregations that ministry is always a contextual event. Christian ministry involves people reaching people and people sharing with people. We must live out the gospel in the presence of other people. There are no easy short cuts to this. This truth is inherent in the very nature of the Christian gospel. Indeed, the cross itself reminds us that our salvation required nothing less than the condescension of the eternal God to dwell in our midst and walk among us and, ultimately, to die for us. This is the paradigm through which an evangelical, globally aware preaching ministry can be effective in the new global context in which we now live.

Conclusion

This chapter has examined the new global context of preaching today. The dramatic changes in the growth of the church in the non-Western world, the hemorrhaging of Christian faithfulness to historic Christianity among various sectors of the church in the West and, finally, the constant and almost overwhelming pressure around us to compromise the gospel message has given rise to a unique opportunity and challenge for preachers of the gospel today. This new context requires an ongoing vigilance to not forget that we have both a defensive as well as an offensive role to play in the church.

We must defend and guard the gospel even while we extend it boldly into the world. This twin truth is illustrated powerfully in the Aboth tractate of the Mishnah where we find the rabbi Johanan ben Zakkai praising two of his favorite disciples all in a few short verses. He praises Eliezer ben Hyrcanus as a "plastered cistern which does not lose a drop," and in the same passage praises Eleazer ben Arak because he is "an ever-flowing stream."[10] Here in the Mishna we find a great metaphor for the global challenge we face as preachers of the gospel. We are to be both cisterns that will not lose a drop, as well as an ever-flowing stream. We have been given the precious heritage of the gospel, once for all delivered unto the saints,

---

10. Herbert Danby, trans., *The Mishnah,* tractate *Aboth* 2:8 (Oxford University Press, 1922) 448 as quoted in A. Walls, *The Missionary Movement in Christian History: Studies in the Transmission of Faith,* (Maryknoll, New York: Orbis Press, 1996), 49.

a fixed revelation which must be guarded, protected and defended. To lose even a drop of this precious treasure known as the Gospel is to lose something which is priceless. Yet the same Lord who gave us and entrusted us with this gospel also called us to be "an ever flowing stream" and to share this gospel boldly in the place where God has called us. Indeed, keeping those two realities in balance is the biggest challenge as well as the greatest privilege of evangelical preaching in this new global context.

Chapter 10
Discipleship and Family

Tim Philpot, Fayette Circuit Family Court Judge
Lexington, Kentucky

Tribute

"And the things you have heard from me in the presence of many witnesses, entrust to faithful men who will be able to teach others also." (2 Timothy 2:2)

Sometime around 1970, men like Robert Coleman and Dennis Kinlaw began to seriously invest in Al Coppedge, who—despite lots of knowledge, including a doctorate in theology—still needed discipleship. And then, understanding the truth of 2 Timothy 2:2, Al began look for 'faithful men'. One of those men was Paul Law, home in Wilmore from the mission field.

As all that was happening in the early 80's, a young lawyer named Tim Philpot was saved but barely hanging on. No one saw the need to disciple this young man because outward appearance indicated he was doing fine. Lawyer, nice wife, teaching Sunday school, no criminal record, good Methodist boy in a church pastored by his brother.

But Paul Law saw him. And called him. And invited him to participate in a 'Barnabas' group, a radical idea from Al Coppedge inspired by John Wesley. That group saved my life. It began a lifelong journey of relationship with Al Coppedge and all of his friends and disciples.

The fellowship of Al's friends has been life-changing for me.

And now, I write this "Discipleship and Family" in his honor. This is especially appropriate because if one needs proof that Al Coppedge is a 'true disciple,' it is found in his family. He is not just a scholar. He is a model husband, father, brother, and son.

One does not think of Al without Beth. And one does not think of Al and Beth without remembering Katy Beth, serving in Hungary as a missionary; or Cricket, serving as the behind-the-scenes formidable wordsmith and editor of Dr. Kinlaw ; or Billy, changing his part of the world in Africa; or the baby Susanna, serving the mission field of Lexington. So, to Al Coppedge: thanks for believing in the truth of 2 Timothy 2:2 and seeing the possibilities that I could be one of those faithful men, walking in your large footsteps.

'Who Are We Anyway?'

As my mother began to lose her memory at about age 86, she began to ask questions that I'm still trying to answer today. In her small room at the retirement center, she pointed to a picture one evening and asked me, "Who is that man?"

I smiled and reminded her that the man was Ford Philpot, her husband and my father. I told her he was in heaven now. I recounted some stories which she pretended to remember, embarrassed by her slow memory. She was able to recall that she called him "Phil," a nickname that started in 1939. I reminded her how much he loved "Ginnie," her own nickname. She smiled thinking of him, because he could make her laugh and I believe she remembered that. The memories were deep, almost hidden.

And then, a few years later, when she was over 90, a second and even more profound question came out of nowhere.

She looked at me with a very puzzled expression and asked, "Who are we anyway?"

It was not "Who are you?" or the philosophical "Who am I?"

It was "Who are we anyway?" Mom knew 'we' were something special but she could not put it all together.

My answer was simple. "Mom, we are family."

Unqualified Author

"*...I am the least in my family.*" (Judges 6:15)

I have never felt more unqualified in my life than to write in honor of a theological scholar on the title that was given to me: "Discipleship and Family." First, I am no theologian and my 2.9 GPA eliminated me as a scholar a long time ago.

Second, I grew up in a home where the word "*discipleship*" was strangely missing. I was at least 30 years old before I even thought about the concept. My father was an evangelist back in the days when it was not a dirty word. But in those good ol' days (the 1950s and 1960s), it felt like evangelism and discipleship were competitors. These were the days before *The Master Plan of Evangelism* spawned a whole new era of cooperation between the two camps.

I grew up with the image that a man of God was someone who, like the Lone Ranger, rode off into the sunset, gone most of the time preaching to sinners in Tampa or Fort Wayne or Africa, or some other place where there were lost souls that needed to be saved. As a little boy, it seemed normal to have an evangelist father who spent his life fighting the devil for every wandering soul. And so, since little boys want to be like their daddy (which explains why I am an unrepentant Cincinnati Reds fan to this day), my first ideas about a "man of God" were connected to evangelism, not discipleship.

Unspoken was the idea that people who disciple other people, in small groups or one on one, are those who do not have the requisite skill or ability to preach to thousands, to draw a big crowd together for the gospel show. My father even had a tent for two thousand people for his evangelistic crusades, not just a small living room or coffee shop. I grew up believing that small groups and discipleship were only for people that could not preach like my dad did. He never said that, but it was what the little son felt.

Then, as I grew older, I heard there was a point that I would need to be "saved," and, even more confusingly, "sanctified." Both experiences would be instantaneous, I was told by my Wesleyan dad and other camp meeting preachers. I was not thinking that I needed to be discipled, since everything was so "instant," almost like microwaving is surely superior to standing over a hot stove cooking all day. Two trips to an altar could cover all the bases for life.

And so, sure enough, I was "saved" at age 18, prayed to be "sanctified" soon thereafter at an altar, and made it all the way to age 31 without really experiencing intentional discipleship of any kind. I was on my own.

From age 18 to 31, no one offered any help. Why? I suppose I looked good on the outside. I was teaching Sunday School, had a nice wife, was a lawyer driving a Mercedes that looked brand new, was the city golf champion, and otherwise appeared to have my act together.

Thankfully, Paul Law and Al Coppedge were two men who saw through the façade and realized there was a young lawyer in town who needed some help. And so, in a Barnabas group in about 1982, I got my first taste of "discipleship." And thus, I am at least barely qualified to discuss the subject.

But third and last, I feel unqualified because in the eyes of some, I have no "family." Sue and I have been married for 45 years but never had children. We have no experience in parenthood. Our family picture is rather empty. A cute little dog never quite fills the picture at Christmastime like children and grandchildren would. When the word 'family' comes up, for Sue and me it means parents who are long gone, plus brothers and sisters and nieces and nephews. Admittedly, there is a small empty space in not just the Christmas card but also the heart. But most of all for an author of an essay like this, there is clearly an empty space in the "family expert resume."

"Discipleship and Family" should be written by someone who has multiple amazing children with success stories to tell, like Al Coppedge, for instance.

Family Chaos

"In the days when the judges ruled, there was a famine in the land." (Judges 1:1)

And so, how did I get this assignment? Simple. Having been a judge in family court for over thirteen years, I am an expert on what not to do. Family Court is certainly no place of discipleship. It is a place of chaos and tragedy. Neglected and abused children, domestic violence, jail for those who refuse to support even their own children, drugs and alcohol involved in virtually every tragic circumstance. And in some ways the saddest of all, the cases of divorce for truthfully no good reason, other than "we've grown apart." Or "we are just really different." Or "the children deserve parents who don't argue all the time." Or, "we're better people apart." Really?

Psalm 68:6 tells us that "God puts the lonely in families." Mankind's fundamental problem is being alone. And God's greatest answer for that loneliness is the family. But that family is so dysfunctional that now we need special courts to handle the load. Half the litigation in America is in family courts. Mostly unqualified judges like me decide where children will sleep at night or what McDonald's will be the pickup and drop off point for the weekend visits.

In some tragic cases, family court is even a place of death. Three recent funerals reminded me of this gruesome fact.

In October, Trinity died. 15 years old. A senseless bullet in a parking lot at 4 am. The bullet was intended for no one in particular, just a way to let the kids hanging out know that someone was cool, someone had a gun. She should've been home, almost everyone said. Her daddy was not there to help her. He lives in another state. The media reported that just ten days before her death, she had tweeted that "*Aww, I can't wait for the day I get married. I already know who I'm marrying, I can see the future...*" She was wrong.

In November, Angel died. 14 years old. Another bullet. But this time, he was at home. He simply opened the door at 11 PM to see who was there. Bullets, intended for one of his brothers who was involved in gangs, were waiting on him. Revenge bullets.

In December, Nova died. 2 years old. She was not in a parking lot at 4 am. She was not opening the door to see who was knocking at 11 PM. She was asleep on the couch in the middle of the day, napping like most two year old toddlers, trying to be a good girl so Santa Claus would remember her in just a few days. But bullets intended for mama's new boyfriend found her instead. No Santa Claus this year for Nova.

And the common denominator? Perhaps many, but one for sure. No one in these families had ever considered marriage or commitment or fidelity. And, of course, there was no father there to protect these little ones.

When marriage disappears, when fidelity is a thing of the past, when commitment to your co-parent is gone, children suffer and even die. Statistics prove this to be true. But statistics are just numbers. The stories are more revealing. Indeed, we are now living in the "days of Noah," where a flood of tragedy awaits our families.

Days of Noah

"By faith Noah, in holy fear, when warned about things to come, built an ark to save his family." (Hebrews 11:7)

So, what was it like in the so called days of Noah? The Biblical record shows that the "days of Noah" meant total depravity, chaos and catastrophe. Isaiah discussed those days (Isaiah 54). Peter mentioned them (I Peter 3). And even Jesus Himself talked about these bad ol' days (Luke 17, Matthew 24).

How bad?

> The Lord saw how great the wickedness of the human race had become on the earth that *every* inclination of the thoughts of the human heart was *only* evil *all* the time. The Lord regretted that he had made human beings on the earth, and his heart was deeply troubled. (Genesis 6:5)

The exaggerated language in this passage gets our attention. Every thought. Only evil. All the time. Honestly, when I hear such extreme language in a courtroom, I presume I am speaking with an exaggerator or even a liar. But this was God Himself explaining the earth as he saw it in the "days of Noah."

Thanks to Hollywood's *Noah*, we got a taste of what that might have looked like. Early in the movie, this earth of total chaos was graphically shown. There were no boundaries. No laws. No courts or government or police to enforce any kind of moral code whatsoever. It was a day when anything went. Our minds cannot even imagine the evil of that day, providing insight into "original sin" and "total depravity."

Every generation of preachers has been sure that their generation is the worst one yet. Listen to the preachers of any generation and you will hear the same tone. Things have finally hit rock bottom, they all say. I still remember my father bemoaning, in the 1960s, that women were smoking and retail stores were opening on Sundays. Liquor was being sold in grocery stores. Even the bookstore at the Wilmore Camp Meeting was open on Sunday afternoon. What was the world coming to?

My preacher dad could not even imagine 2017, when men routinely marry other men. When mothers routinely kill their babies in the womb. When children are permitted to decide their gender in elementary school. And more than male and female, by the way. When divorce is a sacred right. When marriage has virtually died.

So now, as we seek God's direction for these evil days in which we live, can Noah teach us anything? What did Noah do?

He built an ark to save his family.

Not to save the world.

To save his family.

And so, discipleship has something to do with building an ark to save your family.

What is This Ark?

"But I will establish my covenant with you, and you will enter the ark- you and your sons and your wife and your sons' wives with you." (Gen 6:18)

So, what does building an ark to save your family look like? Let us begin with what it is not.

One, the ark is not just sending your kids to Christian schools. Such a place can be a good experience for many children, but it is not foolproof. Drugs and sex are at Lexington Christian Academy in only a slightly smaller version than the public schools. My wife and I both were sent away to a Christian boarding schools at times. And while it all seems so worthy, it leaves the impression that educating and even discipling children is the job of professionals, not parents. Christian schools can be fantastic, but they are not the ark.

Two, the ark is not just attending the right church. Sunday schools and youth groups are fine, but it is not the youth pastor's responsibility to disciple your children. Churches and Sunday schools and youth groups are not the ark.

Three, the ark is not being a politically conservative evangelical. Watching Fox News and checking the box 'evangelical' is not the ark. The ark is not a place for angry ranting and raving by church people about the current culture. I've heard a church person complain about same sex marriage or Obamacare, while the same person whispers quietly that while his daughter is now living with a guy, "at least it is a guy."

Four, the ark is not the government itself. G.K. Chesterton saw this misconception coming nearly 100 years ago, when he wrote about the modern State's role in the family. Socialist and even Communist ideas about family were on the rise when he wrote these words:

> This modern notion about the state is a delusion. It is not founded on the history of real states but entirely on reading about unreal or ideal states like the utopias of Mr. Wells. The real state, though a necessary human combination, always has been and always will be, far too large, loose, clumsy, indirect and even insecure, to be the *home* of the human young who are to be trained in the human tradition. If mankind had not been organized into families, it would never have had the organic power to be organized into commonwealths. Human culture is handed down in the customs of countless households; it is the only way in which human culture can remain human...the king cannot be the nurse in every nursery; or even the government become the governess in every schoolroom. ...*Government grows more elusive everyday.* But the traditions of humanity support humanities; and the central one is this tradition of *marriage.* And the essential of it is that a free man and a free woman choose to found on earth the only voluntary state; *the only state which creates and which loves its citizens.* So long as these real responsible

> beings stand together, they can survive all of life's changes, deadlocks and disappointments which may cut mere political history. But if they fail each other, *it is as certain as death that "the state" will fail them.*[1] (emphasis added).

I often ask parents in Neglect and Abuse cases to look around the room during a hearing and observe all the help being provided by the government. The number is usually upwards of fifteen people, which includes a prosecutor and her assistant, two or three social workers who are backed up by a huge government social system we call the "Cabinet" (not sure how we got such a word for social services), a separate free lawyer for each parent, a free lawyer for the children, two or three deputy sheriffs keeping order in the court, the clerk making the court record, my two support staff filling out orders and paperwork, a lawyer who works for the judge. All paid for by tax dollars, government workers trying their best to save this one family.

We the government usually fail. If we built the ark it would sink.

And so, if the "ark" has nothing to do with schools, churches, politics or government, what is it?

One beautiful thought, although not the focus of this chapter, is that Jesus Himself is the ark. With the waters of death and destruction rising all around, with no hope of salvation seemingly in sight, Jesus Himself becomes the ark that saves us. If we rest in him, if we are "in Christ," just as Noah and his family were in the ark, salvation is available for us. But that is another sermon for another day.

Instead of Jesus as the ark, let me suggest another Biblical idea. Is it possible that a Godly marriage is an ark that saves our families? The ark is a safe and secure place for children and their parents. It is a place of discipleship and family.

Could Marriage Be the Ark?

"..marriage should be honored by all." (Hebrews 13:4)

Marriage is on life support in America, even within the church. Indeed, "evangelicals" led the charge in 2016 to elect a new President who is working on his third marriage after a lifetime of infidelity. How often did we hear, "We love his family," which meant all the kids with all the wives. This is the new normal in America. No candidate willing to speak for Biblical marriage and family had any chance to survive past the first round or two of Republican debates. And so-called evangelicals seem to have totally forgotten or maybe never heard that marriage is essentially the entire message of the Bible.

I have a dear friend who regularly attends a mainline evangelical church. He was divorced thirty years ago, like many people in the pews these days. He knows I probably don't approve of his living arrangements with a so-called girlfriend, a term

---

1. G.K. Chesterton, *Sidelights on new London and newer York: And other essays* (Sheed & Ward, New York, 1932), 80.

which best fits age 13 rather than age 65. The word girlfriend gets upgraded slightly by saying "in a committed relationship," or "significant other" or the favorite of social workers, "paramour."

When I told him I was writing a book about marriage, he reminded me that as far as he could tell the Bible didn't say a word about the subject. He was hinting that even though he was "living in sin," as we said in the old days, it was surely no worse than anything else all the churchgoing hypocrites do. I said:

> Really? You don't think the Bible says much about marriage?
>
> *How about Genesis 1-3 in the Garden, or the story of Noah, or Abraham and all his kin, leading up to Joseph, then Moses and his covenant in Sinai, then the Judges leading up to Ruth and Boaz, and then on to David and Solomon, and all the wedding references in Jeremiah and Ezekiel, plus Isaiah, not to speak of the direct stories about Hosea, and the admonitions from Malachi.*
>
> *And that's only the Old Testament. Go to the New Testament and you'll find John the Baptist calling himself the bridegroom's "best man," and Jesus calling himself the groom, performing his first miracle at a wedding. Not to mention that coming into his kingdom is discussed as being "born again," bringing the family analogy into the picture vividly. Paul and Peter both emphasize marriage in several passages, finally culminating in the wedding supper of the Lamb in Revelation.*

My friend, who thought the Bible said nothing about marriage, mumbled something like, "Well, that was a long time ago."

And so, marriage itself is in big trouble. It is disappearing off the face of the earth. Clearly, it is not seen as an ark that can save a family. If marriage is the ark, it surely will sink, say most modern thinkers. It is seen as the institution that will ruin your life and eliminate your freedom. And of course while many bemoan the arrival of same-sex marriage, it is here only because everyone, including the church, has devalued the meaning of marriage for decades now.

The days of Noah are back with a vengeance in the 21st century. But even 100 years ago, G.K. Chesterton saw the opening blows to marriage coming:

> While I have known thousands of people arguing about marriage, sometimes furiously against it, sometimes rather feebly in favor of it, I have never known one of the disputants begin by asking what marriage is. They nibble at it with negative criticism; they chip pieces off it and exhibit them as specimens, called "hard cases;" they treat every example of the rule as the exception to the rule; but they never look at the rule. They never ask, even in the name of history or human curiosity what the thing is, or why it is, or why the overwhelming mass of mankind believes that it must be.[2]

Marriage can be described in many ways. But certainly it is a place of safety and

2. Ibid, 73.

security, for both adults and children. It is the "first step from barbarism to civilization" *(Maynard vs. Hill [1888, US Supreme Court]).* Marriage is intended to save us from ourselves and the floods of evil that would overwhelm us. As it saves families, it saves the communities they live in, and as it saves communities, the nation is saved.

So, if the ark represents marriage, what should happen inside that ark?

Inside the Ark

"…if you're capable of growing into the largeness of marriage, do it." (Matthew 19:12 - *The Message).*

First, the ark is a large place for just a few people. The ark was 150x75 yards. It had about 100,000 square feet of space, a really large space for only eight people and the animals. Marriage is also a large place.

One of my favorite references to marriage in Scripture (if one can call *The Message* scripture) is Matthew 19, where the Pharisees asked Jesus to talk about divorce and marriage. He ends with a unique statement: "…if you're capable of growing into the largeness of marriage, do it." (Matthew 19:12, *The Message*)

That's it. Marriage is for "large" people. People who are willing to grow, to expand, to change, to get better. While singleness is a specific calling for many, and therefore should not be minimized or criticized, it can sometimes be an excuse to stay the same, to stay "small," to stay unchanged.

And while marriage is a large place, like the ark, discipleship inside the ark is for just a few. Noah built the ark to save only eight people. But that was enough.

Likewise, while marriage is large, discipleship is by definition about the few. In these 'days of Noah,' we need men and women who will stop trying to save the world and concentrate on saving a few, starting with their own families.

Second, both parents are present inside the ark. This ark means that, by definition, both parents are home. Noah was the star of this show, but he was no one without his wife. As any good lawyer, I can make an argument in either direction as to which parent is most important.

It is impossible to exaggerate the primacy of a father in the discipleship process. The father is expected to be the primary protector, the primary provider, the primary professor, the primary preacher, the primary prototype, the primary prayer, and the primary presence in the lives of the children. When that happens, you have the perfect father, even though such a man is actually far from perfect. Being 'present,' not just physically but emotionally and spiritually, covers a multitudes of fatherly failures.

In one of the greatest novels of all time, *To Kill a Mockingbird,* a couple of lines leap off the pages. Talking to Scout, age ten, about her father, Atticus Finch, Mr. Raymond says, "Jean Louise, you don't know your Pa's not a run of the mill man, it'll take a few years for that to sink in."

And isn't that what every child needs, a father who's not just a "run of the mill man": one who stands for right, and even when wrong, does it for the right reasons.

But no matter how good the father may be, kids need mom. Mom's role is arguably even more important. The value of motherhood does not really need scientific proof, but it is there. The Adverse Childhood Experiences ten-question test (ACE) is an assessment tool to help predict future tragedies, like drug addiction, criminal behavior and even a wide range of illnesses. In a twenty-year study, begun with rats and finally confirmed through human families, it was proven that the stress of an adverse childhood made success virtually impossible. There was, however, one huge exception to the rule. The one major exception that overcomes all the stress of adverse childhood experiences? Mom. A good mother figure, even if not the biological mom, could overcome it all virtually all the time.

In the original study with rats, researchers counted every instance of maternal licking and grooming (called L&G). And after 10 days of placing a maternal rat into the lab, they divided the baby rats into two categories: those that got licked and groomed a lot, labeled high LG; and the ones that were licked and groomed very little, which they labeled low LG. The ones that were high LG became better at the mazes; they were more social; they were more curious; they were less aggressive; they had more self control; they were healthier; they lived longer.

Indeed, the presence of the maternal rat who licked and groomed the baby made all the difference. And then they transferred that same principle to real children in a decades-long study of 1200 infants. It was determined that "high quality mothering can act as a powerful buffer against the damage that adversity inflicts on a child's stress response system much as the dams licking and grooming seem to protect their pups."[3]

In fact, despite all the negative possibilities from childhood, a powerful mother figure literally overcomes it all.

The bottom line – inside the ark you need both a mother and a father. Both.

Third, the message and the messenger must be the same inside the ark. Like many parents, mine were not intentional in their "discipleship." However, it was exceedingly important that the same message my father was preaching was lived out at home. My father was the same man at home as in the pulpit. There was no private self and public self for my parents. They were the same in and out of the public eye. There was no confusion about the words and actions being different. Life inside the ark of family and marriage looked the same as outside the ark in public settings.

As Paul said in a different context to the Ephesians, "You know how I lived

3. Paul Tough, *How Children Succeed: Grit, Curiosity and the Hidden Power of Character* (Mariner Books, 2013), 32.

among you….." (Acts 20:18), meaning that his words and his actions were the same. So it must be inside the ark with the family. Message and messenger must match.

Fourth, the kids are not the most important thing inside the ark.

The critical relationship is between husband and wife. The greatest gift that a mother and father can give their children is to love and respect the other parent. Children are obviously important, but they should not be the center of family life. The center must be the love relationship of husband and wife. In my novel *Judge Z: Irretrievably Broken*, Judge Z's eulogy at his mother Beulah's funeral made the point:

> Mother taught me that I was not the most important person in her life. Maybe that shocks some of you. "Of course," you're thinking. "God was the most important thing in her life." Well, yes and no. Beulah loved God. She loved this church and all of us here today. But as Jesus would say, those who have "ears to hear" will understand what I say next. The number one love of her life was her husband, Johnny. By seeing that, I was able to understand that marriage was important and children like me were created by the love of a man and a woman. And I finally realized that to save a marriage is to save a child… I saw them kiss. I saw them hold hands. I saw them love each other. They didn't even know they were teaching me. But they were. I felt secure because of who they were, not just individually, but also together.[4]

Inside that ark of marriage, children are expected to pay attention, to listen in on adult conversations, to learn from them. Discipling children happens "24/7" if the children can be trained to just pay attention to the everyday life and conversations of parents.

Fifth, inside the ark, there is a commitment to never leave. How crazy would it have been for Noah's wife or sons to say, "I'm out of here. This is crazy. The place stinks of elephant dung. I'm getting claustrophobia. I don't care how much water is out there. See you later."

Obviously, that would be insane. But that is exactly what is happening in the 21st-century marriage. It is not "until death do us part" but "until I can't take it anymore." The sense of permanence is gone. And it is damaging children, who need to know that their tomorrow is as secure as their today. Chesterton discussed the security children need in the home:

> The atmosphere of something safe and settled can only exist where people see it in the *future as in the past.* Children know exactly what is meant by having really come home; and the happiest of them keep something of the feeling as they grow up.
>
> But they cannot keep the feeling for ten minutes, if there is an assumption that Papa is

---

4. Tim Philpot, *Judge Z: Irretrievably Broken* (Chilidog Press, 2016).

> only waiting for Tommy's 21st birthday to carry the typist off to Trouville....[5] (emphasis added).

Children need to know that no one is leaving the ark. No one is jumping ship any time soon, they hope and pray.

Obviously, there can be good reasons for divorce. Dr. William Doherty discusses the three A's, the primary "hard reasons" for divorce: affairs, addictions and abuse. But sadly, while divorce was once a tragic exception, it is now seen as a sacred right. And now we mostly hear the soft reasons for divorce. "We've grown apart," or "we're just really different," or "the children deserve happy parents," or "we've moved on," or "we're still friends but we're just not in love anymore." These answers would never be spoken if people understood that the ark of marriage was protecting them and their children from the flood of evil outside.

So, if marriage is the ark that can save our families in these days of Noah, what else can we teach our children about these days? Each time the 'days of Noah' is mentioned in the Bible, marriage is also mentioned. This cannot possibly be an accident. The Holy Spirit is pointing us to a truth about discipleship in such times.

Days of Noah Acccording to Isaiah – "God is Compassionate"

"This is like the days of Noah to me: as I swore that the waters of Noah should not more cover the earth...says the Lord, who has compassion on you." (Isaiah 54:10)

First, Isaiah 54. The theme of the chapter is God's unfailing love for us, His compassion which is beyond our comprehension, and His covenant of peace with us. The chapter reminds us that, while it may seem like God has abandoned us, it is only for a moment.

He reminds us that even the barren one who never bear children can burst into song and shout for joy because of the spiritual children they may produce (Isaiah 54:1). This is a wonderful reminder for people like Sue and me who have no biological children.

He reminds us that our Maker is our Husband and the Lord Almighty is his name (Isaiah 54:5). This is a superb image of the nuptial nature of the Creator's love for us.

He reminds us that the Lord will call us back like a wife deserted and distressed in spirit, like a wife who married young but was rejected. (Isaiah 54:6). What a comforting passage for women who have indeed been through that horrifying experience.

The barren woman and the deserted wife have nothing to fear. Why? The great Maker of the universe is our Husband. And His love is unfailing:

---

5. G.K. Chesterton, *Sidelights on new London and newer York*, 76.

...I swore that the waters of Noah would never again cover the earth. So now I have sworn not to be angry with you, never to rebuke you again. Though the mountains be shaken and the hills be removed, yet my unfailing love for you will not be shaken nor my covenant of peace be removed, says the Lord, who has compassion on you. (Isaiah 54:9-10)

This is the "*hesed*" love of God, unfailing lovingkindness, which we are reminded is even possible in our marriage and family life. When asked about how such "love" could save a marriage, Rabbi Levi testified:

"My answer may not be what you expect. I don't have a policy or a program or a clever counseling gimmick. I have *hesed.* But some of you may still not quite 'get it.' He made air quotes around the words with his long, bony fingers. So let me offer some practical examples.

Hesed is a mother who cuts her career short to be sure her Down Syndrome baby has full-time care. For thirty years or more, as long as it takes.

Hesed is a father who drives all night to bail his drug-addicted son out of a county jail. Again.

Hesed is a wife who stays up praying all night for her husband, who went off on Friday night to have a beer with his friends and came home Saturday afternoon with no money in his pocket. She cooks him dinner.

Hesed is a sister who prays for her alcoholic brother. And then uses all of her savings to send him to rehab.

Hesed is a husband who welcomes his wife even after she has listened to her friends who told her to go back to an old boyfriend.

Hesed does not care what wrong has been done, what sin has been committed, what trust has been violated.

Hesed is a judge...and a lawyer...who have the love in their hearts to fight to save a marriage when it seems like the whole world wants to destroy it.

Hesed is the husband who loves his children unconditionally and refuses, for their sake, to let his marriage be broken.

Hesed is the mother who protects her family by opening her heart to find reconciliation, even after her husband has wounded her deeply and says he wants to walk away from her."[6]

In the ark of marriage, God's love must be present, living inside a mom and a dad who can forgive and cherish and continue. Forever.

---

6. Philpot, *Judge Z.*

Days of Noah According to Peter – "God is Patient"

"God waited patiently in the days of Noah while the ark was being built. In it only a few people, eight in all, were saved..." (I Peter 3:18)

Peter's discussion of these "days of Noah" begins with a lengthy seven-verse soliloquy about wives and husbands. But as Peter goes into some deep theological concepts related to Christ, the key word is *patience.*

Peter reminds us that God was willing to not only wait patiently, but do so for only eight people. Noah worked for 100 years to save eight people, but those eight were his family, and it was worth it all. And God was surely hoping that during that century of building the ark, someone would hear the Voice that Noah heard and repent. Perhaps God even called on thousands of people to build an ark, but only Noah had "ears to hear."

God was patient, waiting a hundred years to send the flood and execute his judgment.

Just like in the historical days of Noah, we didn't get here overnight. In fact, the last century has been a steady decline for the family. From 1917 to 2017 has been quite a ride in the wrong direction.

- 1917 was supposed to be the "war to end all wars."
- The Roaring 20s got us moving.
- The 1930s gave us a depression.
- The 40s gave us another World War.
- The 50s gave us *Playboy* plus "Leave it to Beaver" and Disney.
- The 60s brought us assassinations, free love, Woodstock, LSD, and Vietnam.

All of which led us to the 1970s, where *Roe vs. Wade* confirmed that babies were expendable. The father need not marry the mother any longer, since abortion was now freely available. We began the journey to let the fathers off the hook. An entire generation was freed up to have sex with no consequence. The old fashioned view of marriage began to crumble for real, and brought us no fault divorce as the cherry on top.

And then, like a snowball rolling downhill, from the 1980s until June 26, 2015, the family structure changed so radically and quickly that it was almost no news at all when the Supreme Court of the United States declared that same-sex marriage was a constitutional right.

The inhabitants of the ark were no longer "male and female."

Now, just two years later in 2017, has God's patience been stretched thin again?

It feels again like the days of Noah. Is judgment coming? Or even worse, has it arrived and we barely see it? Or has God again been patient, ready and willing to wait for a few families to be saved and discipled?

Those 100 years also remind us that discipleship in the family takes a long time. The century that it took Noah to build the ark was nothing compared to the hundreds of years it took him to disciple his own family.

Marriage itself is an expression of this patience. Again, as Chesterton said: "The basic idea of marriage is that the founding of a family must be on a firm foundation; that the rearing of the immature must be protected by something patient and enduring."[7]

Marriage, like the ark, is a place for patience.

Days of Noah According to Jesus – "God is Watching"

"Just as it was in the days of Noah, so also will it be in the days of the son of man. People were eating, drinking, marrying and being given in marriage, until the date Noah entered the ark. Then the flood came and destroyed them all." (Luke 17:26-27)

Even Jesus himself weighed in on the days of Noah. In Luke 17 and in Matthew 24, the Pharisees asked him when the kingdom of God would come.

Jesus reminded us that in those awful days of Noah, people were unaware of the impending doom that lay before them. They were going about their basic business, which was "eating, drinking, marrying." The only difference would be that in 2017, people are mostly eating and drinking but not really marrying. Over half of all children are born outside marriage. About 90% of the family court caseload is people who are not married. Marriage is at an all-time low, while eating and drinking is at an all-time high.

These current "days of Noah" require us to be watchful, says Jesus. But we live in a day when families are not watching. We live in a day when families are sleeping.

Today is like December 7, 1941 at Pearl Harbor.

There was much eating and drinking and dancing that Saturday night. And early Sunday morning, after a night of partying, the entire US forces were mostly asleep, recovering from a hangover. The Admiral was playing golf that morning.

While we slept and played, the Japanese nation had declared a silent war and sent planes to Pearl Harbor with the intent to destroy the entire American Pacific fleet. And basically, they did.

We were at war but only the enemy knew it. Sound familiar?

Likewise, the typical American Christian is now spiritually living in those days. Satan is attacking marriage ("it doesn't matter as long as you are committed"), and attacking our kids ("they'll be ok"), and attacking our very souls ("everybody makes it"). We are living in wartime, but we act as if we are living in a sitcom, maybe the Andy Griffith Show, or Seinfeld for a little younger crowd. We wake up and wander down to Starbucks for some coffee or turn on the Today Show. The first voice

7. G.K. Chesterton, *Sidelights on new London and newer York*, 77.

we hear in the morning is not God but NBC. We are actually in the center of a Braveheart-type battle, but we wake up every morning thinking this is Mayberry.

Indeed, we should wake up each day like soldiers on a field in Afghanistan. Alert. Ready. Unwavering.

As John and Stacy Eldredge say in their book, *Love and War*, marriage is a "love story…set in the midst of a war."[8] The devil himself is waging war against all our families. He loves it when Christian people get divorced and move on.

And the answer? As the Admiral said in the movie about Pearl Harbor, the attack happened because "we did not face facts." So, we must face the fact that the devil and his crowd have declared war on our families and marriage. We cannot win a war unless we know the war exists. We cannot defeat an enemy if we pretend there is no enemy. Face the facts – we are at war!

Once the obvious is stated, that we are at war, Christians must act. Those people who do not take this seriously will never disciple their own children, will never develop their own family, will just wake up in another decade or so and see their entire family crumbling around them. Millions are seeing that even today.

Who are We, Anyway?

I started this essay with my mom's question, "Who are we anyway?" I mentioned that my dad did not really intentionally 'disciple' me as I now understand the term. But with a few decades of experience in the rearview mirror, I think I have understated my father's role as a discipler.

I now know that I was honored to grow up in the greatest 'Commonwealth' in the world, and I don't mean Kentucky. It was described quite well by Chesterton:

> The Commonwealth is made up of a number of small kingdoms. In those kingdoms, a man and a woman are the King and Queen. They exercise a reasonable authority, subject to the common sense of the commonwealth, until those under their care, the children, grow up to found similar kingdoms and exercise similar authority .[9]

That's it. The family. The greatest kingdom in the world, where my mother Ginnie was the Queen and Phil was the King, and the subjects were Tim and Danny. Where the authorities were not an unloving judge or government worker. Where this King and Queen actually loved the subjects. Where forgiveness was possible. Where no automatic sentences had to be imposed. Where discipline was applied but subject to the love of the Queen or King. Where we were safe inside the ark of marriage, knowing that no one was leaving this place of safety and security. Where

---

8. John and Stasi Eldrdge, *Love &War* (Colorado Springs, CO: Waterbrook Press, 2009), 3.

9. G.K. Chesterton, *In Defense of Sanity: The Best Essays of G.K. Chesterton.* (Ignatius Press; 2011), 178.

leaving would have been unthinkable.

So Noah, in holy fear, built an ark to save his family.

Not the world.

His family.

Chapter 11
Discipleship as a Lifestyle

Robert Coleman, Professor, Disciplemaker, Author
Wilmore, Kentucky

Tribute

I have known Allan Coppedge for a long time, first as a student, later as a colleague, and also as a trusted and long-term friend. It has always been an inspiration to see how he hasn't been satisfied to teach about and write concerning the life of discipleship. He has always gone much further, seeking to practice the principles he teaches in an effort to be obedient to the Great Commission. Over the years I have watched him gather a small group of young men and lead them in a vigorous discipline of spiritual formation – prayer, fasting, scripture memory, service, small group interaction. An enlarging contingent of these men has gone forth with renewed vision and robust dedication to disciple others in America as well as several nations of the world. The rippling effect of his life as a disciple-maker will be experienced for many decades to come.

Only when teaching is incarnate in flesh and blood does it become convincing. That is why it is such a joy to honor Al with a chapter in this volume. He has lived what he has articulated in the classroom and from the pulpit. His has been a life of discipleship well-lived, and the end is not yet.

Essay

The Great Commission (Matt. 28:18-20) establishes the priority around which our lives should be ordered. It is a command to every Christian. But you may ask, "If I am not a church worker or a missionary or something of that kind, how can I be engaged in ministry?"

The answer lies in seeing disciple making as a lifestyle whatever one's personal calling or giftedness.[1] Jesus was simply asking his disciples or learners to follow the

1. A distinction can be made between a general or primary calling and a unique or secondary calling. For a good treatment of this difference, see the recent book by Todd Wilson, *More: Find Your Personal Calling and Live Life to the Fullest Measure* (Grand Rapids: Zondervan, 2016).

same rule that had directed his life.[2] He knew his way, though slow and not accomplished without great sacrifice, would succeed. For as individuals learn of him and follow the pattern of his life, they will become disciple makers; and as their disciples in turn do the same, some day through multiplication the nations will hear the Gospel.

To understand how the Great Commission unfolds in our lives we need to look closely at the way Jesus made disciples. His way of doing it becomes our book of directions. Adaptations of his approach, of course, must be made in our situation. But his lifestyle of ministry offers guidelines for us to follow.[3]

Become a Servant

One does not need to observe Jesus very long without becoming aware that he lives by a different value system from that of the world. Renouncing his own rights, he "made himself nothing, taking the very nature of a servant, being made in human likeness" (Phil. 2:7; cf. 2 Cor. 8:9). From the beginning, his incarnation established the criteria of a fruitful life.

Jesus came to serve, not to be served (Matt. 20:4). When he saw people in need, "moved with compassion," he reached out to help (Matt. 9:36). He fed the hungry; he healed the sick; he opened the eyes of the blind; he cleansed the lepers; he bound up the broken-hearted; he delivered the demon-possessed; he raised the dead. And through it all, he held forth the Word of life, proclaiming the Gospel of the Kingdom.

Little wonder that multitudes were drawn to him. People always respond to love when it finds practical expression where they hurt. Though his fearless preaching often invoked the disdain of the religious gentry, it generally was received with appreciation by the masses (e.g., Mark 12:12; Matt. 21:26; Luke 20:19).

The same holds true of skeptics today. To reach them we must take the servant's mantle. When they know they are loved, we have their attention. In a generation like this that has lost a sense of objective truth, living by feelings rather than by faith, this may be the only way initially to make sense to them.

Look around and see how you can meet a need. Unassuming as it may be, this is how our witness becomes credible. One who is known as a servant will never lack opportunities to make disciples.

---

2. To clarify, Gerhard Kittel states that "The word *disciple* designates a learner or follower, as in the sense of an apprentice, and always implies the existence of a personal attachment which shapes the whole life of the one described" (Gerhard Kittel and Gerhard Friedrich ed. *Theological Dictionary of the New Testament* trans. G. Bromiley (Grand Rapids, Eerdmans, 1974), vol. 4, p. 441.

3. In my older book, *The Master Plan of Evangelism*, what is discussed as principles in that study of Christ's lifestyle of evangelism are called "guidelines" in this article.

Look for Disciples

Getting the appreciation of people can be misleading. Crowds of people were drawn to Jesus by his healing grace; they even liked his preaching, but they were lost. They were like aimless sheep without a shepherd (Matt. 9:26). Yes, there were many who were supposed to give them direction, likes the scribes and priests. The problem was that these persons in privileged positions of leadership were themselves blind to the truth (Matt. 15:14; Luke 6:39), nor did they truly love the people (John 10:12, 13).

What a commentary on people without shepherds. Lost sheep must have someone to lead them. Jesus was doing all he could to help, but in the incarnation he assumed the limitations of a human body. He could not give attention to all the people. Obviously, unless co-workers could be raised up to multiply his ministry—redeemed men and women with the heart of a shepherd—there was no way the waiting harvest could be gathered. Jesus said to make this the burden of our prayers (Matt. 9:37, 38).

So while ministering to the multitudes, Jesus concentrated upon persons who could learn to reproduce his life and mission.

His first disciples were found largely within his own home environment in Galilee. In culture, education, and religious orientation, they had much in common. To be sure, they were not the most socially astute people, perhaps most religious. None of them appear to be from the Levitical priesthood. Yet Jesus saw in these untrained lay persons the potential for turning the world upside down. Though often superficial in their comprehension of spiritual reality, with the exception of the traitor they were teachable.

This is going to require a long-term approach to reaching the nations. Too easily we have been satisfied with short-term efforts to see the multitudes turn to Christ without assuming their discipleship. In so doing we have inadvertently added to the problem of evangelism rather than its solution.

Discipling is best accomplished with a few people at a time. Notice them. Likely they are persons with whom you already have much in common; begin with your family, and reach out to neighbors and friends. Within this natural sphere of influence, you will have your greatest potential for changing the world. Though you are not the only person involved in their discipleship, for a period of time you may be the most significant influence on their Christian growth.

Build a Relationship

As the disciples grew, Jesus chose twelve to be "with him" in a special comradeship (Mark 3:14). Of course, he continued to relate to others as the fellowship of believers increased through his ministry, but it is apparent that he gave a diminishing priority of attention to these outside the apostolic company. Within this select group,

Peter, James, and John seemed to enjoy an even closer relationship.

Notice the deliberate way that Jesus proportioned his life to persons in training. It also illustrates a basic principle of teaching: the more concentrated the size of the group being taught, the greater the opportunity for learning. In a profound sense, he shows us how the Great Commission can become the controlling purpose of every family circle, every small group gathering, every close friendship in this life.

For the better part of three years, Jesus stayed with his pupils. They walked on the streets together; they sailed on the lake together; they visited friends together; they went to the synagogue and temple together; they worked together. Have you noticed that Jesus seldom did anything alone? Imagine! He came to serve the nations—and finally, he dies on the cross for all humankind; yet while here he spends more time with a handful of disciples than with everybody else in the world put together.

There is nothing new in this pattern, of course. He simply incorporates in his lifestyle the dynamic of family, the foundation of all learning. It was God's plan in the beginning when he instituted marriage and ordained that the home become the center of religious training. Making disciples is like raising kids.

Close personal relationships are especially crucial if persons are just starting out with Christ. Like newborns in the physical world, beginning disciples need spiritual guardians to regularly meet together, inquire about their needs, answer questions, encourage their witness, and make them feel a part of the family of God.

The more informal and unpretentious the association, the better. Some of this fellowship can be arranged in small group meetings, periods devoted to testimony, Bible study, and prayer. Such casual activities do not take the place of formal church services, but learning comes most naturally in more relaxed, family-like settings.

Teach Obedience

What assured the disciples' ongoing relationship with Christ and continual learning from his teaching was to "obey everything (he) commanded" (Matt. 28:20). This was spelled out in the Great Commission, Indeed, it is what made them disciples. Jesus did not ask them to recite a creed; he said, "Follow me" (John 1:43, 46; Mark 2:14; Matt. 9:8; Luke 5:27; cf. John 18:19). Faith in Christ was evidenced by following him.

This was the means by which those with him learned more truth. He did not ask the disciples to follow what they did not know to be true, but no one could follow him without coming to learn what was true (John 7:17; 8:31, 32).

What made them want to obey was their love for Jesus. "If you love me," he said, "you will keep my commandments" (John 14:15; cf. 14:21, 23, 24; 15:10). Putting this in perspective, he added, "This is my commandment, that you love one another, as I have loved you" (John 15:12).

Obedience to the will of God, of course, was the controlling principle in the life of Jesus. Calvary was the crowning climax of his commitment. The cross, having already been accepted in advance (Rev. 13:8; Acts 2:32), made each step Christ took on earth a conscious fulfillment of God's eternal purpose for this life.

Just as he found his blessedness in doing the Father's will, even so his followers will find theirs. From the standpoint of strategy, however, it was the only way that Jesus could mold their lives by his Word.

One might ask why so many professed Christians are stunted in their growth and ineffective in their witness. Is it not because there is a general indifference to the commands of God? Certainly if we are to make any impact on this indulgent generation, the obedience of the cross must become more evident.

Lead by Example

Following Jesus, a lifestyle of holiness was always on display. By practicing before them what he wanted them to learn, they could see its relevance and application.

Take, for example, his discipline of prayer. Surely it was no accident that Jesus often let his disciples notice him praying. Inevitably the time came when they asked, "Lord, teach us to pray" (Luke 11:1). Having awakened their desire to learn, he could now teach them how. Notice that in this beginning lesson he did not preach them a sermon or assign them a book to read; he gave them an example (Luke 11:2-4; Matt. 6:9-12).

In the same way, he taught his disciples the importance and use of Scripture; the essence of worship; the stewardship of time, social responsibility, and every other aspect of his personal life. At the same time, he was showing them how to care for the needs of people, how to feel their sorrows and burdens, while always seeking their ultimate welfare in the Gospel. Evangelism was so woven into daily experience that it did not seem contrived or programmed. Through it all, he was demonstrating how to make disciples. When finally he gave the Great Commission, there was no confusion in their minds about its meaning. They had seen it lived out before their eyes.

When it all boils down, those of us seeking to disciple people must be prepared to have them follow us, even as we follow the Lord (1 Cor. 11:1). We are the illustration of our teaching (Phil. 3;17ff; 1 Thess. 2:7, 8; 2 Tim. 1:13). They will do those things they see and hear in us.

Growing this kind of leadership, of course, puts us on the spot. Persons we let into the inner working of our lives will see our shortcomings and failures. But let them also see a readiness to confess our sins when we understand the error of our ways. Weaknesses need not impair discipleship when there is transparent sincerity to follow Christ; an honest exposure may tarnish our halo, but in seeing our humanness, others may more easily identify with our precepts. Furthermore, if we learn from our failures, as abundant as they are, there is no end to the lessons we will derive.

Involve in Ministry

Jesus was always preparing disciples to carry on his work. So, as they were able to assume some responsibility, he gave them things to do suited to their gifts and talents.

First duties were small, unassuming tasks, like providing food and shelter for himself and the group. After a while he began to have the disciples more actively assist in his ministry. They were enlisted, for example, in baptizing believers who responded to his preaching (John 4:2). For another setting, he has them distributing food to hungry people that had come to hear him teach (Mark 6:30-44; 7:31-8:9).

The work assignments increased with their self-confidence and skill. Before long they were sent out to do much the same kind of work that Jesus was doing with them—healing, teaching, and preaching (Matt. 10:1-10; Mark 6:6-9; Luke 9:1-3).

Lest they forget the priority of equipping leadership, however, he stipulated that above the public ministry they were to search out "worthy" persons to spend time with wherever they went (Matt. 10:11-15; Mark 6:10, 11; Luke 9:4, 5). They could work across the community all day, but in the evening they were to return to the house where there was someone interested enough in their mission to offer hospitality. In effect, the disciples were instructed at the onset to build a relationship with a promising person who could follow up their ministry when they were gone. If no one could be found with a desire to learn, then they were to shake off the dust of their feet and move on to the next village. We do not have the luxury of going through the motions of ministry when no one is being discipled.

As a leader, it is your business to help a follower take the next step. For those not yet believers, get them involved in Christian fellowship. Hopefully, as they come to faith, you can help them get started on a discipling ministry of their own with some new believer at home or in the marketplace. Many programs of the church may also afford new opportunities for service.

Whatever form ministry takes, whether informal or structured, God can work through it to make disciples. When the Great Commission is seen as a lifestyle, everyone can be involved. The priesthood of all believers becomes a reality. Nothing is insignificant; nothing falls outside the work of helping learners fulfill their role in discipling the nations.

Monitor Progress

Checking on their progress, Jesus would get back with his disciples after some attempt at ministry to see how things went (Mark 6:30; Luke 9:10; 10:17). By asking questions, responding to their queries, he was making them accountable for what they learned, teaching them that "from everyone who has been given much, much will be demanded" (Luke 12:48). Moreover, the experiences the disciples were having in their work became illustrations for him to teach some new or deeper truth (e.g., Luke 9:37-43; 10:14-24; Matt. 15:37-16:12; 17:14-20; Mark 8:10-21; 9:17-29). It was on-the-job training all the way.

Problems were dealt with when they came up. Though their progress was painfully slow, Jesus patiently kept them moving towards his goal. He did not ask more from them than they were capable of giving, but he did expect their best, and this he expected to improve as they followed him.

To me, the most awesome aspect of Christ's concern for the disciples' growth comes out of his prayer. John 17 is the greatest example. Have you noticed how most of the prayer turns to these men "given" to him "out of the world" (John 17:6-19)? He prays for their protection from the evil one; he prays that they might have his joy in doing the will of God; and as they are sent into the world on a mission like his own, he prays that they will be sanctified even as he sanctifies himself. Nothing must be allowed to distract them from the work to which they are called, for "through their word" the world will come to believe on him (John 17:20ff)!

Think of it! Though he knows that in a few hours they will forsake him, even that his chief spokesman will openly deny him, yet his love will not let them go. He believes in them when they cannot believe in themselves. This is the test of a real shepherd. However weak and faltering his disciples may be, Jesus cherishes for them the highest that he knows in spiritual communion, "that the love you have for me may be in them, and that I myself may be in them" (John 17:26).

Jesus is teaching us never to limit what he wants to accomplish in and through his disciples. Likewise, those persons entrusted to us need continual nurture. Innumerable things can happen to sidetrack the best of intentions, and unless these matters are faced realistically, young disciples can easily become defeated.

Probably the most deceiving problems in human relations come out when the ego is offended, giving rise to various expressions of self-centeredness, like pride or bitterness. When these fleshly traits are recognized, they must be brought to the cross. Rebuke will not be resented when offered in love.

Though we are perceived as leaders, let us make clear that Christ is the authority. Avoid any authoritarian role of a master guru. Jesus alone commands. In subjection to him, discipler and disciple learn together.

In this joint experience of growth, I have come to see that the Great Commission is more than our Lord's plan to reach the world; it is his way to encourage the sanctification of his church. You cannot sincerely lead another person to learn more of Christ without being disciple yourself in the process.

Expect Multiplication

Life inevitably reproduces its own kind. Careless persons who let the cares of the world choke the Word of God will reap the folly of their ways. On the other hand, those growing in conformity to Christ develop the qualities of his character and ministry.

His parable of the vine and the branches is a beautiful illustration (John 15:1-17). Jesus likens himself in the analogy to the vine and the disciples to the branches. The branches are conveyors of the life in the vine, and when properly functioning produce a harvest. Any branch not fulfilling its purpose is cut off by the very watchful gardener. Even producing branches are pruned by the gardener in order that they may be more fruitful. "This is my Father's glory," Jesus explained, "showing yourselves to be my disciples" (John 15:8).

When fruit-bearing is seen in the larger context of producing Christ-likeness—first in ourselves and then in others—practically everything Jesus did and said pointed to this truth. The Great Commission brings the principles into focus, phrasing it in terms of discipling. The disciples were taught to live always with the harvest in view. "Open your eyes and look at the fields," he said, noticing the men coming to hear him in Sychar, "they are ripe for harvest" (John 4:35). The disciples could see what he meant and could also appreciate its spiritual application to "eternal life" (John 4:36).

The key to the final harvest centers on the quality and supply of laborers obeying the mandate of Christ. It does not matter how few their numbers in the beginning provided they learn to reproduce and teach their disciples to do the same. As simple as it may seem, this is the way his church will ultimately triumph.

He has given us a model every believer can follow. As those close to you realize how they fit into this multiplication strategy, you can dream with them about their place in the coming harvest. God can use their unique personalities and gifts in ways beyond your own.

The time comes when they are so occupied in their own discipling that our relationship takes on a different quality. Though you are not needed as before, a bond of love remains, perhaps even deepens. As these men and women move on, others will take their place, and the process begins again. With each succeeding spiritual generation, anticipation of the harvest grows, looking joyously to the day when disciples will be made of all nations.

Trust the Spirit

Having given the disciples his last command, Jesus assured them, "I am with you always, to the very end of the age" (Matt. 28:20)—the promise of the Great Commission.

The Holy Spirit puts it all together. What God administers as the Father and reveals as the Son, he accomplishes as the Third Person of the Holy Trinity. We are introduced to him in the Book of Genesis (1:2) as he created the cosmos and later breathes life into the men and women God made in his image (2:7). When persons turn to their own way, the Spirit seeks to bring them back and effect reconciliation with God. Throughout the Old Testament he can be seen at work making a nation to be his witness in a fallen world (Isa. 43:10; 44:8; 49:6). Though Israel fails her calling, a day is envisioned when one would come on whom the Spirit would rest without measure (Isa. 11:2; 42:1).

In the fullness of time, the Holy Spirit planted the seed of the Father in the womb of the virgin, so that she conceived and gave birth to the only begotten Son of God (Matt. 1:18, 20; Luke 1:35). Thereafter, the Spirit directed Jesus during the days of his incarnate life. Everything he said and did was in the strength of the Spirit of God (Luke 4:18, 19).

By the same mighty power, Jesus taught that persons who believe on him would partake of his ministry. He would guide them into truth (John 16:3); he would help them pray (John 14:12, 13; 16:23, 24); he would give them utterances to speak (Matt. 10:19, 20); he would enable them to do his work, "even greater works than these" (John 14:12). Supremely the Spirit would glorify the Son, and as he is lifted up, people are drawn to the Father.

It is not difficult to understand why Jesus told his disciples to tarry until they were empowered by the Spirit (Luke 24:49; Acts 1:8). We see how this begins to unfold at Pentecost (Acts 2:4). The witness of the church now becomes the acts of the Holy Spirit.

The same is true today. It is the Spirit who creates Christ in us, reversing the self-centered value system of the world so that we begin to live as servants. He it is who draws out disciples, planting in their hearts the desire to learn; our part is to respond to his initiative. The same Spirit forms the body of believers, the church, even in our daily associations with one or two followers. Through the Spirit's infusion of love, our faith comes alive in obedience. By his regenerating grace, we become a demonstration of what Jesus teaches. The indwelling Spirit calls us to ministry and disperses gifts for service. He supervises our growth—reproving, encouraging, enlightening—always leading on to something better. Finally, it is the Spirit of God who brings forth the harvest.

Just as those first disciples needed a heavenly endowment, so do we. The sanctifying power from on high, by whatever name it is called, must be a reality in our lives—not as a distant memory, but a present experience of the reigning Christ. Though we can never contain all of him, he wants all of us.

May I ask, where do you want your life to count? Though the way Jesus made disciples does not produce immediate gratification, we are not living primarily for the present. Our satisfaction is in knowing that in generations to come, our witness will still be bearing fruit in an ever-widening circle of disciple makers to the ends of the earth and the end of time.

Chapter 12
Discipleship and Orality

William A. Coppedge, Missionary, Uganda

Tribute

Whether reading Al Coppedge's work or listening to his conversations, it does not take long to pick up on one of his preferred life themes: fatherhood. He argues persuasively that before God was a king, shepherd, or even creator, God was a Father. To know God the Father through Jesus his Son by the power of the Holy Spirit is to know the very essence of the triune God. Furthermore, it is only when God is understood as father that perfect love can be properly understood and even more remarkably, experienced.

Dr. Coppedge also continues to play numerous roles, including teacher, scholar, discipler, friend, husband, and even cowboy. Like many others, I have known him or observed him in close proximity in many of those roles. I have sat in his classroom, participated in his Bible studies, and even ministered alongside and adventured with him in places as unique as Australia, St. Vincent, South Africa, and South Sudan. However, while I can call him "teacher," "discipler," and even "friend," my unique privilege is that I also call him father.

Let me share several significant features of Dad as a father. First, I was often reminded, the only legitimate response to the goodness of our heavenly Father is obedience. According to Dad, "His track record is good, so we want to keep saying 'yes' to Him, whatever He asks." Second, because of His consistent goodness, Dad has been fiercely committed to trusting the Father's provision. I continually witnessed a man not afraid to pray BIG, asking the Father for the impossible.

Third, the only response to the Father's remarkably faithful provision is gratitude. Thanksgiving, Dad says, shifts the focus off of one's self and reminds one of what He has already done. Finally, this life orientation of obeying the Father, trusting in His provision, and cultivating a thankful heart has led Dad to cultivate the presence of God throughout each day. Therefore, as I now father my own five children, I am recognizing more and more the value of imitating my own earthly father, even as I seek to represent our heavenly Father to my own family.

Essay

This essay explores the interconnectivity between discipleship and an interesting phenomenon that is occurring in contemporary missions today: orality. For those who have had the privilege of knowing Al Coppedge, whether personally or through his writings, one immediately recognizes the golden thread of discipleship that runs through all of his relationships and labors for the Kingdom. "God wants to be known"[1] and discipleship describes the process whereby people can know God and be known by God. Whether in his writings or through meetings in his living room, his passion has been to disciple men (and women, albeit indirectly) into more intimate relationships with the triune God.

Coppedge's passion for discipleship is mirrored in the Orality Movement, a movement of people from around the world who have become enthusiasts, practitioners, and champions of employing oral communication strategies in contemporary mission endeavors. The International Orality Network (ION) has come to represent this groundswell of evangelical fervor for removing any communication hindrance to people encountering the good news of Jesus Christ, including communication barriers such as print. ION's motto, "influencing the body of Christ to make disciples of all oral learners," captures the twin emphases within the movement, namely discipleship and oral-preferenced communicators.

The desire of this essay is to consider the points of connection between orality and Al Coppedge's own thinking. Due to the ambiguous nature of orality and perhaps its unfamiliarity for some, this essay begins with an elaborated description of this phenomenon. After establishing a basic framework regarding orality, we will turn our attention to two central dialogue points; namely, discipleship and the roles of God. Since discipleship is a natural bridge between ION and Al Coppedge's own work, we consider the inherent "oral" nature of the "LAMB" principle followed by a slightly more ambitious, albeit brief analysis of the "Portraits of God" from an orality perspective. Bringing a systematician's biblical theology, which by definition requires considerable propositional (and highly literate-shaped) thinking, into conversation with orality may initially prove incongruous. However, I submit that these paradigms can be helpfully engaged in promoting oral communication strategies.

Orality

In the early 1980s Trevor McIlwain, a missionary with New Tribes Mission, began to promote what he called *Chronological Bible Teaching* (CBT). Working in the

1. Allan Coppedge, *Portraits of God: A Biblical Theology of Holiness* (Downers Grove: InterVarsity Press, 2001), 1.

Philippines among people with limited formal education, he had encountered communication frustrations in presenting the gospel message among the Palawano peoples. He found that people responded well to beginning with creation in Genesis, not with Jesus in the gospel of Matthew. Instead of having to constantly stop and explain the background leading up to Jesus, he decided to start at the beginning of the Bible and allow the Palawanos to encounter the biblical narrative as it unfolded.

While remaining highly expository in nature, McIlwain and other missionaries following his lead began to recognize the power of having the "big picture" in mind and, furthermore, the power of story itself for connecting with oral reliant communities. In time, missionaries discovered that instead of merely referring to the biblical episodes, what proved most effective for engaging with audiences was an oral storytelling performance of the biblical narrative. Thus, for example, instead of requiring everyone to read Genesis 1-2 and then write down their observations, interpretations, and applications in their notebooks, missionaries began to story the creation narrative and facilitate discussion through questions around the story, enabling local audiences to understand and apply the biblical truth that was relevant for their cultural context. Early adapters among the International Mission Board of the Southern Baptist Convention (IMB) joined the NTM innovators, and by the 1990s, Bible storytelling was beginning to circulate among Protestant evangelical mission agencies as legitimate currency for conducting evangelism among oral-preferenced peoples.

By 2005, numerous leading mission groups, including IMB, Youth With A Mission (YWAM), Campus Crusade (now Cru), and Wycliffe Bible Translators came together to form the International Orality Network. The use of the term "orality" instead of "storytelling" was intentional. Numerous practitioners within the movement had begun to recognize that while storytelling was a key genre of oral communication, it was only one of various other oral communication methods (i.e. music, dance, etc.).

Orality is defined by those within the movement as "the complex of how oral cultures receive, remember, and replicate (pass on) news, important information, and truths."[2] The movement has borrowed from Walter Ong's differentiation between primary and secondary oral communicators.[3] *Primary oral communicators* are those who are reliant on the spoken word for communication, with a strong appreciation for songs, proverbs, and stories. *Secondary oral communicators* prefer to receive information orally through electronic media, although the message itself may have been shaped by written texts. In counting both primary and secondary oral communicators, ION claims that over 80 percent of the world's population, a

---

2. Charles Madinger, "Coming to Terms with Orality: A Holistic Model," *Missiology: An International Review* 38, no. 2 (April 2010): 204, doi:10.1177/009182961003800211.

3. Walter J. Ong, *Orality and Literacy: Technologizing of the Word* (New York: Routledge, 1982).

stunning 5.7 billion people, are oral-preferenced communicators.[4]

The increasing breadth of ION's vision is worth further explanation. Avery Willis, the first executive director of ION, described ION's mission as to

> radically influence the way oral preferenced communicators are evangelized and discipled in every people group. ION exists to accelerate the process of making the Gospel available to all oral learners in their mother languages and to do it better, faster, cheaper, and more effectively than when literate methods alone are used. The orality movement mobilizes mission organizations and denominations around the world to work together to share oral strategies, to disciple oral preference learners, and to accomplish the vision of reaching all unreached people groups.[5]

Willis' description communicates the intentional passion within ION for reaching the unreached, a group which has traditionally been understood as living primarily in "oral" rural communities. However, participants within ION have begun to acknowledge that digital media, increasingly the communication currency of today's globalized world, while influenced by print, bears many similarities to oral communication. While speaking in generalizations, oral communication and digital communication share several similar characteristics, including an emphasis on story over proposition, an appreciation for the concrete over the abstract, an accent on the community instead of merely the individual, and a mutual interest in image and ritual. As more of the globe turns to digital media, the scope of ION's vision continues to broaden to include not only remote Majority World oral communities but also western *digit-oral* communities. Therefore, instead of dealing with communication issues that might relate only to small, marginalized communities in rural corners of the world, participants within the Orality Movement sees themselves as probing critical communication issues related to whether people can hear, understand and obey the gospel message.

However, detachment of the biblical message from black ink on white pages has not transpired without considerable questions, none less important than whether the Bible, understood as the Word of God, is being manipulated, diluted, or corrupted. One issue that has raised evangelical eyebrows has been the discussion within the movement of an "oral Bible." While controversial for some due to the supposed undermining of the integrity of the Bible, early missionary practitioners were probing the issue of how much Bible is necessary for people to understand and make an informed decision regarding the Christian message. Naturally, for evangelicals, the whole of the Bible is understood as God-breathed and valuable

4. Significantly, secondary oral communicators often can read themselves but their communication preference is oral. Madinger, "Coming to Terms with Orality: A Holistic Model," 201–2. Lovejoy acknowledges ION's number as a rough estimate, and yet he argues that even if his figures are off by a billion, the results beg considerable attention. Grant Lovejoy, "The Extent of Orality: 2012 Update," *Orality Journal* 1, no. 1 (Spring 2012): 11–39.

5. Samuel E. Chiang and Avery T. Willis, Jr., eds., *Orality Breakouts: Using Heart Language to Transform Hearts* (Hong Kong: ION/LCWE, 2010), viii.

for teaching, reproof, correction, and training in righteousness.[6] However, the traditional process of translating the entire Bible takes decades. What are communities to do while they wait for that literate miracle to unfold? Furthermore, translation agencies have struggled with an unanticipated phenomenon of what to do when a translation is completed, but then the intended audience has little to no interest in it due to its literate packaging.

These and other related uncomfortable issues have raised thorny questions for mission organizations and translation agencies alike. None of these evangelical groups want to give away their commitment to the authority of the entire Bible and its importance for missional activities such as evangelism, discipleship and church planting. The alarming question that has emerged is whether ultimately the evangelical commitment to the importance of the whole Bible requires a proficiency in the technology of reading to be a disciple of Jesus Christ. This essay is not the place for unraveling all those complex communication and theological tensions. However, a cursory glance at an episode in Jesus' own communication strategy could provide some initial points of reference and will allow for raising some issues that are relevant for later discussion regarding orality and Al Coppedge's own ideas.

In Luke 10:25-37, an expert in the Jewish law tests Jesus, "Teacher, what must I do to inherit eternal life?" Immediately, regardless of the motive of the lawyer's heart, one recognizes that this question probes into the very heart of human existence itself. An argument could be made that every community raises questions about the possibility of life after death and, if possible, how it might be attained. Although, in theory, evangelicals often discuss questions of "eternal life," caution is necessary here lest the weightiness of this potential standoff between Jesus and this religious expert be overlooked. This is a high stakes encounter, and it requires careful consideration of how Jesus handles this situation. Furthermore, while a theological lens will provide a particular view of this conversation, I would like to propose looking through a communication lens. How does Jesus handle this communication event and what communication choices does he make?

First, Jesus does not respond directly but counters the lawyer's question with his own line of inquiry. "What is written in the Law? How do you read it?" Jesus could have chosen to seize this perfect setup question and provide a detailed exposition of the "Roman Road" or the "Four Spiritual Laws." At least, he could have given the lawyer and the presumably present crowd a 1-2-3 step process for confessing, repenting, and praying for forgiveness. However, Jesus does not answer a direct question with a direct answer. He turns the man back to his own area of expertise, namely the law. There is an accommodation or conversational hospitality being extended by Jesus. Instead of rebuking the lawyer's antagonistic heart or trying to impress him with an unexpected answer, Jesus allows him to be the expert and talk

6. 2 Timothy 3:16.

about what he knows.

What needs to be recognized is that Jesus meets this man on his communication terms. Presumably, this lawyer would have known much of the law by heart, but he also would have been an expert in reading the Torah. This is a literate and learned communicator, and so it is worth highlighting the literate approach that Jesus' questions imply: "What is *written* in the Law? How do you *read* it?" Jesus does not turn to storytelling or a proverb, or even a first century chorus or hymn to initially engage this educated and literate communicator. He begins by meeting this lettered religious expert where the expert felt comfortable – discussing the written text.

We could stop there and reflect on the simple but profound communication example that Jesus is beginning to unfold. But the communication event is only just beginning. The lawyer responds by quoting from the Torah: "You shall love the LORD your God with all your heart, and with all your soul, and with all your strength, and with all your mind; and your neighbor as yourself." The man does not respond by telling the Abraham saga or reiterating the Exodus narrative or recounting the giving of the Torah on Mt. Sinai. He sums all those up in a short-handed propositional summary, a literate crafted response to Jesus' question.

Jesus, having gently led the man to answer his own question, now affirms and encourages him to obey the information he already knows: "You have answered correctly; do this and you will live." The significance of this moment in the conversation from a communication perspective is tremendous. The man has asked and answered a primordial question and thus far the engagement, while orally transmitted, has been shaped by the written text and propositional dynamics.

Technically, the interchange could have ended and yet Jesus' literate and hospitable responses, oriented towards the lettered lawyer, fail to connect with his heart. Something in the man remains unsatisfied with the propositionally correct answer of how to attain eternal life. The episode continues, "But wishing to justify himself, he said to Jesus, "And who is my neighbor?"

It is at this point that Jesus shifts communication strategies. He could have chosen to expound on what loving God with one's "all" really means. He could have given a definition of a "neighbor." He could have provided additional propositions to clarify the already established sound doctrine. But what communication strategy does Jesus adopt? To this religious lawyer, this expert in Jewish Torah, this highly literate and lettered scholar, Jesus tells a story.

Several points are worth highlighting within this communication interchange. First, Jesus adopts the appropriate communication strategy for the particular audience he is engaging. With a highly literate lawyer, he initially adopts a literate-oriented or propositional approach. Second, one communication strategy was not enough to handle the realities that emerged in the conversation. The man knew the correct propositions; he did not need more information. So Jesus switched tactics and turned to more of an oral-oriented approach – he told the story of the Good

Samaritan.

Propositions communicate information succinctly, but they offer very little emotional or experiential engagement. Stories, on the other hand, afford the possibility for emotional and experiential engagement. For example, not only does the story communicate the hopelessness of the man attacked by thieves, but it also highlights the cost the Samaritan endured to ensure the man's recovery. Stories invite the imagination to depict the broken and bleeding victim, to notice the sneer of disgust by the priest and Levite and hear the jingle of the two denarii coins being handed over. Furthermore, story can be a powerful tool for memory, as evidenced by popular title given this account. It is not referred to as, "Jesus and the Academic Heckler" but "The Good Samaritan."

Throughout this conversation, Jesus seems to be modeling an integrated communication approach, one that validates both literate-shaped engagement and oral communication methods. One is not necessarily better than the other, but they do lend themselves to accomplishing different purposes. Naturally, it is worth consideration that if Jesus met a lettered scholar on a literate communication level, would the natural implication not be that he would meet an oral reliant communicator on an oral level? Jesus certainly did not force the lawyer into a communication interchange beyond his communication expertise. The relevant question for missions, church planting, theological education and even children and youth ministries is whether our communication strategies are as sensitive to our intended audiences as Jesus was to the lawyer.

The question begging to be asked is how evangelical missions' adoption of orality and Jesus' own validation of orality relate to Al Coppedge's understanding of discipleship and his own systematic approach to theology. I propose that even as a trained systematic theologian gravitates towards a propositional or highly literate-oriented theological paradigm, there emerges within this understanding of discipleship and his proposal of the roles of God a distinct desire to effectively communicate. Furthermore, characteristics of oral communication can be identified within his thinking, which deserve to be highlighted. Such an analysis will enable a greater appreciation for this theologian's contribution to the Church and the academy. It will also contribute to reaffirming the potentially fruitful line of inquiry regarding how these rich ideas can be adapted for communicating the gospel in today's globalized world.

Orality and the "LAMB" Principle

Al Coppedge, as he has labored alongside others in *The Barnabas Foundation,* has developed numerous resources related to discipleship, but one that provides a natural "on-ramp" into his theology and philosophy of discipleship is the LAMB principle. This section provides a brief overview.

Life-to-Life

The LAMB principle begins with "life-to-life sharing," and a personal anecdote illuminates its effectiveness. While discipleship happened for Dad[7] at the seminary, on weekend discipleship retreats, and hosting discipleship group meetings on weeknights, he recognized that something different was possible when the discipler and disciple shared life together. I have vivid memories of him discussing the difference between engaging men in classroom settings or even in the living room and when he would invite one of them to go in the truck to pick up a load of hay for our horses. It was in the drive out for hay, where the formal seminary attire of coat and tie was exchanged for the informal Levis and cowboy boots, that life was shared together.

Part of this sharing of life on life resulted in Dad never traveling alone. My first short-term mission trip was as a twelve-year-old boy to Australia, and I, along with two other men, was a part of his team. We all watched and learned from him as he was busy praying, teaching, and preaching, and he courageously invited all of us to participate and contribute in a variety of ways. But another level of learning went on in the playing of chess on the flight together, trying out new foods together, or exploring the Australian snowy mountains together. The model for this life-to-life sharing was Jesus, who boldly invited twelve men to live with him for three years. Dad was convinced that this life sharing was essential for any true discipleship to actually take root, not just in the head, but also in the heart and imagination.

Accountability

The second LAMB principle is accountability. The "lone ranger" Christian man or woman is the most vulnerable to attack. Therefore, it was stressed for disciples to hold one another accountable for particular Christian commitments. In good Wesleyan fashion, these commitments were not to be taken lightheartedly. Al Coppedge and the Barnabas Foundation regularly invited people to enter into a signed discipleship covenant that detailed spiritual and other personal commitments and goals.

Not insignificantly, accountability was only effective if sufficient relational capital had been accumulated through life-to-life sharing. Without this personal connection, asking hard accountability questions week in and week out could quickly deteriorate into legalism. What should not be missed is that both of these principles situate the discipleship process within community. Discipleship is about growing in communion with God, and that was not possible without communion with other people.

---

7. While "Al Coppedge" seemed appropriate throughout much of the article, several points felt very awkward and I beg your forgiveness for digressing to more intimate references.

Means of Grace and the Band

The "means of grace" was the third LAMB principle. This included scripture reading, scripture memory, attending worship, tithing, fasting and praying. Jesus was the model for these spiritual exercises, and Dad strongly encouraged any disciple to recognize that some combination of these, if not all of them, was necessary for cultivating a greater spiritual awareness of God and his grace in one's life. Finally, as already alluded to, the fourth LAMB principle was the "band" or group of like-minded men or women who were serious about following after Jesus.

LAMB and Orality

An initial communication assessment of the LAMB principle is immediately forced to acknowledge that any acrostic, such as LAMB (**l**ife-to-life, **a**ccountability, **m**eans of grace, **b**and), is by definition a literate construct. Furthermore, the written and signed discipleship covenants, the high value placed on Bible reading, and even the accountability reports, although given orally, amounted to a propositional checklist. For a seminary audience, such a communication strategy seems to mirror Jesus' own accommodating approach as seen with the lawyer. The question that we want to ask is, in light of the increased interest in discipling oral-reliant communicators, in what ways can oral communication characteristics be identified within text-oriented ideas? What are some initial ways to consider harnessing the wealth of literate constructs for discipleship among oral-preferenced disciples?

First, the stress on the importance of interpersonal relationships within the discipleship process is inherently oral. While speaking broadly, it is worth reiterating that oral-preferenced communicators are typically communally oriented. Traditionally, without the technology of writing to help remember, persons within the community preserved messages, truths, and information orally, by speaking them to each other. This is changing today with the increase in education and digital technology, but one needs to recognize that literate communication events, where a person or group of persons read a text, isolate persons. The attention shifts from *I-Thou* to *I-It*, even if a group reads out loud together. They have to momentarily all "look to the text." Thus, while texts make communication possible across time and space, they can have a tendency to depersonalize.

While the LAMB discipleship model stresses personal and even corporate reading, it also recognizes the value of community. All four elements of the LAMB principle contain either explicit or implicit communal expectations. Discipleship and spiritual transformation does not happen in isolation but in the interchange between persons walking the journey of life together.

Second, a natural corollary to this stress on community is that when persons are in community together, they use spoken, not just written, words to communicate with one another. Even with the written Word of God at the center of this discipleship paradigm, each group came together in our family living room to speak orally about what was happening in their lives this week, how God was working, and where prayer was needed. They did not write letters, send email, or message their weekly reports. They looked each other in the face and talked, laughed, cried, and prayed together. While often taken for granted, it is worth reiterating that one of orality's greatest assets for creating transformational moments is in the humanness of the spoken word.[8]

Across the years of these discipleship groups unfolding, something else was happening in personal relationship and in the interchange of spoken words. Not only did people hear from each other, but they had that many more ears attuned to hear God speak. This Trinitarian God is an oral and creative communicator. Therefore, for this understanding of discipleship, one has to believe God speaks. While that can happen independently between God, his Word, and a person, the helpful balance to any single interpretation was one's community who knew the person best and could help filter what one believed God was saying.

A third oral characteristic emerges from considering the LAMB principle, namely ritual.[9] In certain contexts, ritual conjures certain negative connotations. We want to be aware of those, and yet there remains a tendency to associate discipleship primarily with articulating true doctrine or attaining "more" spiritual information. God changes people's thinking, but a privileging of the mind over and against one's heart and body creates misshapen disciples. Ritual provides a category that may helpfully balance any overemphasis on rationality as it tends to speak to the embodied activities of the person or community. God wants to transform the whole person – a disciple's head, heart, and body – and in that spirit the term ritual can be reclaimed and imbued with constructive qualities.

Part of the reason for this is that in large measure participants within the orality movement have noted the importance of ritual and liturgy for communities which value the spoken word.[10] These rituals or behavior practices not only cultivate a sense of belonging but also help give meaning to and interpretation of circumstances.[11] Within many discipleship paradigms, there is a certain ritualistic pattern where one chooses behavior practices that then begin to influence and shape one's spiritual experiences and maturity. For example, many discipleship efforts encourage the

8. Not incidentally, while being leveraged for the Kingdom of God throughout the world, this remains one of the inherent limitations to digital discipleship – no screen can replace the humanness of orality.

9. While I do not agree with Smith on numerous theological points, I have found his discussion of ritual and liturgy very intriguing. James K.A. Smith, *Desiring the Kingdom (Cultural Liturgies): Worship, Worldview, and Cultural Formation, Cultural Liturgies* (Grand Rapids: Baker, 2009).

10. Hans-Ruedi Weber, *The Communication of the Gospel to Illiterates: Based on a Missionary Experience in Indonesia* (Edinburgh: Edinburgh House Press, 1957).

11. See chapters 2 and 3, Smith, *Desiring the Kingdom (Cultural Liturgies): Worship, Worldview, and Cultural Formation.*

daily behavioral ritual of concentrated time in the Bible study. This behavior practice, embodied by the disciple in reading, studying, praying, and even singing, becomes a liturgical form for shaping one's spiritual desires. Likewise, the weekly discipleship group is itself a ritual, an embodied activity that oriented the disciple towards other people and then communally towards God. Even the annual discipleship weekend retreats we watched our Dad conduct played this formational role, providing an occasion for serious disciples to "conference" together in true Wesleyan fashion for the purposes of worshiping, exhorting, and learning together.[12]

It needs to be clarified that performing these rituals does not guarantee spiritual growth or maturity. We want to guard against an inadvertent step into considering certain spiritual disciplines as either magical or a means of attaining salvation. We neither control God through these activities nor seek to earn God's favor by demonstrating certain behaviors. These ritual behaviors are "methods," voluntary habits that afford opportunities for disciples to grow in intimacy with Jesus. While identifying activities like daily quiet time or discipleship meetings as rituals may be uncomfortable for some, even a cursory consideration of the means of grace connotes ritualistic components. Therefore, identified methods like tithing and Scripture memory ought to be embodied practices with value to engage the mind, body, and heart – forming and shaping a disciple's actions and desires.

The LAMB principle, while initially designed with seminary audiences in mind and thus perhaps not considered an oral perspective, offers a natural place for considering discipleship among oral-preferenced communicators. A few suggestions might be helpful for generating additional creativity for how these ideas could be employed among oral communities.

The emphasis on community and relationship as being the place where discipleship transformation happens cannot be overemphasized. Among oral-preferenced communicators, the relational context, more than the discipleship content, influences real spiritual change. The discipler, not the instruction or even the discipline, is what makes the most difference in provoking spiritual change in other people. This can be hard to accept for some trained in western educational systems that specialize in knowledge transference (with positive and negative results). Unless care is taken, one can too easily assume that more knowledge will just naturally result in greater spiritual maturity. While direct spiritual teaching can be tremendously helpful, one must be reminded that the disciple is learning through the indirect, the informal, and often the unintended. Hence, some have suggested that discipleship should be considered more of an apprenticeship,

12. For a season, these weekend retreats were held consistently in Wilmore. They came to have a liturgical meaning for my younger sister and me as after the Saturday morning breakfast, any leftover doughnuts were brought home. While I cannot say that we gleaned much spiritually from the extra maple-glazed treats, the power of ritual to reinforce memory can be discerned in that neither of us have forgotten what became affectionately dubbed the "doughnut retreats."

wherein one learns but also lives the craft of following after Jesus.[13]

Another area that has tremendous potential but needs reconsideration is the ritual of daily quiet time. Allow me to explain. Early one morning, while living in northern Uganda, I was out for a walk with my wife and daughters. We passed a church and could hear a chorus of voices praising God in the local language. It was not a Sunday morning and one of the girls asked what was happening. To my surprise, the unconscious response that came out was, "They are having their quiet time." It was not until later, upon reflection, that I realized how true that is for many oral communities. Daily quiet time may not be individuals cuddled up with their Bibles, journals, highlighters and cups of coffee. Instead, it may be small clusters of people joining together to communally consecrate the day to God. Bible engagement may happen through a public reading, but it may also take place through listening to an audio Bible or engaging in an oral Bible story performance. While for some evangelical western Christians such community devotions would not "count" as personal time with Jesus, I submit that the typically individualized and usually highly literate quiet time being "me, my Bible, a workbook, and Jesus" needs careful reconsideration. While tremendously helpful for particular communicators, this method will not work for many oral-reliant communicators. We can either fault them (and consequently applaud our own preferences) or we can hospitably consider alternative oral options.

Among oral-preferenced communicators, checklist accountability is another area that needs attention, and specifically contextualization. In many communities where the spoken word is valued, traditionally understood accountability, where one acknowledges whether one maintained or failed to uphold personal spiritual commitments, is likely to encounter problems. This relates to the issue of honor and shame that remains a highly valued cultural dynamic in many traditionally oral communities. To acknowledge before a group of peers and an elder that one failed to fulfill one's commitments could be incredibly shame inducing. From a stereotypical western guilt-innocence perspective, an argument can be made that shame is the point of the accountability – to keep one from failing. However, in a culture with high considerations for issues of shame and honor, there may be tremendous cultural pressure to either lie to keep hidden failed commitments or just not appear at the arranged meeting. While this could be seen as a lack of interest on the part of the disciple to really grow spiritually, it could also be interpreted as a weighty cultural dynamic that many western educated persons might fail to fully appreciate.

Certainly, this does not mean that the emphasis on accountability cannot work among oral disciples. What it does mean is that his emphasis on life-to-life sharing

13. See the forthcoming article by Randy Arnett, *Discipleship in the Face of Orality*, in the Orality Journal, 6, 1, Spring, 2017, https://orality.net/library/journals/.

will need to be even more pronounced, perhaps exaggeratedly emphasized, so that deep emotional and relational deposits can be made by the discipler into the lives of his or her disciples. Furthermore, the dynamics of the group may need to be adjusted. Accountability may need to be done more on a personalized level, where the discipler visits the disciple and can gently inquire about the commitments they have made. This will allow for accountability but in a safe context for people to acknowledge where they fell short. Once again, the typical western mentality may want to associate such action as failing to be transparent. But issues of failed transparency have at times had to do with the cultural differences regarding how much one values issues related to honor and shame considerations. If nothing else, an awareness of matters related to shame and honor needs to be in every discipler's paradigm.

Orality and the Roles of God

Finally, a word is necessary regarding the roles, or portraits, of God which were a major interest in the seminary classroom for Dr. Coppedge.[14] This has potential to be a very helpful tool for approaching the breadth of the biblical material, particularly for oral-preferenced communities. The *Portraits of God* has to be considered a highly literate, systematic, propositionally-oriented text, complete with detailed diagrams. This is appropriate and valuable within a seminary context where mastering such tremendous amounts of biblical and theological data is necessary. But can such a highly literate-oriented work serve oral-preferenced communicators?

The roles of God can serve discipleship in oral communities in several ways. Initially, it is important to recognize that the "roles" are essentially a communication paradigm. Coppedge wants to enable people to know God personally. Personal relationships are built on personal communication, and thus the biblical data was mined for communication clues that might enable disciples of Jesus to understand God's communication to them, and likewise to know how they can communicate God to others. "Personal revealer" is the most amorphous of the portraits, but the inclusion of this role was an attempt to highlight that this God speaks, and He speaks in every major role and in all the sub-roles.

The "roles" also offer a holistic paradigm. What is attempted is to produce a holistic biblical theology that can likewise provide categories for interpreting classic systematic theological doctrines. Along those lines, vivid biblical images are thus recognized, portraits that very helpfully concretize much of the abstract and usually propositional tenets of both biblical and systematic theology. This appeal

14. In the seminary classroom "roles" was the original use for these God-given pictures for the holiness of God. They were later designed "portraits" in the *Portraits of God: A Biblical Theology of Holiness* (IVP). The major roles/portraits were the Good Shepherd, Sovereign King, Loving Father, Transcendent Creator, Personal Revealer, Righteous Judge, Powerful Redeemer and Pure Priest.

to holism and imagination through pictures aligns itself well with oral-oriented communities, as many cultures all over the world can identify with roles such as shepherds, priests, and kings. Therefore, while each of these could be elaborated, I submit that this issue of orality and interpersonal communication lies not on the fringes of either theology or missional activity but at the very heart of serious theological reflection and discipleship engagement.

In conclusion, I want to suggest that one of the challenges of theological education in oral-preferenced communities is coming to grips with the reality that not as much information can be disseminated in the same amount of time because the tools of memory, particularly note-taking and reference books, are less prevalent. Things need to be packaged in such a way that they can be remembered, whether through story, song, or other symbols. This means that introducing a copy of *Portraits* into a discipleship group among oral-reliant communicators would not be necessarily fruitful. But what deserves further exploration is the key stories that could be shared from Scripture that could enable oral disciples to discover the various roles of God within the grand biblical narrative. A cache of key stories needs to be adopted, tried, and adapted so that over time a discipleship set of stories, centering on the roles of God, can be compiled. In true oral fashion, these stories should then be put to song and drama and made accessible to entire communities.

Al Coppedge, along with other systematic and biblical theologians, has provided us with helpful tools for theological engagement and disciple-making. With a little creativity and courage to think outside the literate categories, I submit that these contributions continue to hold tremendous value for discipleship *both* among print-oriented audiences and oral-preferenced disciples.

Chapter 13
Church History's Greatest Missed Opportunity

Thane Hutcherson Ury, Scholar in Residence for Intercultural Studies
Asbury University, Wilmore, Kentucky

Tribute

I landed on "Planet Asbury" in 1982—clueless and nervous—lurching in the wake of a recent spiritual awakening. The plan was only to disambiguate my beliefs, little else. Cheap grace, shallow thinking, and a casual faith had been the norm for far too long. That was about to change when I fell in with The Barnabas Foundation, and its laser-focus on discipleship and accountability. Its premises were basically that "Christian maturity does not happen by accident," and the Holy One still longs for hearts in community *to pant after His; tenets so simple that even I could grasp them.*

Barnabas was one of your many gifts to the Church, Al. And the invite to join your group marked your guys forever, as we caught more theology in your home and on road trips than in most seminary degrees. What a rare ob portu *to observe a piety well-tempered, a family well-raised, and a faith well-calibrated to Scripture. In time we more fully absorbed the wisdom of the Barnabas formula.*

But such really is China's only path to becoming the China she was meant to be. Waking from its Confucian slumbers and disencumbered from the State church, this dragon won't be tamed by stadium evangelists and jumbotrons. It will only come by tracing the Master's blueprint; the one you showed us whereby a mentor, with a life worth emulating, commits a huge chunk of his/her heart to guide unpolished souls along the ordo solutis, *thoroughly grounding us to repeat this "life-to-life transference." Why? Again, godliness does not happen by accident!*

Al, no superlative does justice to capture the gratitude we contributors have for your having poured your heart and mind into ours. May the rumblings you hear of the Asian harvest be just one reminder of your continued global impact through discipleship. Work is underway here to undo an ancient mistake, and your input has been part of the correction!

Essay

Henri Charrière's life was immortalized in the 1973 movie *Papillon.* Falsely convicted of murder, Henri was sentenced to a work camp in the penal system of French Guiana, a living hell aptly dubbed the "Dry Guillotine." After years of failed escape attempts he was moved to his Patmos, the allegedly inescapable "Devil's Island." The film's final scene is epic. From high atop sheer cliffs Henri had long studied the deadly waves below. Over time he made a liberating observation, noting that every seventh wave into the rocky inlet below rebounded out a little further than the others. From this he projected that if timed perfectly, the seventh wave might be just enough to carry him past the jagged rocks and out to the open sea. He calculated correctly, made the 80-foot leap, and floated twenty choppy miles to liberty, buoyed by only a burlap sack filled with coconuts. This emancipation did not come by mere sea gazing—or even by correctly exegeting the waves. No, it came in actually having the courage to personally take a huge leap of faith.

Intriguingly, the English word *opportunity* has nautical origins. It refers to right timing, as skippers of old often had to read the flood tide just right to get a ship to port. When a harbor was approached from far off, experienced captains knew they had to come in at the right window. Arriving at an inopportune time often meant having to wait outside a port until the right (safe) time. The ancients called this the '*ob portu*,' referring to 'standing off port.' And as with Charrière, merely knowing the *ob portu* principle (i.e. reading the waves) was not sufficient. Commanders had to have the patience to wait for the right moment, and then also ultimately to commit to action. Spiritual applications here are legion.

The entire flow of human history might be likened to episodic bursts of one *ob portu* after another—separated by long periods of "what ifs." The weight of these opportunities is seldom fully realized as matters are happening, sometimes taking centuries to fully fathom. Consider Constantine's conversion, Athanasius' defense of the Trinity, Luther's 95 theses, colonial America's break from Britain, the Scopes Trial, a risky amphibious landing at Normandy, or nineteen undetected boxcutters on 9/11. These represent countless *kairos* events whose historical scales could have dipped either way. The subject of this chapter focuses on just such an occasion: a missed opportunity considered one of the most lamentable in all of Church history.

Historical Context

Napoléon Bonaparte referred to China as a sleeping giant, saying "Let her sleep, for when she wakes she will move the world."[1] In these opening years of the 21st century China dominates the world stage. Pundits generally concede the merit of

1. Napoléon allegedly said this while pointing to China on a map. Some sources read 'lion' instead of 'giant;' all known references have been traced only to secondary sources.

Newsweek's May 2005 cover, labeling this as "China's Century." In the last thirty years her economic surge has been nothing short of breathtaking.

But eight centuries ago China was already the world's largest free-trade zone. In those days Kublai Khan, founder of the Yuan Dynasty, governed the largest land bloc in history and a quarter of the world's population. His domain spanned from Poland to the Pacific, and from Russia down to India, a land grab that dwarfed the exploits of Alexander and the Roman Caesars. The main trade artery, the Silk Road, connected much of this astounding 12 million square miles of commerce. And China's mercantile dominance (among other things) is the new normal for us.

An Unexpected Journey

It was onto this mid-13th century stage that Niccolò and Maffeo Polo stumbled. Normal trade took these Venetian brothers as far east as Soldaia (a Crimean peninsula port), then Surai and the Volga river (both in present-day Russia). A civil war unexpectedly broke out, blocking their return path, so the brothers were shunted further east than planned. They found sanctuary in a city on the Silk Road—famed Bukhara (now in Uzbekistan). Bukhara was no backwater town—second only to Bagdad as an intellectual center in the Islamic world. This haven offered new openings for trade and also for language and culture acquisition. Little could Marco's father and uncle imagine they would be marooned there for three full years. And their confinement might have continued had it not been for a chance encounter with one of Kublai Khan's noblemen. Meeting the Italians, and knowing of his ruler's insatiable appetite for learning, the envoy encouraged them to come visit his liege. With little to lose and a prospect for a new trade stream, the Polos consented. Taking advantage of the *Pax Mongolica,* they launched out on a challenging eastward trek, with only God knowing of the *ob portu* waiting on the horizon.

After a perilous trip they reached Shangdu—known as *Xanadu* due to Coleridge—and Kublai warmly received them.[2] Europe was only familiar with the bloodthirsty exploits[3] of his grandfather, Genghis Khan, so the civil manner of his grandson was unexpected. Kublai had an avid interest in anything occidental and probed the Polos about Europe's legal and political system, about Latin Christianity and its doctrines and Pope, pressing for any minutiae about their world.

Discussions on faith matters did not take place entirely in a vacuum. Kublai's

2. The Polos were not the first Europeans in Mongol territory. Pope Innocent IV sent Giovanni da Pian del Carpini in 1245 and Willem van Ruysbroeck in 1253. While the Papal motive was to forge an alliance with the Mongols in the crusade against Islam, Willem had a heart to evangelize the steppe empire.

3. 4 millions souls perished in the onslaught: 10% of the world! The Khans marked territory in other ways: 1 in 12 Asian men today carrying a Y chromosome traced back to this Mongolia era.

uncle was a convert to Nestorian Christianity,[4] as was his mother, Sorghaghtani Beki.[5] And Nestorians had also been appointed as governors throughout the Khanate realm. Kublai himself embraced an odd hybrid of Nestorianism and Lamaist Buddhism, while his wife was a devout Buddhist. Of all the Mongol Khanates, he was most tolerant toward other beliefs. But Kublai's neutrality did not mean he viewed all religions as equally credible. Wildman notes that Kublai's people could freely

> ...worship as long as their faith was moral; and as for himself he worshiped by turns in Buddhist, Confucian, and Mohammedan temples; Marco Polo tells us that he likewise favored the Christian religion. As for the Taoists, they were so openly corrupt and fraudulent that Kublai ordered a public examination to ascertain whether there was any truth in their writings on geomancy, necromancy, and astrology.[6]

Thus, after a year of discourse with the Tartar chief, the Polos hit an open spot in his heart.[7] We see this in Kublai's astonishing request that the Polos return home and solicit the Pope to marshal one hundred "wise men" from the West to come and share their faith in in his kingdom. Specifically, he asked for

> ...a hundred persons well skilled in your law, who being confronted with the idolaters shall have power to restrain them, and showing that they themselves are endowed with similar art, but which they refrain from exercising, because it is derived from the agency of evil spirits, shall compel them to desist from practices of such a nature in their presence. When I am witness of this, I shall place them and their religion under a ban, and shall allow myself to be baptized. Following my example, all my nobility will then in like manner receive baptism, and this will be imitated by my subjects in general. In the end the Christians of these parts will exceed in number those who inhabit your own country.[8]

It would pay rich dividends for the reader to go back and digest the request a little more slowly. The thesis of our chapter depends on grasping just how unprecedented and astounding this appeal really was. Here from the East we have the head of history's largest empire essentially opening the door for the West to permeate his world, asking for the best apologists to come and commend their Christian world-

---

4. Nestorius (386–450) advanced the view that Christ's human nature (the man Jesus) and his divine nature (the divine Son of God) were so distinct as to be two persons, instead of two natures unified in one person. This Christology was declared heretical at Ephesus (430 AD) and Chalcedon (451 AD).

5. She longed for oil from the lamp at Christ's tomb, thinking it had healing properties. Her son sought other rare artifacts, even acquiring a beggar's bowl from India thought to have belonged to Buddha.

6. Rounsevelle Wildman, *China's Open Door: A Sketch of Chinese Life and History* (Boston: Lothrop Publishing Company, 1900), 98. Geomancy and astrology will be factors in the Ricci section.

7. The Bukhara stay helped the Polos in Turkic and Persian, trade languages in China. As merchants, not scholars, speaking Kublai's own tongue allowed conversations beyond mercantile interests.

8. Marco Polo, *The Travels of Marco Polo*, edited with an introduction by Manuel Komroff (New York: Garden City Publishing Co., 1930), 122. See also page 8.

view. Is there any more remarkable *ob portu* in Church history?

Not just 100 Men, but 100 Scholars

What type of men did Kublai seek? They have been variously labeled as wise men of learning, teachers, teachers of science and religion, evangelists, missionaries, philosophers, and learned men. Kublai was clear that this class of thinkers be ones

> thoroughly acquainted with the principles of the Christian religion, as well as with the seven arts, and qualified to prove to the learned of his dominions, by just and fair argument, that the faith professed by Christians is superior to, and founded upon more evident truth than, any other; that the gods of the Tartars and the idols worshipped in their houses were only evil spirits, and that they and the people of the East in general were under an error in reverencing them as divinities.[9]

Men grounded in all seven arts were wanted who could argue the merits of Christianity to the Mongols. The arts were arithmetic, astronomy, geometry, grammar, logic, music, and rhetoric (or dialectics),[10] widely considered the sum of human knowledge.[11] But what Kublai could not have fathomed was the radical paradigm shift in education he was courting. For these arts were not only fundamental to the European university system, but also the nurturing soil for the birth of science *qua* science. We will unpack this daring notion a little further below.

You Can't Con a Khan Man

Discerning readers by now have wondered about Kublai's intentions. While he saw some aspects of Christianity as weak,[12] he still vowed to his Venetian guests to be baptized provided one condition be met. He was conflicted over which of the four great sages was true, so in part he wanted the West to prove its faith. He is said to have had sorcerers who could alter the weather and magically move objects. In particular, Marco observed Tibetan lamas at meals levitating goblets right in front of Kublai's mouth.[13] Given this, it is only natural for Kublai to wonder if the West could match these signs and wonders. If the God of the West could not contend, what would be the point? All China needed was one Elijah—any more would be a

---

9. *The Travels of Marco Polo*, 8.

10. The initial three are referred to as the *trivium*; the last four, the *quadrivium*.

11. See Otto Willmann, "The Seven Liberal Arts," *The Catholic Encyclopedia*. Vol. 1. (New York: Robert Appleton Company, 1907).

12. Nestorians came to China in 635 AD. Marco later noted that various communities had survived across the empire six centuries later. He also relays that far from being anti-Christian, Kublai actually sensed the superiority of Christianity. Yet it was the low level of learning among some Nestorians that put him off. So some nuance is needed here, as 13th-century Nestorians blanched in contrast to their more gifted precursors in the T'ang Dynasty; ones who had earned the trust of Emperor Taizong, mastered the language, and were given freedom to translate Christian works into Chinese.

13. *The Travels of Marco Polo*, 108-109, 121.

bonus. Just one who knew the power of the Holy One and the toothlessness of the Baal. Just one who would trust God to decide how wet to soak the wood.

What a hinge moment! Bevington notes Kublai "hadn't been able to choose among . . . Christ, Mohammed, Moses, or Buddha—respecting them equally because he didn't know which" was the true god.[14] Echoing Wildman above, Marco Polo agrees that the Khan had a discernible predilection toward Christianity.

> Upon being asked his motive for this conduct, [Kublai] said: "There are four great Prophets who are reverenced and worshipped by the different classes of mankind. The Christians regard Jesus Christ as their divinity; the Saracens, Mahomet; the Jews, Moses; and the idolaters, Sogomombar-kan,[15] the most eminent among their idols. I do honor and show respect to all the four, and invoke to my aid whichever among them is in truth Supreme in Heaven."[16]

Marco adds that "from the manner in which his majesty acted towards [these worldviews], it is evident that he regarded the faith of the Christians as the truest and the best."[17] Just imagine if Kublai had one or two scholars trained in the seven arts that could provide reasonable answers. The very year the Polo returned to Kublai, 1274, was the same year Thomas Aquinas died. What if a lesser luminary like Aquinas' disciple, Remigio dei Girolami, had answered the China call? What if just one with the stature of a Bonaventure, a Fibonacci, or a Lombard came?

Among the many moving parts here, it is probably a safe assumption that Kublai's initial motive was not that his subjects hear of Calvary's love. His first inkling was likely political. In asking for the hundred he was being tactically ecumenical, like his ancestors, using religion as an opiate to tame the masses. Such, of course, reduces the Polos and the hundred to little more than *useful idiots.*[18] Additionally, the crusades had garnered the attention, if not respect, of the East, so maybe Khan's gesture was an olive branch of sorts. And an alliance between East and West would benefit both against their arch foe, Islam. Others argue that Khan never intended for Jesus to replace other deities—as Rome would insist of infidels—but that he was only willing to add Christ to the Mongol pantheon. Or maybe he was just seizing his own *ob portu* to stock Mongol administrative posts with foreign advisors.[19] To save time we can cede part or all of these conjectures and quickly add, "So what?"

These proposals miss the more salient parts of the narrative. First, it seems

---

14. Helen S. Bevington, *The World and the Bo Tree* (Durham, NC: Duke University, 1991), 118.

15. Most likely this is scribal corruption of "Shakyamuni," another name for Gautama Buddha.

16. *The Travels of Marco Polo*, 120-121. Discussed more below; for the moment know that these sentiments were expressed years after the Polos had returned, and without the hundred.

17. *The Travels of Marco Polo*, 121.

18. Used initially to denote Western sympathizers of Marxism, the term now refers to ones unaware that they are being cynically used as mere tools for leaders or causes.

19. Not trusting native Chinese, Khanates filled most administrative posts with non-Chinese.

obvious that there were *also* some religious motives at play. Second, at the end of the day, top-notch apologist-missionaries were being invited to settle in China indefinitely. To this point, thirdly, given that the trio of Venetians ended up having about two decades of unfettered access to the Mongol empire, what reason is there to think that the hundred would not have had comparable access at the highest echelons, maybe even greater? Fourth, these outsiders were given the green light to proselytize, denoting an astonishing level of confidence on Kublai Khan's part. And lastly, at least in principle, Kublai was open to having his own views challenged. As mentioned above, he was at a crossroads, weighing the four key faiths. If the hundred had come, or even just Nicholas and William—whom we will meet in a moment—Kublai would have had a much better opportunity to assess the truth claims of Jesus.

While Khan's motives can and should be debated, in the end no other ruler has ever invited adept apologists to flood his nation en masse. Cultured despisers of providence can balk all they wish, but what is not in dispute is that this was a huge *ob portu* for the West to slip in the front door and tell the East of Calvary's amazing grace and Pentecost's purifying fire. The sacrificial act alone of making the three-year trek would have earned the respect for the hundred to be heard. All that was needed was for the West to read the waves and leverage this *kairos* moment.

The Polo's Grueling Return Mission

While it is tempting to play the spiritual warfare card, such would require tracing out a much different trajectory. Having said that, would any God-fearing Christian seriously doubt that the enemy would spare any effort to keep light out of this darkened empire? Merely asking for a hundred top-shelf evangelists was easy, but concrete steps toward making it happen would be overwhelming. So, not surprisingly, snags arose for the Polos at every turn. We will highlight a few.

Above we referred to the regional turmoils and threatening events leading to detainment in Bukhara. But the real obstacles began for the Polos on their return home. Khan, for example, had charged a bodyguard to accompany the Polos back to Italy. But barely 20 miles into their course he took deathly ill and bowed out. What a way to start their 1,000-day trudge to Italy. When they arrived home they were shocked to learn that Pope Clement IV had died during their long absence. A two-year long sede vacante followed—the longest wait in papal history—until Gregory X was chosen! The Polos entreated him about the squadron of sage-evangelists requested by China. Gregory's response was underwhelming as he deployed only two Dominican friars.[20] But since God has a long track record of using outli-

20. The men were Nicholas of Vicenza and William of Tripoli; both of "the order of preachers." The Pope gave them authority to ordain, along with letters and gifts for Kublai.

ers,[21] maybe two was enough. However, they had to get to China first.

The Polos set their sights back toward Xanadu, now with teen Marco joining them. The 5,000 miles ahead would sap 40 months of their lives and began one of history's truly phenomenal adventures. After detouring to the Holy Land to secure oil from Jesus' tomb, the caravan then wove its way east toward Asia Minor. And here is where the two monks' true colors showed. Only 800 miles into their mission, somewhere around Armenia, Nicholas and William encountered a threat and quickly deserted. So not even 1/5 into the trip, they traded away certain sainthood for virtually complete anonymity. We shall see below just how much more was lost.

Undeterred, the three pressed on to Baku (now Azerbaijan), Georgia, Hormuz, Balkh (Afghanistan), and over the Pamirs. Here Marco became so ill (malaria?) that the three stayed in Badakhshan an entire year to take advantage of its fabled "healing" air. Once recovered, it was on to Kashmir, Kashgar, and Khotan (modern Xinjiang) and the murderous Taklamakan (place of no return) and Gobi deserts. They would encounter Saracens, bandits, sandstorms, floods, and bone-numbing winters along the way.[22] These are only a few known factors—and we can only imagine the unrecorded obstacles—but it seems this huge *ob portu* was met with resistance at every stage. Eight years passed between the Khan's request and the Polos' return. Their reunion was hearty, gifts were exchanged, and Marco quickly won the Khan's admiration. But the hundred were nowhere to be found.

A Costly Dithering

There is no extant record of the Pope taking Kublai's request seriously. And no data survives spelling out Kublai's response to the no show. In truth, the silence of both men speaks volumes. After years of waiting for the hundred to come, think how nonplussed Kublai might have been regarding Rome's token gesture of two spineless monks. We can envision him asking something like, "Given all we have heard of the God of the West, a little better response might be expected . . . *any* response! Surely a quarter of the world's population merits more effort than this!"[23] Or, "How can my people be drawn to Rome's Christ when she is so anemic about spreading the Truth?" And who could blame him? The non-response was deafening.

In the annals of squandered opportunities, this one is hard to surpass. What excuse could possibly justify such a feckless reply? Was it because the Polos failed

21. Gideon sought 32,000 to defeat the Midianites; the Lord whittled it dowb by 99%. Think of Elijah vs. Baal's 450 prophets, a boy's sling to fell Goliath, and 12 fishermen to shake the world. If God used 5 loaves and 2 fishes to feed the masses, China could be changed with 5 Italians and 2 monks.

22. I write these words while aboard a domestic flight to west China. This cloudless day gives perspective on how challenging it would be to travel by donkey through this mountainous land. and amplifies how natural barriers kept East from West for so long—indeed a brutally slow road to China.

23. The empire's population at this point is estimated to have been nearly 60 million.

to convey a sense of urgency? Did Rome suspect ulterior motives? Was she too suspicious? Did this diplomatic debacle carry any hint of xenophobia? Did concern for advancing an earthly kingdom eclipse building a heavenly one? Maybe she was too engrossed in the Crusades, building projects, etc. Was there infighting? And surely a three-year trip—dragging such a huge band over 5,000 miles—would be too dangerous, right? Too costly? Too embarrassing?[24] Only two friars! Seriously?

Some may give Gregory a pass, saying that it was God's will, or even that He was protecting China from a nascent Romanism that would require reform. China had warped Buddhism into something new, so perhaps Christianity also would have morphed into something blasphemous. We could surmise that Providence foresaw that the persecuted Church in modern China would ultimately bear more fruit? But for those not prone to rearranging the deck chairs on a head of a pin, Rome's costly dithering will be seen as one of the most critical miscues ever—not just in China, but across the entire 10/40 window.

Spiritual Nature Abhors a Vacuum

Considering how the Good News initially swept across Europe, there is no reason to doubt that this same fire could have spread to adjacent Asian countries. The strongholds of Islam and Communism might never have gained a foothold if Christianity had become the predominant religion in China. H.G. Wells rarely gets thing right, but was correct when describing this aborted mission as one of several "feeble and feeble-spirited attempts, with nothing of the conquering fire of the earlier Christian missions."[25]

Rome later tried amending the blunder,[26] but too late. Gone were any "golden passports," and a once fertile opening became arid again. It would be ages before missionaries returned to China in any significant way. But that is only a single domino in this tragic drama. The hundred not coming is one thing; what filled the void is another matter entirely. The well-known axiom, "nature abhors a vacuum," has a corollary. Spiritual nature *also* abhors a vacuum. Due to Rome's inaction, Kublai allowed two of Christianity's chief rivals—Buddhism and Islam—to fill the void and spread their views throughout his court. The Buddhist response was swift, and within mere decades, Tibetan Buddhism and Shamanism infiltrated China. Buddhism shed its stigma as a foreign import, and in just two centuries half of all males in the Middle Kingdom converted. Half a billion lay claim to

24. Could Gregory have been threatened at the prospect of Asia having more Christians than the West? Xenophobia may also have been in play as China was mostly unknown to Rome. It was unthinkable to Europe that this "barbaric" place could have been just as culturally advanced. Ironically, China felt the same about Europe. But the writings of Marco Polo would explode this misconception.

25. H.G. Wells, *The Outline of History*, 3rd edition (NewYork; MacMillan Company, 1921), 677.

26. Pope Nicholas IV sent the Franciscan, John of Montecorvino, to China in 1294. The efforts of the latter cannot be disparaged (thousands were converted), but they pale to what might have been.

the same general dharma today. The century after the Polos, the whole Mongol Golden Horde turned to Islam. Oversimplifications are unavoidable as so much more was at play, but such are the basic contours of how China gave entrée to two non-indigenous religions. The reader must assess the verity of whether this is how the East was lost.

Our hearts should feel crushed; a nauseating weight for the throng of post-Yuan dynasty souls that slipped into a Christless eternity, in some measure, because of the hundred no-shows. Imagine the spiritual rock China might have become if the West had seized upon this opportunity with the same fervor as the Buddhists. What if the Kublai had received an army envisaged 500 years later by Wesley, who longed for

> ...one hundred preachers who fear nothing but sin and desire nothing but God, and I care not a straw whether they be clergymen or laymen, such alone will shake the gates of hell and set up the kingdom of heaven upon earth.[27]

The mother of all opportunities to influence many nations for Christ was squandered when the Church failed to send its best apologists to harvest the Silk Road. Would we have ever heard terms like Two-China Policy, Red Guard, Cultural Revolution, Bamboo Curtain, Three-Self Church, one-child policy, "bare branches," 10-40 Window, or *River Elegy*?[28] The Silk Road that became a corridor for wielding the sword of Islam could have been one for spreading the Sword of the Spirit. Instead, monks from India and Burma, and later Persian Islamists, jumped at the *ob portu* and planted the seeds for worldviews that still entrap those along the Silk Road. That ancient path now threads through places the Church long forgot and long feared. Due to a lethargic and anemic response to Kublai's request, we now have countless people who have never once heard the Name.

Armed with centuries of hindsight, historians and missiologists label Rome's stinginess as *the* biggest missed opportunity in Church history. The unanswerable conjecture—relatively trivial in the economy of the Kingdom—is just how close history came to remembering Kublai Khan as the Constantine of the East. What should gnaw at the soul of the modern-day believers is the lost potential. What if Nicholas of Vicenza and William had any genuine discipling impulse? The prospect

27. Letter to Alexander Mather, Aug. 6, 1777. Kublai sought the same rarified men as Wesley. See "An Address To The Clergy." *Works of John Wesley*, 3d ed., 7 vols. (Grand Rapids, MI: Baker, 1996), 6:217-31. Wesley challenged pastors to be skilled in the Scriptures, logic, geography, and conversant in the philosophy, history, and the science of their time. Are these not reminiscent of the seven arts? To be clear, Wesley was not after mere philosophes. Both East and West have strained under the curses of rationalism and an over-cerebralizing of the faith. No, he was longing for those with those with pure hearts, who also grasped the power, grandeur, and efficacy of the principles of biblical discipleship.

28. As is widely recognized, the 10/40 Window is the least-evangelized area in the world and a contemporary stronghold for Islam, Hinduism and Buddhism.

for multiplication is both hard to imagine and impossible to deny. Ponder the spiritual footprint left on Scotland by one person in the 5th century or the impact of just one obedient soul in Ireland a century later. And those two missionaries had nothing like a Khanic imprimatur. What if Nicholas of Vicenza had harbored a burning concern for lost Cathay souls like St. Patrick had for the Scots? Could Xi'an have been his Scotland? Imagine if William of Tripoli had possessed the tenacity that Columba had for the Irish. Could Hangzhou have been his Ireland?

A REPRESENTATIVE AND NECESSARY EXCURSUS:
Needham's Question, with Principle Reference to a Latent Derivative of Monotheism

We have examined the spiritual costs when the West failed to leverage a pivotal *ob portu*. But the Asian Church is not the only context that would have been radically reframed. Manuel Komroff suggests that the cultural and ideological scythe would have cut both ways, with Europe benefiting from China's numerous technological advances. The hundred from the west, he contends, coming to

> China at this time and returning home at various periods would have changed the course of human events. Europe was just awakening from a long, barbaric sleep, while China was already cultured in many fields. Marco Polo came to exchange merchandise, while a hundred cultured men would have returned to exchange ideas. It is the traffic of ideas that is of greater profit to humanity.[29]

So many cognate areas beg exploring. Think how a cluster trained in the seven arts could have emulated for China the ideas giving rise to the liberal arts.[30] And the storied Chinese penchant for discipline, creativity, and technology would have helped the West in so many ways. An incomparable symbiosis was lost.

All this leads us to the thorny question of why an indigenous science never developed in China as it had in the West.[31] Cambridge's iconic sinologist, Joseph

29. This network of routes dates to the Han Dynasty, fostered a cross-pollination of ideas, beliefs and practices between Europe and Asia. Its real legacy is cultural exchange, not merely trade.

30. Huff notes that China had "no autonomous institutions of learning independent of the official bureaucracy; the ones that existed were completely at the mercy of the centralized state." Toby Huff, *The Rise of Early Modern Science: Islam, China and the West* (Cambridge: Cambridge University Press, 2003), 234. Confucian underpinnings prevented imagining (much less tolerating) a model of higher education where learners had autonomy to pursue independent lines of research. We are not saying that had the hundred come, China would have switched; we are only suggesting the far more modest idea that had they come China would have more likely benefited by being exposed to the fruits of a highly contrarian and (if scientific output is an accurate litmus) academically superior model.

31. Some scholars have demonstrated a causal nexus between the Judeo-Christian cosmology and the genesis of scientific realism. See J. Hannam, *God's Philosophers* (London: Icon Books, 2010); Peter Harrison, *The Bible, Protestantism and The Rise of Natural Science* (Cambridge: Cambridge University Press, 2001); and R. Stark, *For the Glory of God* (Princeton, NJ: Princeton University Press, 2003), 121-197. E. Grant, S. Jaki, and D. Lindberg have also accented the Needham question.

Needham, was a biochemist, prolific researcher, and Marxist. Referred to as a 20th century Erasmus, this remarkable scholar was fixated on pinpointing what factors hindered the rise of modern science in China.[32] In fact, he was so absorbed with this issue, it is simply known as *The Needham Question*.[33] While he gave decades to the search, such a full-orbed treatment is beyond our scope. But since a case can be made that the Pope's non-response to Kublai's request played some part in delaying the advent of science in China, we must lodge a few reflections on this matter.[34]

Some Key Philosophical Impediments

First, of all the causes for science being stillborn in ancient China, an organic view of nature and a cyclical view of time were her great philosophical walls. No post-Sinaitic culture holding such views ever independently cultivated an empirical investigative mindset. Cathay culture saw nature as a singular thing, self-governed, subjugated to an impersonal treadmill of birth, maturity, and death. Man saw himself as inseparable from nature and its internal harmony. This perspective suppressed any bent to transcend, analyze, and understand ordering principles of reality. Such metaphysically-bound frogs trapped in a "waterless well"[35] have no yen to escape, let alone methodically vivisect the natural realm. On this gloomy view, Chesterton noted,

> For most of Asia the rhythm has hardened into a recurrence. It is no longer merely a rather topsy-turvy sort of world; it is a wheel.... a sort of cosmic rotation, of which the hollow hub is really nothing. In that sense the worst part of existence is that it may just as well go on like that forever.[36]

Cyclical thinking was so imbedded in eastern thought that it fostered, in Eric Snow's words, a "metaphysically-induced hopelessness and passivity since no matter how hard humans may struggle to achieve, work, and think, the results of all efforts will be destroyed."[37] Pantheism and animism, in concert with the Asian view of time,

---

32. Joseph Needham, *Science and Civilisation in China, General Conclusions and Reflections*, vol 7 Part II, Kenneth Girdwood Robinson, ed. (Cambridge: Cambridge University Press, 2004), 208. Needham and his team produced a herculean 17 books, researching and contrasting how East and West interacted with the natural world. The project continued posthumously, now up to 7 volumes in 27 books. This scholarly output is so breathtaking that Needham is cemented as *the* authority in the field of "the history of science in China." Nathan Sivin, however, would make anyone's short list.

33. Alfred North Whitehead and Bertrand Russell also mused over this question.

34. Venturing into deep waters here means a few oversimplifications and generalizations. Thus, this section serves only to point to issues requiring further research and reflection.

35. This famous metaphor is lifted from a passage in the Maitrayaniya Upanishad.

36. G.K. Chesterton, *The Everlasting Man* (New York: Dodd, Mead & Co., 1925). George Bugg captures this fatalism as the "the wanton and wicked notion of the Hindoos, viz., that God has 'created and destroyed worlds as if in sport, again and again'!!" George Bugg, *Scriptural Geology*, 2 vols. (London: Hatchard and Son, 1826-27), 2:44.

37. Eric V. Snow, *Christianity: A Cause of Modern Science?* Unpublished essay, 1997.

deadened any notion of *succession*. So a basic rubric of science—the law of cause and effect—was a nonstarter. As foot binding limited normal growth, the view that all reality was endlessly cyclical stunted the Chinese mind from thinking linearly. Science *qua* science was literally implausible within the philosophical constraints of Asia's collective psyche. This reduces Bertrand Russell's assertion that nothing in ancient *China was "hostile to science" to little more than paradigm-laden dogma.*[38]

Amnesia of Earlier Monotheism

Second, this epistemological millstone was not China's original lot. Data has long mounted that monotheism was observed in ancient China. Needham blamed China's scientific blind alley on an "*early vanishing*" of a rational, law-giving Creator from the Chinese mind.[39] Oxford's James Legge, a sinologist every bit Needham's equal, unequivocally affirmed that "five thousand years ago the Chinese were monotheists," a monotheism under constant threat of being corrupted by nature-worship and divination.[40] Sadly, such corruption had crept in eons prior to Kublai's day. The idea of a cosmos regulated by knowable laws—vital to the genesis of science in the West—was now irrational to the Chinese mind. C.S Lewis contends, in contrast, that the patriarchs of science in the West "became scientific because they expected Law in Nature, and they expected Law in Nature because they believed in a Legislator."[41] A.N. Whitehead concedes that "faith in the possibility of science, generated antecedently to the development of modern scientific theory," even seeing such as an "unconscious derivative of medieval theology."[42]

There was unrest in Needham. His biases had him looking for economic, racial, geographical, or political factors, so loath was he to cede theistic convictions as having any hand in the advent of science. But in the end he extrapolated to the best inference: that Judeo-Christian premises enabled (not caused) the birth of science. Finally, he saw that it was the Occidental embrace of a *personal* Creator that was science-enabling, while the *impersonal* cosmogony of the East was science-inhibiting. In the West there was liberty to decode the created order for personal use, while the East was reined in for fear of disrupting the Tao. In the Western view,

> ...the ideas of natural law in the juristic sense and of the laws of Nature in the sense of

38. Bertrand Russell, *The Problem of China* (London: George Allen & Unwin, 1922), 193.

39. Stanley Jaki, *The Road of Science and the Ways to God* (University of Chicago Press, 1978), 14. Italics added. The phrase "early vanishing" points to something forgotten that had existed long ago.

40. James Legge, *The Religions Of China: Confucianism and Taoism Described and Compared with Christianity* (London: Hodder and Stoughton, 1880), 16. Ancient Chinese referred to theirs as the "Land of God" (Shen Zhou) and those familiar with rituals (like the border sacrifice) at the Temple of Heaven see Old Testament parallels (no idols, etc). On China's primordial monotheism, see John Ross, *The Original Religion of China* (Edinburgh: Oliphant, Anderson & Ferrier, 1909), 18-25.

41. C.S. Lewis, *Miracles: a Preliminary Study* (London: Collins, 1947), 110.

42. Alfred N. Whitehead, *Science and the Modern World* (New York: The Free Press), 3-4, 12-13.

> the natural sciences can easily be shown to go back to a common root.... [One] of the oldest notions of Western civilization was that just as earthly imperial law-givers enacted codes of positive law to be obeyed by men, so also the celestial and supreme rational Creator Deity had laid down a series of laws which must be obeyed by minerals, crystals, plants, animals and the stars in their courses. There can be little doubt that this idea was intimately bound up with the development of modern science at the Renaissance in the West. If it was absent elsewhere, could that not have been one of the reasons why modern science arose only in Europe; in other words, were medievally conceived laws of Nature in their naïve form necessary for the birth of science?[43]

After decades of careful thought, Needham decided that the main obstacle preventing the birth of science in China was a theological one. The highest deity known and worshipped in China was sharply different from the Creator known to the Hebrews. The supreme deity of the Chinese was not a celestial law-giver who created the cosmos and imposed ordinances on it. The Chinese had lost the concept of *He who is*—a God who was *personal*.[44]

Needham's research helps us see that while the Chinese did have an idea of order in nature, it was not an order born of a rational Creator. And minus this, what assurance was there that other "persons" would be able to lay out in their own languages any pre-existing divine code of laws that had been previously formulated? Gone was any certainty "that the code of Nature's laws could be unveiled and read, because there was no assurance that a divine being, even more rational than ourselves, had ever formulated such a code capable of being read." For Taoists this remains "too naïve to be adequate to the subtlety and complexity of the universe."[45] Western Trinitarian convictions held man as an image bearer of a three-personed God: One who was relational, revealed Himself propositionally, and wanted to be known. Viewing the natural realm as the work of a personal and transcendent God paved the way for man to turn his ear to the canyon of the cosmos in loving pursuit of divine echoes (Rom 1:20). This made all the difference.[46]

Matteo Ricci Notes a Lack of Foundation

Third, about four centuries after the Polos left China, another Italian came and invested about thirty years of his life for the Asian harvest. Matteo Ricci was the first Westerner ever to be invited into the Forbidden City. He was a brilliant

43. Joseph Needham, *The Grand Titration* (Toronto: University of Toronto Press, 1969), 35-36.

44. Needham, *The Grand Titration*, 327.

45. Ibid.

46. It bears mentioning in this context that until 2015, no homegrown Mainland Chinese citizen had ever won a scientific Nobel Prize, while those self-identifying as Christians have won 78% of all the Nobel Prizes in Peace, 72% in Chemistry, 65% in Physics, and 62% in Medicine. Further, though Muslims account for a significant portion of the world's population, they have won only 0.8% of all Nobel Prizes. Jews, in contrast, make up less than half a perce nt of the world's population, but have won an astonishing 22% of the prizes.

16th-century Jesuit missionary with a passion for science. But despite China's centuries of impressive inventions, Ricci was taken back by her scientific backwardness. In teaching geography, he found that the Chinese had "had practically no contact whatever, with outside nations, and consequently they are grossly ignorant of what the world in general is like."[47] This gap signaled a deeper deficiency, namely, the inability of the Chinese to assess the natural world. Ricci immodestly noted,

> [If] China was the entire world, I could undoubtedly call myself the principal mathematician and philosopher of nature, because it is ridiculously and astonishingly little what they know; they are preoccupied with moral philosophy, and with elegance of discourse . . .[48]

A few years later, Ricci dolefully added that the Chinese had

> . . .no science at all; one may say that only mathematics is cultivated, and the little they know of it is *without foundation*. . . . They just manage to predict eclipses and in that they make many mistakes. All are addicted to the art of divination, which is most unreliable and also completely false. Physics and metaphysics, including logic, [are] unknown among them.[49]

The phrase "without foundation" is telling, as a rational Creator, in contrast, was foundational in the West. Ricci goes on to show that due to all of their knowledge being rooted in tradition, the Chinese were weak in mathematics,[50] wanting in logic, autocratic in ethics, and stifled in geography.[51] Further reflection is needed on Ricci's lament that the Chinese were addicted to divination and astrology,[52] but at

---

47. *China in the Sixteenth Century: The Journals of Matthew Ricci: 1583–1610.* Translated from the Latin by Louis Gallagher (New York: Random House, 1953), 327. Hereafter, *Ricci Journals.*

48. Matteo Ricci, personal letter to Jesuit general, Claudio Acquaviva, November 4, 1595. *Opere Storiche del P. Matteo Ricci*, S.I., ed. Pietro Tacchi Venturi, S.J. (Macherata, 1913), 2:207.

49. See Henri Bernard, *Matteo Ricci's Scientific Contribution to China* (Westport, Connecticut: Hyperion Press, 1973), 52. Italics added. *The I-Ching*, a Confucian classic, was China's main divination guide. The present writer's closest confidant in China sees Confucianism as a curse on his nation. Needham, no friend of the Church, would have concurred, saying that it would have been to China's eternal benefit to "tie a millstone about the neck of the *I-Ching* and cast it into the sea." Interestingly, Kublai Khan at one point ordered all Confucian literature be burnt, except the *I-Ching*.

50. "Geometry as a systematic deductive system of proofs and demonstrations" writes Huff, "was virtually nonexistent in China." In disciplines core to scientific inquiry (astronomy, physics, optics, and mathematics) he adds, "the Chinese lagged behind." *The Rise of Early Modern Science,* 242-243.

51. Since the Chinese had virtually no contact with the outside world, Ricci saw that they were "grossly ignorant of what the world in general" was like. *Ricci Journals*, 166.

52. A 1988 series on CCTV, titled *River Elegy*, caused a furor. I targeted Confucianism culpability in hindering modernization in China. In contrast to the *scientific* West, China's millennia of introversion left it isolated and backward. Confucianism had carved out deep, freedom-inhibiting philosophical ruts (cleverly disguised as *tradition*) which the Chinese have slavishly followed. Harmony, stability, and submission became sacrosanct, while independent and critical thinking were anathema. See Thane Hutcherson Ury, "Confucianism: A Humanistic Wisdom Tradition," in *World Religions and Cults*, vol II, Bodie Hodge and Roger Patterson, eds. (Green Forest, AR: Master Books, 2016), 432-33.

face value this reminds us of Legge's thesis above, when he inferred that divination was culpable in the decay of China's early monotheism.

But What About China's Ancient Technological Advances?

Lastly, the Chinese were wise before their time with unparalleled creativity. No one disputes that, prior to Ricci, China was far beyond *any* previous civilization when it came to applying practical knowledge to basic needs. Her list of inventions is voluminous, with the "big four" being gunpowder,[53] papermaking, printing, and the compass. All had huge roles in the West but had comparatively little impact in China. So it is a fair question to ask why such innovation does not count as science? Snow addresses this common misnomer as follows:

> We must avoid assuming technological advance proves a given civilization has science, or modern science, for most inventions that affected daily life in the pre-modern world economically were "empirical" discoveries by craftsmen and other pragmatic types, not true scientists meditating on the laws of nature.[54]

Stanley Jaki adds that "practicality, craftsmanship, and organizational talent do not . . . qualify as science."[55] Reading between the lines, Snow and Jaki infer that while China was deft at applied technology and engineering, she was stunted when it came to theoretical science. Most moderns miss this by confusing activity with progress. Egyptians, Mayans, and early Chinese notched many amazing engineering feats—but no alchemy ever matured into chemistry, no obsession with stars ever advanced past astrology to astronomy, and the phenomenal algebraic skill of the Chinese never led to a mathematized science. Given how they excelled in practical knowledge, and in fact exceeded the West, we are astonished (like Ricci) that the Chinese never felt the need to spell out an intelligible scientific view of the cosmos.[56]

The Chinese gained knowledge—skills, crafts, technology and engineering—but did not "do" science. To Stark, such "empiricism was quite atheoretical, and their theorizing was nonempirical."[57] Technology develops through trial and error, while Science involves a search for natural laws, and hypotheses are advanced to

53. Since guns were not invented until the 14th century, 'gunpowder' is an anachronism. The powder was invented in 9th century China, and it was used only for fireworks.

54. Eric V. Snow, *Christianity: A Cause of Modern Science?*

55. Stanley Jaki, *Science and Creation* (Lanham, MD: University Press of America, 1990), 14.

56. Yu-Lan Fung refers to China's 4,000-year "failure" as a warning to seek happiness not "in the barren land of human mind" but in the external world. "Why China Has No Science—An Interpretation of the History and Consequences of Chinese Philosophy," *International Journal of Ethics*, Vol. 32, No. 3 (April, 1922), 263. Fung is significant since he predates Needham and posits different philosophical triggers for why the natural sciences never developed in dynastic China.

57. Rodney Stark, *For the Glory of God*, 126.

explain observations and then tested. Science arose in Christian Europe because Christianity pollinated this kind of thinking. This is why Hinduism did not cultivate (indeed *could not* cultivate) a Kepler, why Buddhism birthed no Mendel, why Greece gave us no Galileo, and why Islam never nurtured a Newton.[58]

The redemptive impact of the hundred coming to China would have been profound, not just in pointing hearts to Christ but also in reminding China of its roots. The above excursus shows how much more was likely lost in the missed *ob portu* of the Polo era. Other theses could be added, but such is enough to help us envision the profound domino effect when the West did not answer Khan's call. The "*earlier vanishing*" of a rational, law-giving Creator fostered a "theological orientation" for China that became her seminal hindrance in grasping and developing scientific realism and, indeed, the Savior of science.

Aslan is Once Again On the Move in China

We close with a bit of good news. Our God specializes in second chances. While access to China was notoriously difficult in the last century, the Silk Road is open again. Travel from Europe to Xanadu once demanded 2-3 years, but the author's flight this month took 13 hours. There are many opportunities for modern visionaries to till the soil and spread the Truth in this vast empire—that is, if we learn from history's mistakes. The Church is rapidly growing in China. Estimates vary, but there are likely more than 100 million Christians in China. Missiologists tell us that more than 22,000 Chinese convert to Christianity *daily*! A decade ago, Marvin Olasky dared assert, "If recent trends continue, the major religious story of the 21st century will be China's becoming the global center of evangelical Christianity."[59] Outrageous, you say? Well, the trend *has* continued, and in the next 15 years China is on pace to boast nearly 300 million Christians.[60] They know how to evangelize. But China's great cry is for teachers, disciple makers, apologists. What a critical window for Christendom to reap an unprecedented harvest. James Hudson Taylor III, whose sinological DNA is unquestioned, confirmed this when he wrote,

> Church history can be understood as the history of apologetics. . . . Because of the uniqueness of the Chinese people and their culture, there is an unparalleled need in China for a bold, biblical apologetic. Unless Chinese apologists are raised up who are well trained in Chinese thought and culture as well as the truth of the Bible and the power of the Gospel, Chinese hearts and minds will remain highly resistant to the Word of God.[61]

---

58. The author is indebted to Michael Bumbulis for inspiring this sentence.
59. Quoted in *Unfinished*, a publication of The Mission Society, Fall 2007 (38), 5.
60. See Rodney Stark and Xiuhua Wang, *A Star in the East: The Rise of Christianity in China* (West Conshohocken, PA: Templeton Press, 2015), 1-12.
61. On file with author, no date.

Taylor does not specify a hundred apologists, but his call dovetails with Kublai's request—namely, needing apologists who are bold, "well trained in Chinese thought and culture as well as the truth of the Bible." The future will judge how effectively our current generation responded to this 21st-century *ob portu*. Surely the modern Church will not commit the second greatest mistake in Church history. She should relearn ancient and essential lessons. When God opens a door, don't dither, bicker, bargain, or retreat. Our world is vastly different due to the non-response to Kublai's request. As a result, the 10/40 Window—stronghold of Buddhism, Islam, and Hinduism—is our biggest challenge today. We are in desperate need of radical souls who can look past creed, ethnicity, hardships, and personal safety, and like Jesus, cry hot tears for the lost. The cross bears the Message, Pentecost provides the power, discipleship becomes the means, and missions is the mandate: tenets so simple that we should all grasp them.

The Rest of the Story

In our opening cliffhanger about Henri Charrière, we omitted a few details from the film's dénouement.[62] If you saw the picture you recall that Henri was not alone on the jagged cliff that day, but flanked by his best friend and fellow prisoner, Louis Dega. Movie buffs recall that there was a second sack of coconuts atop the precipice. The original plan had been for both of them to seize the opportunity for freedom *together*. But at the moment of truth, Dega's nerves got the best of him. Not only did Louis get cold feet, he even tried to talk Papillon out of jumping. Nonetheless, after a last embrace, Henri took his leap of faith. And there atop the cliff, Dega cast a long, long poetic farewell gaze at his friend drifting away on the waves of emancipation. Louis cocked his head, pondered further, stared down at his bag of coconuts, and then silently shuffled away.

God gives each dispensation, each generation, each person an *ob portu*. Unfortunately, many are not watching or praying for their chance. Many may be concerned about their safety, like Nicholas and William. Others, like Dega, will just stare quizzically, even trying to dissuade others, before hobbling back to the safety of their garden. There aren't enough tears to correspond to the lament of why 13th-century Europe had so many like Degas and so few like Henri. Who will you be? What bold opportunity is God is calling you to embrace? He will certainly provide an *ob portu* for you. Are you readying yourself? Have you acquired the wisdom and courage to read the waves? When you are ready, He'll open the door. But when that moment comes, you must take the leap of radical obedience. Such will be a hinge moment in your life and perhaps even for history as well.

62. The film clip can be viewed at https://www.youtube.com/watch?v=4XGWXmxmaoE

"There is a flow to the biblical principles of discipleship. Discipleship is designed to be a part of the accomplishment of God's purposes in the world. It is a means, not an end in itself. Its chief function is to draw men and women to God so that He might do with them as He pleases.

"Since discipleship's primary purpose has to do with relating to God, it is not surprising that the nature of God determines its role. As the Bible unfolds the purposes and plans of God for His people, so the nature and character of God are also progressively revealed throughout history. Particularly in the unfolding drama of salvation history, God makes Himself known as a triune being: Father, Son and Holy Spirit. In a unique sense, our grasp of discipleship principles is closely tied to our increasing understanding of the holy Trinity throughout Scripture. This should not surprise us. As God makes Himself known, His design for mankind becomes clear. At the same time He more crisply identifies His means for accomplishing His purposes. As a result, when we get to the climax of God's purposes through the person of Jesus Christ, we understand more clearly the design and implementation of the discipleship process."

Allan Coppedge
The Biblical Principles of Discipleship
1987

66141912R00121

Made in the USA
Lexington, KY
04 August 2017